LEADERSHIP IN MODERN WAR

LEADERSHIP IN MODERN WAR

FROM WW 2 TO THE WAR AGAINST ISIS

JAMES BROOKS

FRONTLINE
BOOKS

First published in Great Britain in 2023 by
PEN & SWORD MILITARY
An imprint of Pen & Sword Books Ltd,
Yorkshire – Philadelphia

ISBN: 978-1-39906-729-4

A CIP catalogue record for this book is available from the British Library

Typeset in Chennai, India by Lapiz Digital Services.

Printed and bound by CPI UK

Pen & Sword Books Ltd incorporates the imprints of Pen & Sword Archaeology, Atlas, Aviation, Battleground, Discovery, Family History, History, Maritime, Military, Naval, Politics, Social History, Transport, True Crime, Claymore Press, Frontline Books, Praetorian Press, Seaforth Publishing and White Owl

For a complete list of Pen & Sword titles please contact
PEN & SWORD LTD
47 Church Street, Barnsley, South Yorkshire, S70 2AS, England
E-mail: enquiries@pen-and-sword.co.uk
Website: www.pen-and-sword.co.uk

Or

PEN AND SWORD BOOKS
1950 Lawrence Rd, Havertown, PA 19083, USA
E-mail: Uspen-and-sword@casematepublishers.com
Website: www.penandswordbooks.com

To
Josh, Matt, Car, Sully,
and the students of EMW81: Perspectives in Modern War,
who taught me to tell stories

CONTENTS

Foreword

BY SETH MOULTON

I made the same mistake that thousands of generations of boys have made before me: I wanted to go to war. My parents objected, of course, just like thousands of generations of parents. My mom famously told a Boston newspaper, when asked if she was proud of her son for joining the Marines: "I would only have been more disappointed in Seth if he had chosen a life of crime." She protested the Vietnam War in college. She couldn't understand why anyone would want to go to war.

My motivation was not the savage glory of battle. I didn't have a particular penchant for getting in fights or playing violent video games. My motivation was not to get out of life back home. I had a great life back home. My motivation was rooted in admiration – admiration for the young men, boys often, who have fought and died for our freedom. My motivation was rooted in selflessness – I wanted to do my part, too. But it was also self-serving: I thought the experience would make me a better person. I was insecure enough in myself to recognize that war might teach me things I didn't really understand: leadership, decision-making, and perhaps a bit of self-awareness. I made the final decision to join about three months before September 11, 2001, unaware I would go to war, but hoping that I might.

When I returned from war, I didn't talk much about it. There is a healthy disrespect among combat veterans for those who tell war stories. An investigative reporter once dug up my war record to see if I was hiding anything. He found a few awards I hadn't mentioned to anyone, not even my parents. Too many guys I served with did heroic things and never got recognized themselves. When I returned from war, I was lucky: I had no major scars, at least not that I could see. But nobody returns from war the same person. Some of the best days of my life were in the war, and some of the worst days were there, too.

When I made the decision a decade after I returned to tell a story that haunted me and contributed to my post-traumatic stress, I learned for the first time how telling war stories can help others. That, ultimately, is the core of this book, written by a fellow veteran I admire for his own service, his own selflessness, and his own dedication to making his experience meaningful to others.Through a collection of thoughtful, emotional, powerful, and occasionally entertaining accounts of great Americans and Brits from several wars of the past century, James "Jay" Brooks welcomes the reader to step into the shoes of multiple generations of our country's military leaders. From his great uncle's battle from Normandy to Berlin in the Second World War to his own service in Iraq in the War Against ISIS, Jay asks us to act and think as those key decision-makers. The questions range from the vast to the personal: What would you do in the face of an oncoming ambush? Would you cross a narrow, dangerous bridge first to lead the way, or last to ensure nobody is left behind? How would you help a friend get clean in a matter of days so that he could ship home? By seamlessly intertwining his own story throughout the book, Jay grounds his own experience in these very questions. He tests his audience in a way that many authors do not, asking us to think about the lessons of war for our country, for our world – but most of all, for ourselves.

Sometimes people ask if I would be proud to have my daughters join the Marines. My answer is always the same: Yes, I'd be proud. But I'd be even more proud if they didn't have to. It's through the careful retelling of war stories that combat veterans hope we can share the powerful lessons of something that should never have happened. Extracting something worthwhile from horrific experiences, we hold out hope that everyone else might understand why we never want others to have to learn these lessons the same way we did.

Seth Moulton
Marine veteran and US Congressman
April 2023

Preface

FINDING MEANING

"Can't wait to read your book."

A burly, former football player named Ben jeered at me about my potential future in writing as we took advantage of a pause during an urban-warfare exercise. We were sitting against a wall inside a large shipping container that was meant to prepare us for buildings we might encounter in Iraq. Where I looked disheveled in my dusty assortment of combat gear, Ben seemed to wear his much more naturally. Ben had earned the nickname "Rock" not only from his physical stature, but also from a moment in another urban-warfare training exercise. He had run out of training grenades while clearing a building, so he rolled a rock into a room to make the role-playing enemy take cover. A usually reticent instructor gave him what amounted to a high compliment afterwards: "That was pretty smart."

Ben and I were in the middle of a force-on-force, free-play battle that set us against other Marines in our training company. "Rock" was one of my platoon's squad leaders. He, more than anyone I knew, was born to be a Marine. When I saw him years later as a platoon commander, I only wished more Marines would be as lucky to have leaders like him. In this exercise, I was leading our platoon and got to pick who would take key leadership roles below me. "Rock" was one of my first choices.

"I'm not writing a book."

"Sure, man."

Well, Ben, you were right. What started as a manuscript for a high-school English and history class called "Perspectives in Modern War" has turned into this book. Since the book has broken out of the circle of family and friends I originally intended it for, I am now called to explain more who I am and why I wrote it.

My journey started almost exactly twenty years ago. I was 10 years old and sitting in fourth-grade class. The school administrator called my name over the loudspeaker and told me to pack up my bags since my mom was there to pick me up early from school. I gleefully jumped up and let out a "Yay!" My teacher did not question my early departure and simply gave me a pained nod.

My mom met me in the school lobby. I could tell immediately she was distraught. "They bombed the World Trade Center," she said as she turned away to lead me out of school. My 10-year-old brain had trouble understanding where that was or why it mattered so much, but my 10-year-old brain also had trouble forgetting the image of a business lady sitting on the sidewalk in high heels covered in dust and blood that I saw in the newspaper the next day.

As I grew up in the shadow of those memories, I felt the call to serve in different ways. I looked up to my pediatricians and wanted to help people like they had helped me. I admired my teachers and coaches and wanted to pass on their lessons of growth to the next generation. I revered my grandfathers, who both served in the Navy, one in the Second World War and one during the Korean War, and the quiet wisdom they seemed to carry so naturally. Once I started to understand more about that fateful Tuesday, their service seemed even more meaningful. Stories of veterans who died in the attack as heroes like Rick Rescorla solidified that meaning further.

Those varied callings found outlets in high school and college through tutoring, coaching, and playing sports. I found fulfillment helping others learn and grow both academically and athletically. I found purpose challenging myself and leading teams in the arena. Boxing became the outlet I enjoyed the most: my time in competitive sports culminated in college coaching boxing in downtown Boston and fighting in the ring at Harvard. I would remember these years of leadership, physical, and mental challenges in sports when I faced my own challenges at war.

Fifteen years after 9/11, I followed my calling to serve into my first deployment to the Middle East as a Marine scout sniper platoon commander. For seven months from September 2016 to April 2017, I supported my sniper teams spread out across Iraq, Kuwait, and Syria from a command center in Western Iraq. Though day-to-day, my primary mission was to enable Iraqi soldiers and US special forces actively fighting the Islamic State of Iraq and al-Sham (ISIS). My most impactful memories came targeting ISIS fighters through air strikes and evacuating Iraqi casualties from the battlefield.

After less than a year home, I would return to the Middle East for a second seven-month deployment from March to October 2018, this time as an intelligence officer. I facilitated counterterrorism missions across Syria, Afghanistan, Iraq, and Kuwait and analyzed all edges of the US's multifaceted war. My career would culminate with a third "deployment," based at home, fighting ISIS propaganda online from 2019–21.

I returned then to my high school to teach and coach like I imagined I would years before. It would be a short stop along my way to medical school, as I had already been accepted and planned to start that coming fall. I never thought my path was that interesting or unique, especially compared with veterans from previous generations of war and the many before me who had left to journey into medicine. Yet leaving the military and talking more openly about my path made me face its apparent rarity. I once briefly described the transition I was undertaking from the military to teaching and medicine to a friend of a friend at a wedding. He smiled, looked around at the group we were with, and said, "Damn, man. When you're a grandpa, people are gonna say, 'This guy lived life.'"

I could only laugh and say I've been lucky, which is true. Any stumbles I have had outweigh any success, and luck means more than circumstance. Luck includes race and the advantages I had growing up that not everyone has.

9/11 might have been the first push on this winding path in service. The people I have encountered since are what drive me still to spend my whole life trying to make the best of everything I have been given.

In writing this book, I try to capture the gift I had to teach a course to eighteen young men and women in spring 2021. My students' passion for the lessons of modern war called me to provide the course to a larger audience. Yet as a teacher is not the center of a classroom, I am not the center of this book. Through stories, I thread lessons in self-awareness, decision-making, and leadership from my experiences at war and those of the men and women with whom I was lucky enough to serve. I can only try to pass on our lessons through writing after leaving the classroom, and I can only try to grasp the true meaning of our service.

Part of that meaning is left up to you to determine yourself, to decide how and why these lessons on the traits and skills of self-awareness, decision-making, and leadership can apply to your life and offer meaning to your own experiences. All of our journeys intersect at the basic, fundamental need to try to make sense of what we have experienced and will experience.

So, here's to trying.

ACKNOWLEDGMENTS

Teaching a senior elective on modern war was never my intent. The truth is I had only wanted to be an assistant golf coach and walk around with the coach who had coached me eleven years prior. After securing the assistant golf-coach role two years ahead of time in 2019 (which consisted of a text and an immediate response of "you're hired"), I asked the headmaster that fall if I could be a long-term substitute to help pay for rent. He responded by saying, "Why don't you teach your own elective?"

I initially, and stupidly, thought that would be less work than re-learning high-school math or science and agreed. While my time coaching was extremely meaningful, the class became an outlet to learn and grow that I never thought I needed. I had eighteen dedicated and impressive students, who engaged with my guest speakers' and my experiences of war more than I could have ever imagined (and only sometimes turned in late assignments as second-semester seniors). For four months, I learned and grew with all of them.

Before leaving for the summer and starting my journey to New York City and medical school, I helped lead a small group during the annual senior retreat. A secular retreat, yet built on the Jesuit model, it served as another mark for learning and growth I did not know I needed. On that retreat, a student not in my group came up to me and asked me how I could describe my time in the military in three words. I thought for a moment and then said, "Pride, pain, and memory." Even having had much more time to think, I would not change my answer. "Pride, Pain, and Memory" was the original title for this book and remains for me the easiest way to summarize my service.

Leaving retreat and seeing the seniors graduate, I was called to continue to pass on the lessons from the course. As I was entering medical school, teaching a high-school elective was not feasible, but I knew I could write and collect the stories in a book. The book encapsulated all I had started to learn from teaching, the retreat, and the memories in service I had not yet faced. How much I needed all this growth hit me when I finished the first draft the night before my first medical school classes. Weeks of reflection later, I am more grateful than ever to have had these opportunities to learn from my experiences and put them in order behind me. I know many veterans are not as lucky to have all the support and opportunities I had when I finally came home. And with all that encouragement, I know it also took me too long to grow and move on.

With that delay first in mind and as winding as this path was to teaching and writing, I have many, many people to thank who have supported me along my journeys, through all my mistakes, lapses in judgment, and inattentiveness. I would not be here without you.

First to my family, especially my parents, sisters, brothers-in-law, Papa Jim and Laura B., the Smiths, and the Tuckers, you are the village that it took to get me here. I do not want to imagine what my deployments and transition into civilian life would have been like without all your support.

Second to my guest speakers who gave their time to the course and allowed me to attempt to communicate their stories through this book. Without you, the class and this book would never have existed. I wish I could have had Toby Finney in the class to speak to my students, but I am greatly indebted to him for allowing me to include some of his story as a Vietnam veteran. Veterans like Toby from different generations welcoming me home and treating me like a brother have been a critical part of my transition out of the military. A special thanks also to Robin Dreeke, who spoke to my class about his book *It's Not All About Me* and his life of experiences in influence and leadership.

Third to Carly, my steadfast partner through my last job in the military to transition as I began to put my experiences behind me. You deserved, more than anyone, to be celebrated at the awards ceremony for officer of the year in September 2021. You were also the first to help me turn my memories into stories and then turn my stories into lessons. The first moment I finally started to grow might have been when you sat with me and watched the Gran Torino scene a few times over. I will never stop feeling blessed for your impact on my life, and I will never stop trying to be more like you.

Fourth to the teachers, staff, and parents of Gilman School in Baltimore, who welcomed me back after college and military service to teach. Thanks especially to Rob for having the idea for the course and placing faith in me to make it happen. Dr T. provided necessary early encouragement and historical corrections. Steve was always a friend and mentor and helped catch a lot of my missing words as one of my most dedicated editors. Thanks to Jeffrey and LCDR Holley for their support and mentorship through the year. Thanks to Coach Wally and all the amazing parents of the Gilman golf team who made me feel like I was finally home.

Fifth to those I served with. Realistically only a slice of our experience is saved in this book. The rest remains close in memory. To my mentors, who saw more in me than I did in myself. And to my Marines, who taught me more than I could ever have hoped.

Sixth to my friends, in and out of service, who carried me every step of the way but especially during the transitions home from deployments and finally to civilian life. I feel endlessly lucky to have been able to lean on you and have your support all through the ups and downs of service and moving on. I will be repaying that for the rest of my life.

Seventh, to the team at Frontline and Pen & Sword for allowing me to save the class I loved teaching so much, especially John, who took a chance on a first-time author with a hastily written pitch, and my editor Alison, who patiently led me through each step of the process so well.

Finally to the eighteen young men and women I called my students. I was burned out and questioning why I had joined and served at all when you met me. You all helped me remember my "why." I will hold onto that closely as I continue on my path into medicine now.

LIST OF PLATES

I sat upon the shore
Fishing, with the arid plain behind me
Shall I at least set my lands in order?

"The Waste Land," T.S. Eliot

Introduction

THE NIGHT OF THE BASE BLOOD DRIVE

"Hey, Sir, do your parents know you are out here playing war?"

I stared blankly back at the overweight civilian drone operator, who smiled at me through a gangly beard. The room full of Marines, soldiers, and civilians ostensibly conducting modern war seemed to focus all energy on my response. I stood on a raised platform in the rear of the room, facing the jeering faces ahead turned back to me.

"Yes, they do. And they are very proud."

The drone operator took a sip of his non-alcoholic O'Doul's beer as he turned to sit down two rows ahead of me. The response seemed to stymie any more laughs from the room. The room's attention returned to the maps and live feeds of Western Iraq displayed prominently on the wall forward, and the standard din of a stalled command center started to take back over. As I sat down, my radio operator Paul Kitter to my right leaned over. He was a young, talented, junior enlisted Marine and had sat next to me every day for nearly five months of deployment.

"That's cute, Sir. Are you proud of me?"

"Yes, Kitter. I am. Now let's ..."

"Then my dad is proud of me, too."

Kitter paused, waiting for me to respond as he smiled with a fist on his chin and stared up towards the ceilinfg. I shook my head and turned back to my keyboard and computer screens. In memory more than the moment, my computer and the screens in front broadcasting life and death would begin to represent what I would know as modern war. The Iraqis fought and died warring against ISIS only a few miles away, but I sat with my team removed in support, in relative safety with functioning air-conditioning.

I had to remind myself it was real, the first time I saw a truck explode on one of those screens. A missile from an unmanned aircraft had made quick work of three ISIS fighters in a pickup truck careening through the desert. I was brand new to the command center then, still days away from starting my first shift as the junior officer in charge of the room. I would learn my job would include facilitating strikes exactly like that one and reporting the kill count in daily briefs. When I got home seven months later and watched the new Star Wars movie with a friend, I had to tell myself to stop counting the deaths in exploding ships; I had to remind myself it wasn't real.

I shook that night with each fantastical explosion that killed incomprehensible numbers when compared with modern war, hoping my friend wouldn't notice and hiding, for the first time, a pain of moral injury I did not fully understand. But how could I? I was 25 and baby-faced enough to be called out for looking too young to be at war. I was trained before deployment for two short years in decision-making and leadership, leadership that called me to shoulder the burden of my Marines, whether physical, mental, or moral. Shouldering the former two was taught well, by testing decision-making and training competency during endless hikes under sleep, food, and water deprivation. But what was I supposed to do after I shouldered my Marines' moral burden? And how would I shoulder a moral burden that belongs to me?

When home, years later, I would say I was lucky to have the experience making life-and-death decisions so young. Facilitating kinetic strikes against ISIS were decisions of death. The hunt for ISIS fighters brought moments of excitement in chase and relief in destruction. Everyone in the room knew explicitly that every fighter we killed was one fewer fighter who could attack and kill Iraqis or attack Americans on base. The reasons I knew explicitly then begin to seem odd only back in a civilian world where killing again becomes illegal.

Supporting casualty evacuations from the battlefield were decisions of life. Enabling the treatment of a wounded Iraqi changed the climate of the command center from a group of stadium spectators cheering on a gladiator to a stressed family in a living room awaiting a call from a doctor. These moments would be most impactful for me and serve as the clearest markers of doing "good" in the face of the jarring reality of war, especially the moment from one night when our base medical center ran out of blood.

It was early 2017, and I was several months into my first deployment. The Battle of Mosul raged to the north, and our forces were struggling to liberate key ISIS strongholds in Western Iraq. Targeting ISIS fighters, supporting casualty evacuations, completing the administrative tasks of leading a command center all had become routine. The day had begun as many had before, supporting an Iraqi operation aimed to seize one of the last towns ISIS held on the Euphrates River. The Iraqis had met resistance on their push forward and took several casualties, some of whom were wounded badly enough to be transferred for treatment on our base. The Iraqi generals, watching and controlling the battle from our command center, still considered progress had been made and had given orders to their soldiers to create defensive positions at the new forward line. The command center slowly began to transition from the heightened excitement of an active operation to the dull administrative work of operational analysis. My shift was ending, and I was sitting with Lance, a junior officer like me who was to take over leadership of the command center into the night. I then started to hear muffled words come from the Iraqi radio behind me. The only word I understood was "jahal" or "child."

"Jay, Jay, come here," my interpreter Louie said, and I stood up immediately to talk to him and the Iraqi liaison officer next to him. I met eyes and smiled at Louie, an Iraqi-American who had patiently re-taught me how to lift weights over the past few months so I could get jacked like he was. It had not worked, but we had become good friends.

"A boy stepped on an IED near the river. Can we treat him?" Louie said, firm but caring in his delivery. I glanced over at the Iraqi liaison officer to Louie's left, still on the radio yet staring steadily at me.

"Yes. We'll make it happen. I'll call the med center."

As a junior officer, I was a powerless middleman for almost everything I did in the command center, and this moment was no exception. I had no authority to accept anyone into the medical center, but I could make the calls and start the approval process. In this case, nearly two hours after the last casualty from the day had been treated and stabilized, I felt confident that the medical center would be able to take on one more casualty. Even though I could pass off the job to Lance, I stayed through to see the boy transferred onto base and into the medical center. Lance deliberately gave off a lackadaisical air, but he was actually deeply thoughtful and intelligent. He seemed to relish in his resemblance, both in looks and attitude, to Peter Gibbons from *Office Space*. Lance therefore never seemed to mind when I stayed late into his shift, and the extra time together made us faster friends. It also kept me away from the gym where I wasn't making much progress anyway and the texts and calls which were altogether unhelpful to me in my off time.

Just before I was to leave, the medical center called to say they were running out of blood. This event too was routine, and one of the few things I could do without anyone else's approval. I walked back behind the Iraqi radio to talk to the contractor who ran the base defense loudspeakers.

"Blood drive activated. B-POSITIVE. B-POSITIVE."

The loudspeakers that pumped the announcement across the remote Iraqi base always seemed slightly too loud for the command center where the call originated. In a break between repetitions, I asked Lance if he was ready to take over shift. "Yeah, thanks. You going to donate?" he asked.

"Nah. I'm A-POS."

The day had ended with more casualties on the enemy side than friendly, which gave me some comfort as I donned my gear to leave. It was, however, just one operation of many, and the day following would add to the blur of memories of enemy destroyed and friendly casualties treated. This last casualty stuck out because he was a boy, a noncombatant away from the front line who arrived at the base through the misfortune and circumstance of living in a war zone where bombs still lived latent in the sand.

Walking out into the night, I adjusted to the winter chill and near complete darkness of the vast desert. As I passed the medical center, I saw a queue of people outside already waiting to donate. I paused staring at the line of people who formed out of the blackness of the night to support a nameless Iraqi. I was proud to be with those people supporting the Iraqis in their war, and I fell asleep feeling like I was a part of something meaningful and worthwhile.

I woke up a few hours later and returned to the command center. I asked for details about the boy and learned that he had died in the night. I hid any reaction and got to work.

* * *

I have only told that story, about the night of the base blood drive, in two general contexts. First, I told the story for several iterations of a medical school application, one that lamented my position staring at the queue when I wanted to be on the other end, serving in medicine and supporting healing during conflict. Those feelings in the moment were true and continue to push me on my path into medicine now. Though for an essay or interview, I always left out the ending, the truth that the boy died. The painful reality seemed to distract from the truth I wanted to communicate, the truth that I wanted to be a doctor.

Second, I told the story in full to my high-school class, the opening of an English and history senior elective built on story-telling I created and called "Perspectives in Modern War." Seven years in the Marines led me to that classroom to teach and drove me to communicate lessons from my experience at home and in modern war. This book, capturing the lessons of modern war for a wider audience, begins as the class did with a story meant to question what "good" we can ever find in war.

Questioning the moral of war is now solidified as that story's purpose, far different from its first use simply to convince someone to admit me into medical school. Giving a story purpose, though, begins to separate it from reality. I do not remember whether the queue I saw that night was for the boy who stepped on an improvised explosive device (IED, or bomb) not too far from base. It might have been for an Iraqi soldier who had a negligent discharge and shot himself in the leg. Even the call of "jahal" that I heard on the Iraqi radio could have been the description of a young junior enlisted Iraqi soldier, rather than for the boy. The memories intertwine as both Iraqis died after a base blood drive as they were transferred to Baghdad for higher care; often the main truth of the story is what you wish you had to invent. For the stories in this book, I have changed some places and names, but they are based on the truth of experience.

After telling the story of the night of the base blood drive to my class, I read these passages aloud from Tim O'Brien's "How to Tell a True War Story" in *The Things They Carried*:

> A true war story is never moral. It does not instruct, nor encourage virtue, nor suggest models of proper human behavior, nor restrain men from doing the things men have always done. If a story seems moral, do not believe it. If at the end of a war story you feel uplifted, or if you feel that some small bit of rectitude has been salvaged from the larger waste, then you have been made the victim of a very old and terrible lie. There is no rectitude whatsoever. There is no virtue. As a first rule of thumb, therefore, you can tell a true war story by its absolute and uncompromising allegiance to obscenity and evil. . . .
>
> You can tell a true war story if it embarrasses you. . . .
>
> In a true war story, if there's a moral at all, it's like the thread that makes the cloth. You can't tease it out. You can't extract the meaning without unraveling the deeper meaning. And in the end, really, there's nothing much to say about a true war story, except maybe "Oh."

Over the semester, I chose stories and readings to communicate and improve the traits and skills I would have wanted as a high-schooler and continue to seek today: self-awareness, decision-making, and leadership. Perhaps in contrast to Tim O'Brien's work, the purpose of the class was to "instruct" what we can learn from experiences at war and "suggest" how those lessons apply to life in and out of the military. This book is a teacher's attempt to communicate lessons, the didactic approach parallel to a writer's attempt to communicate feeling. Some of those lessons are overt in the form of "what-would-you-do" self-awareness, decision-making, and leadership exercises; some are more open-ended, like from the night of the base blood drive. The exercises range from tactical, "on-the-ground" decisions my friends and I faced to the strategic policy our leaders had to navigate. Distilling complex tactical and foreign-policy decisions into short exercises is meant to draw out decision-making methods and encourage a deeper inspection of tactics, history, and policy.

This book collects the major stories and lessons from the class, from my service and the service of veterans I am lucky to call friends. Fellow Marines and soldiers, British and Australian officers, members of the intelligence community, men and women of all races and backgrounds shared their perspectives over the course of the semester. I focus on the stories we told, but like "How to Tell a True War Story," I reference the readings that influenced the stories, either as they happened or in memory. References, additional decision-making exercises, and a map depicting where the book's main characters served are included in the appendices.

Organized under three parts dedicated to self-awareness, decision-making, and leadership, each chapter highlights moments as thought experiments to test and improve those traits and skills. Some stories have elements of all three. The traits overlap and intersect, each representing fundamental aspects of what makes us successful in our lives at work, at home, and in all human interactions. Self-awareness and decision-making specifically build the foundation for successful influence and leadership, the section that culminates the book and provides its title. Self-awareness focuses generally on communicating, understanding, and experiencing human dynamics, the battlefield, and trauma; decision-making on facing ethical dilemmas, seizing the initiative, and incorporating wargaming, probability, and chance; and leadership on shouldering responsibility and influencing others.

History is interwoven throughout the stories, as we all experienced battles that molded territorial lines and affected the strength of nations. I include references for further reading on specific events and historical facts highlighted. Part I begins with memoirs from the Second World War and Vietnam to serve as initial comparisons of war across generations. Part II outlines the history of the US's involvement in the Middle East through conflict with Al Qaeda, Iranian-US relations, the Gulf War of 1990–1, and the Iraq War of 2003–11. Part III traces the rise and fall of ISIS in Iraq from 2014–18 and examines the War in Afghanistan from 2001–21. I also include postscripts on the August 2021 attack in Kabul and the ongoing War in Ukraine.

For a brief moment in spring 2021, I was a high-school teacher. Before that, I was a Marine. My experience in modern war started supporting active combat against ISIS in Western Iraq and ended fighting ISIS propaganda online. For seven years, I served with extremely impressive people who took up the mantle to fight in modern war. At war, we learned about ourselves, our society, our biases, and our influence. Our defining moments I capture here serve to inform and teach, as reconciliation for the haunting elements of war we all experienced in our own ways. Through this book, I hope to communicate more broadly some lessons of modern war with the incessant hope that others do not have to experience it.

The winding path ahead now pulls me into medicine, with a purpose to heal those areas stricken by conflict and poverty. Yet, I have learned these memories will walk with me on that path forever. Teaching and writing them, these fragments of stories shored together, is my best shot to learn from them too.

PART I

SELF-AWARENESS

The capacity to understand yourself, others around you, and how you are perceived by them

Ask for help, but salvation lies within

"You have to carry the fire."

Cormac McCarthy

"Take the foot."

USMC saying

Chapter 1

DON'T GO TO WAR

John Randolph Tucker, Jr was a Richmond boy. Born in 1914, he remembered watching Civil War veterans walk down Monument Avenue on Decoration Day and thinking that they looked old. Still, witnessing the strength and honor of those old veterans may have led the young Tucker eventually to seek the challenges of a military life. As a young man, he shunned the college that generations of his family had attended – Washington & Lee University – to attend Virginia Military Institute, a military academy a stone's throw away from W&L. If he ever regretted his decision, he could easily see "how the other half lived" on the W&L side of Lexington, Virginia. Though even during Rat Year at VMI, the first year of military schooling with a level of discomfort incomprehensible to modern dispositions, Tucker was happy and proud to be on his side of town.

Graduation in 1937 then propelled him to work in sales in London where he lived and began to witness the grumblings of another world war. Holding a commission in the US Army reserve as a First Lieutenant, Tucker watched intently, and on December 7, 1940, the Army called him up for a year of active-duty orders. His service would last five.

In the year training before the US's entrance into the war, Tucker found a home with 83rd Armored Reconnaissance Battalion, a unit that would serve as the lead element for 3rd Armored Division. With vehicles ranging from six-wheeled armored cars, light tanks, halftracks, jeeps, and motorcycles, Tucker quickly learned the intimate details of mounted operations. He even spent a month observing assembly lines in Detroit, as the civilian sector raced to support the burgeoning war effort in the months after Pearl Harbor.

In summer 1942, Tucker and his unit trained for Operation Torch, the Allied invasion of North Africa that would take place that fall.

The best place to train for a desert invasion was the Mojave Desert in southern California, with its heat, jackrabbits, scorpions, and endangered desert tortoises. Sixty years later, Marines chose the same desert to prepare for the invasions of Afghanistan and Iraq. Tucker trained with his men for four months and left in the best physical shape he would be in for the entire war. Then on a rare, magical weekend off, he and other bachelor officers from his unit were invited to party in Beverly Hills with some celebrities, including Judy Garland. Years later, Tucker's son found pictures of that night that seemed to show Tucker had enjoyed the open bar slightly too much. Tucker requested that the photos be destroyed and he be absolved for low alcohol tolerance after months in the desert. Such invites likely escape most troops training in 29 Palms or Ft Irwin these days, yet the low alcohol tolerance excuse is still widely used.

After Tucker and his unit completed their tour of desert training in November 1942, Operation Torch kicked off and was a success, without 83rd Armored Reconnaissance Battalion or 3rd Armored Division. Tucker's orders then changed, and he prepared to go overseas to England for the eventual invasion of France, arriving less than a year later in September 1943. "Lord Haw-Haw," a US-born German propaganda radio host, welcomed 3rd Armored Division to Southampton, England, the day they landed in an impressive and seemingly successful use of psychological operations. Tucker had to laugh at the secrecy and censorship of the trip that had failed to prevent German spies from realizing who they were upon arrival. Yet perhaps Tucker laughed again at the largely innocuous work of "Lord Haw-Haw" a year and a half later when Tucker himself employed psychological operations – in his case, the use of loudspeakers and a US soldier fluent in German – to convince the Germans to surrender the town of Beckum without firing a shot. "Lord Haw-Haw" certainly was not laughing then.

Tucker and his unit trained more intensely in southern England as the date for the invasion of France approached, spending hours on the rifle range and crawling on their stomachs under barbed wire to simulate reconnaissance infiltration. Tucker also experienced some British hospitality, as many Brits were welcoming to the US combat troops from across the pond. On one occasion while being entertained with fellow officers on a horse farm by a duke who lived near their camp, Tucker attempted to make small talk by remarking, "It must be a lot of work for the groom to polish all the brass on the harnesses."

"Brass?? It's gold!" the duke said, standing straighter and turning indignantly towards his ignorant guest.

Tucker's friend and fellow 83rd Armored Reconnaissance Battalion officer kept from laughing but shared the story of the brusque American all over camp when they returned. Needless to say, Tucker did not return to the duke's farm again before the invasion.

Tucker also traveled to London and experienced some of the last vestiges of the Luftwaffe air raids that had terrorized England during the Blitzkrieg. While having tea with the family of a British officer in a flat in London, anti-aircraft guns exploded into action and shook the windows of the apartment until Tucker thought they would fall out. Tucker was certain they would head for shelter or to the Tube immediately. The sole response from Tucker's host was, "I say, old Jerry is out again tonight." They kept on with their cocktails. His host's steadfast determination to have a normal "tea" is one small example of British resilience during the German air raids, which is also captured in Sebastian Junger's *Tribe* in "War Makes You an Animal."

The D-Day invasion on June 6, 1944 left Tucker and 3rd Armored Division in England. They made final preparations for landing once the infantry had secured the beachhead. On D+6, Tucker led a small element across the Channel to Omaha Beach as the advance party for 83rd Armored Reconnaissance Battalion. Approaching the shore on a Landing Ship Tank, Tucker wondered how many men had survived the first climb to the line of German pillboxes on the cliff above the beach. Tucker surveyed the carnage of the invasion, evident in the debris left on the beach and in the surrounding area, and guessed that number was painfully low.

Tucker's foray into combat began in earnest that first evening bivouacking near Omaha Beach when his element was attacked by a German tank unit that had broken through the line. Outgunned and outmatched, he radioed the advanced headquarters element of 3rd Armored Division, who contacted fighter planes to attack the German tanks. His instant recognition of his own element's limitations and humility to ask for help saved his unit from certain destruction. Several of the men he was with were seriously injured and evacuated from the front line that morning, including the best officer he ever served with, who could never return to combat.

Adaptation and innovation were also key to the early success of Tucker's 83rd Armored Reconnaissance Battalion. The Germans had taken advantage of the many hedgerows around Normandy and used them as natural defenses to protect machine-gunners who could levy devastating fire on the advancing Allied troops. Tucker's men attached fabricated plowshares to the front of their tanks, which allowed them to burst through the defenses and attack the Germans from their flank. The Germans also employed various land mines, which could blow off a leg or a tank track, to slow the Allied advance. Tucker's men innovated once more and attached heavy chains to the tanks that would swing forward and detonate most land mines a safe distance from the tank. Tucker thought as his men faced down these first attacks from the Germans in the hedgerows: "Here were two armies whose soldiers looked like each other, whose countries were leaders in the world and who were apparently civilized, using every invention of the devil to try to kill each other." Those thoughts would remain his first impression of combat, a memory he held onto decades after the war. As 83rd Armored Reconnaissance Battalion pushed forward, his experience with combat would only sharpen and harden his perception of war's contradictions.

During the Battle of Saint-Lô in July 1944, Tucker and his men had front-row seats for what he would think would later be re-created in a Hollywood movie. The sky was blackened to almost darkness by hundreds of Allied and German aircraft. The German bombers and Allied planes caught fire and fell towards earth. The silhouettes of men stood out marked against the sky as they attempted to parachute to safety.

The early skirmishes after Normandy connected Tucker with some more British counterparts. Tucker received a warning from a British officer who had just been "put off by bit of sniping" not too far from their current location. Almost on cue, a shot from a German tank exploded near Tucker's men. Tucker had never heard of a tank shot referred to as "sniping." It seems understatement was as ubiquitous within the British military as it was among the civilians facing the Luftwaffe back home.

The push forward through France was exhausting and stretched the limits of logistical support for Tucker's tanks, jeeps, and other vehicles. Tucker, then stepping up to lead 83rd Armored Reconnaissance Battalion as battalion commander, a billet above his rank at the time, would remember the importance of keeping on the tail of the enemy when the enemy is retreating. Allowing the Germans to rest and form up in defensive positions only increased the Allied casualties in eventual attack.

Putting continuous pressure on the Germans required movement at night without lights, except a small slit of red for a taillight which allowed the column to follow each other forward. This pace of battle paid off during the Battle of Mons Pocket in September 1944, as 3rd Armored Division moved ahead of the retreating Germans and enveloped the Belgian town. Through a fierce, three-day battle, the Allies killed or captured over 30,000 German troops, including 3 German generals. At one point in the battle, Tucker had a line of his tanks on a hill with a column of Germans soldiers and a large number of horse-drawn artillery in sight. Tucker's tanks opened fire and decimated the Germans. Tucker would remember the moment of firing on man and horse, "As a former cavalryman, I remember sadness about the killing and wounding of the horses, but no sympathy for the troops who were killed. That is how hardened combat veterans react to the killing of enemy troops."

One of Tucker's tanks had been the first to enter Mons at the start of the battle. The appreciative and dutiful mayor of Mons had noted its serial number when it first pulled in. While 83rd Armored Reconnaissance Battalion and 3rd Armored Division would move on to continue the battle towards the Elbe River and Berlin, the people of Mons would not forget their liberators.

Tasked by his command at 3rd Armored Division to reconnoiter the path east from Mons, Tucker determined the safety of passage and then liberated the town of Verviers under minimal resistance. There, Tucker met a well-dressed and stately looking officer, riding in britches and boots, who identified himself as a member of the Belgian underground resistance. The officer led Tucker to a room within the town's city hall and showed him maps of German positions east of the city. Tucker then took his men to the outskirts of town and observed a column of Germans retreating to the east.

Self-Awareness Exercise – "P-47s On Station": The retreating enemy in column outside of Verviers presented Major Tucker with an opportunity to inflict significant casualties on the Germans. A swift attack would also protect his men from the further harm they would face if the Germans were allowed to make defensive positions. There were several P-47 fighter aircraft on station nearby who could attack the German column. Major Tucker had worked with some of these P-47s before and knew their competency. Standard procedure required that Major Tucker radio back to headquarters and request an attack on the German column. Major Tucker worried that the Germans would get out of range by the time the call was made to headquarters and approved. However, usurping protocol and acting without his command's approval could result in Major Tucker's relief from command. The P-47s could be required for a more significant engagement later in their flight, and this task could distract them and put others at risk. How would you analyze the situation?

An age-old lesson, the adage of "it is easier to ask for forgiveness than ask for permission" likely was on Tucker's mind in some form. Tucker radioed to the P-47s directly, using the callsign "Dixie" of a pilot that he had observed in action and asked them to conduct a strike on the fleeing Germans. When "Dixie" called back that he could not see the column, Tucker's tank marked the column with smoke. "Dixie" and his fellow pilots then decimated the German column with .50 caliber machine guns. Tucker had taken a risk to act without his command's approval, but the attack's success had proven worth the breach in protocol. Tucker's battlefield awareness, understanding the ongoing missions of adjacent units and the capabilities of his tanks and the P-47s in flight, was key to the success of his decision.

Tucker's unit then turned further east from Verviers and faced significant urban conflict in a town called Butzbach. Tucker's men used similar techniques to defeat the Germans there that Marines and soldiers would use in urban conflict in Afghanistan and Iraq: Tucker's tanks would blast holes in the buildings and the infantry would throw in grenades and clear the buildings, room by room, house by house. The work was slow and dangerous.

During this engagement, Tucker, who had been serving as battalion commander, was relieved of command of 83rd Armored Reconnaissance Battalion, since he was only a Major and had not achieved the rank of Lieutenant Colonel. 3rd Armored Division had sent down a Lieutenant Colonel to take command of the battalion, a man who faced the difficult task of taking over a successful unit in the middle of active combat. Taking an aggressive leadership posture, the new battalion commander decided to relieve one of Tucker's favorite company commanders, due to the perceived lack of discipline of the men in that company. Tucker implored that the young company commander was one of the best combat leaders in the unit but could not change the new battalion commander's perspective. The new battalion commander then asked Tucker to show him the front line at the Battle of Butzbach.

Self-Awareness Exercise – "Crossing the Street": The new battalion commander and Major Tucker were in a building that had been cleared through dangerous, house-to-house fighting. The battalion commander then turned to Major Tucker and said he would like to see from the perspective of a house across the intersection. Major Tucker responded that the houses on the far side of the intersection had not been cleared, and it would be too dangerous to attempt to cross the street without waiting for the infantry to clear ahead. The battalion commander did not see the threat and said they should move forward. Already at risk of coming off as insubordinate since he stood up aggressively for one of his company commanders, Major Tucker thought that disobeying this order could have him court-martialed, fired, and removed from the battlefield. However, walking out into the street could also mean death for him and his battalion commander. How would you analyze the situation?

This decision seemed to pain Tucker for the rest of his life, and he never knew what decision would have been right. He agreed to attempt to cross the intersection with the battalion commander. Almost immediately, a German soldier fired a submachine gun at them that missed and hit the wall behind them. Luckily, they both dove through an open door to safety in another building. The battle continued, and Tucker could never believe that the German had missed from such close range.

After Butzbach, 83rd Armored Reconnaissance Battalion continued to push east until mid-December 1944. The Battle of the Bulge, the Germans' last-ditch effort to break the Allied line, then forced Tucker's battalion into a full-scale retreat. Tucker and his men faced some of the most intense fighting at Ardennes where there was no real sense of a front line with SS Panzer tanks and SS infantry troops, the best in Hitler's army, attacking from all sides. Once reestablished in an assembly area, Tucker and his men were put back into combat almost immediately. Due to lack of manpower during the battle, Tucker was ordered to take charge of a small task-force element in part of a larger defense. Several of the elements were overrun by far superior German forces, and Tucker was forced to consolidate his men until infantry reinforcements could arrive. An infantry Lieutenant Commander, serving as reinforcement, then took control of Tucker's task force in the heat of the battle.

Tucker was then transferred to a battalion within 2nd Armored Division, where he would serve for the rest of the war. The battalion fought through the Battle of the Bulge into early January 1945, when elements of 3rd Army came up from the south and sealed off the "bulge." After a brief lull to refit men and equipment, the push to the Elbe River and Berlin continued.

At the end of March after crossing the Rhine River, Tucker and his battalion would face the challenge of liberating Beckum, a German town ostensibly defended by ardent German troops. Here after surrounding the town with his tanks, Tucker used an attached psychological operations team, like those depicted in the Rick Beyer's *Ghost Army*, to broadcast loudly into the town in German that if the Germans did not surrender, they would flatten everything. The soldier fluent in German managed to exaggerate the size of Tucker's unit. Tucker then drove into the town in one of his jeeps, unsure if he would have to take the town by force.

Tucker and his driver came across a German Major, who led the forces in Beckum. The German officer had burned the records in their headquarters and seemed to have imbibed slightly too much alcohol. Tucker tied him to the hood of the jeep and continued to drive through the town, radioing back to the psychological operations team that they could enter the town via the same road with their loudspeaker. Tucker then ordered the German Major to tell the town to surrender over the loudspeaker. Almost immediately, some of the citizens began to hang sheets out of their windows as a sign of surrender. Tucker radioed back to his headquarters that the battalion could move in and take the town without a shot.

Tucker and his driver then reconnoitered east of Beckum in his jeep where it was suspected the German forces had moved. Driving through almost complete darkness, his jeep came face-to-face with a German tank. Tucker jumped out of the jeep and lay quietly waiting for the sound of German soldiers. When he heard nothing, he jumped up to spike the German tank with a thermite grenade. After the explosion, Tucker and his driver retreated back to their defensive line. Tucker would receive the Silver Star, the US military's third highest award for valor, for his actions at Beckum.

Tucker and his men would face intense fighting less after the Battle of the Bulge, as many Germans realized the war was edging closer to its end. Tucker also had to return to Belgium after Beckum to check on the status of some damaged tanks. In this brief visit, Tucker remembered seeing a light in a window: "I saw a light in a window for the first time in almost 2 years, and it was the most beautiful sight I had ever seen. It made me think of home and the possibility that it might not be long before I would see lots of lights in windows. I suppressed my homesickness and traveled back to war."

Tucker experienced what many more would in modern war, the painful collision between feelings of home and feelings of war. Tucker returned fully to war in that moment and back to the front lines.

Only days later, Tucker would receive his second Silver Star and a Purple Heart for his actions leading the clearance of pockets of resistance outside Oschersleben.

The speed of the Allied advance to the Elbe River again surprised the Germans and allowed Tucker and his battalion to destroy an airfield and two German trains. The captured Germans from the trains said that they had thought the Allied troops were more than 100 miles farther to the west than they had been.

Tucker would witness one final moment that could be re-created in a Hollywood movie during the Battle of Magdeburg in April 1945, as planes saturated the town with bombs to soften the German defenses. With Tucker's tanks in a holding position south of the town, they watched as fighters dropped bombs on unseen ammunition depots on the outskirts of the town. The secondary explosions caused when the bombs hit live ammunition threw Tucker from his seat, even as he sat watching more than 2 miles away. The secondary explosions appeared to kill both German soldiers and civilians caught in the midst of battle. After Magdeburg fell, the Allied governments and politicians decided the Soviets would take Berlin, and most US forces would not cross the Elbe River. For Tucker, gratefully, the war was finally beginning to end.

Tucker would listen to the announcement of Victory in Europe Day on May 9, 1945 on the radio from his position west of the Elbe River. He and his men did not celebrate much at all though, because they felt they had won the war much earlier. Before heading home, Tucker was tasked to hold the US sector with his battalion and 2nd Armored Division in Berlin. The Soviets, their wary allies, had lost 80,000 more men in the fight to liberate Berlin, but they still handed over half of the city to Allied Forces. Restless Soviet soldiers would prove particularly troublesome to Tucker's men and not respect these newly created borders in a city they had fought so hard to liberate. Tucker's men reported violent and petty crimes within their sectors carried out by the Soviet troops against German civilians. Tucker went to the Soviet command center and attempted to rectify the situation but was turned away by a Soviet commander who said he had no authority to hold back his unruly Soviet troops. Tucker reported the danger of the situation to 2nd Armored Division, who cautioned him with restraint, as everyone wanted to avoid an international incident after Victory in Europe Day. Nevertheless, the order came down that US troops could defend their sector using any force necessary.

Self-Awareness Exercise – "Troops Breaching the Line": Soviet troops still attempted to breach the US line, even after Major Tucker received the order that he was authorized to use any force necessary to deter Soviet incursion. Major Tucker could pass the order to his men and allow them to shoot Soviet soldiers who broke the line. This action would prevent further disruption of the US sector and protect the German civilians from more violent crimes. Any Soviet casualties, though, could create an international incident and put two allies at odds. If Major Tucker did not pass on the order to shoot Soviet troops, the German civilians could still be terrorized by unrestrained Soviet soldiers. How would you analyze the situation?

Without much hesitation, Tucker passed on the order to his troops and told them to be prepared to fire on Soviet soldiers breaking into the US zone. One night, two Soviet soldiers attempted to breach the line. Tucker's men fired on them and wounded them, forcing them back to their own sector. There were no further Soviet attempts to break Tucker's line, and there was no strategic breakdown of the relationship between the Americans and the Soviets. Tucker likely foresaw that there would be no strategic issue between the allies due to his experience at the Soviet command center. The Soviet leaders themselves did not seem to support or control their own soldiers. This moment represents one more example of the importance of Tucker's own battlefield awareness and understanding.

Tucker would leave Berlin for redeployment camps, the first major step on the way to the US. Priority in the line to leave was given to those with more time abroad and those with decorations. Tucker had been abroad for almost two years and had received five decorations: two Silver Stars, two Bronze Stars (one with a V, meaning he received it for actions in combat), and a Purple Heart. After some boredom in the camp and an impromptu, unapproved VMI reunion in Paris, Tucker's name was called and he boarded a boat at Le Havre that arrived in Newport News, Virginia, in September 1945. Tucker was promoted to Lieutenant Colonel before picking up his discharge papers from Ft Meade, MD, the following January. When he returned to Richmond, he was greeted by his family who had long awaited him.

Tucker would marry, start a family, and follow the family tradition into law. He graduated from law school at Washington & Lee in 1949, served eight years as a representative in the Virginia House of Delegates from 1950–8, and became a judge of the Circuit Court in Richmond from 1960–80. Tucker's tenure as a judge was well respected, and he helped the state recover from Virginia Governor Harry Byrd's political machine that until 1960 had attempted to prevent integration in Virginia public schools through the court system.

In 1983, Pierre Deghaye, a resident of Mons, Belgium, wrote to the 3rd Armored Division Association and asked if John Randolph Tucker, Jr was still alive. Mons residents had worked for years with requests to the US Army to receive that first tank that had driven into Mons so they could display the tank in their museum as a monument of liberation. Almost forty years later, the resident Pierre began a search for the tank's commander and found Judge Tucker. Judge Tucker would make a trip with his wife to Mons, Belgium, and meet Pierre during a battlefield circulation sponsored by VMI in 1984. He found it funny that Pierre had not even been alive during the German occupation.

Pierre and Judge Tucker kept in touch, and Pierre invited him back in 1989 for the forty-fifth anniversary of the liberation to serve as the honored guest of the ceremony. Judge Tucker and his wife returned for the ceremony, although refusing Pierre's offer to pay for all expenses for the trip. When he arrived, to his horror, Judge Tucker saw posters up around the town with his picture in uniform that said, "Our Liberator Returns after Forty-Five Years." He laughed and enjoyed the ceremony, reminding everyone at every moment he could that his men and the rest of 3rd Armored Division and 1st Infantry Division were the real liberators.

The people of Mons brought the celebration to Richmond in 2000, since Judge Tucker had said he was too old to make the journey back to Europe. He marveled that successive generations of Belgians continued to show so much gratitude and appreciation for what the Allies had done so many years before. They paraded together one last time down the streets of Richmond, not far from where the young Tucker had watched the old Civil War veterans march on Decoration Day.

In 2014, sixty-nine years after pulling home into Newport News, Judge Tucker sat in his apartment in his retirement home in Richmond, waiting for the arrival of two young Marines who wanted to meet him. They wore Dress Blue Charlies, the recruiter's uniform in deference to the war hero he was. They asked questions about his service and his lessons in life and leadership. Judge Tucker, as ever, avoided talking about the blood and guts of war, yet before the day ended, he looked at his great-nephew and said, simply, "Don't go to war."

I smiled, somewhat confused, and said, "We'll do what we have to, Sir."

"Well then be ready. I just hope we can manage to stay out of any other dumb wars, not only while you're in service but afterwards, too."

Meanwhile, ISIS had already swept through Iraq, threatening Baghdad, and President Obama had made his speech declaring the application of the 2003 Authorization of Use of Military Force to this new enemy in a familiar country.

Two-and-a-half years later, I returned from seven months in that country. I thought my experience was light-years away from anything my great-uncle experienced at war, far removed when pain and suffering are viewed via screens and not felt in person. Still, I felt closer to him than ever, having shared the bizarre experience of life in a combat zone. Closer still, even though he had passed away a year before I deployed.

My great-uncle's advice stayed with me, and I started to realize why he said what he did. I became grateful I had only seen war indistinctly, as if through a mirror, and could not imagine the emotion of seeing war face-to-face. I only wished I could say thank you to a family member and veteran from another generation for passing on that enduring lesson of war.

I do thank him though, by passing on his advice. I don't always tell young, idealistic Marines, "Don't go to war." But I do always tell them, "Be careful what you wish for."

"Don't Go to War" Summary and Discussion Questions

P-47s on Station

Judge Tucker had a fleeting opportunity to attack retreating Germans and protect his troops from future assaults. He had to predict whether his command would support his quick decision and initiative or perceive him as brash and untrustworthy for usurping the proper channels of approval.

1. In what scenarios could you "ask for forgiveness" rather than "ask for permission"?
    a. What would you need to understand about your leadership or the people working with you?
    b. What would you need to understand about their perceptions of you?
    c. What would you need to understand about yourself?

Crossing the Street

Judge Tucker faced a difficult situation: a boss who already perceived him as insubordinate was about to make a terrible decision that would put both of them at risk. He had to decide whether the risk was enough to put his career in jeopardy by speaking up and telling his boss he was wrong.

1. In what scenarios would you have to speak up if you saw a boss, superior, friend, or colleague making a bad decision?
    a. What would you need to understand about the person you are correcting and their perception of you?
    b. What would you do if you were wrong?
    c. What if they knew something you didn't that led them to their decision?

Troops Breaching the Line

Judge Tucker had a problem defending his perimeter from unruly Soviet troops. He had to decide how forcefully he would defend his perimeter and analyze the intended and unintended consequences of that force.

1. When do you have to hold people accountable for their actions, even if that means hurting them?
2. What are the larger implications of holding someone accountable and hurting them?
3. How does this "use of force" decision compare with some of the tragic encounters between police and people of color in the past decade in the US (2010–20)?
4. Why do soldiers and law enforcement never "shoot to wound"?

Emotional Cost of War

Judge Tucker was a war hero with a flawless record of military and civilian service. He was celebrated in Europe and in the US for his role in the Second World War.

1. Why would Judge Tucker still tell me "Don't go to war" after I signed up to serve in the Marines?
2. What about war compels some people to want to serve in war and conflict?
3. In what scenarios does a country have to go to war?
4. Why do we thank war veterans for their service?

Chapter 2

YOU GOT HEART, KID

"Why do they call you Blood?"

I looked up from the solemn, pre-bout routine of wrapping my hands. I had found an empty chair to sit a few steps away from the boxing ring set up in the middle of a large plaza just outside of Harvard Yard. My opponent looked down at me. He was an early thirties, well-built man about my height, who happened to teach a section of the dreaded Harvard class "Expository Writing," or "Expos," that was mandatory for freshmen. "Just stuck I guess," I shrugged as I held a fist out to bump his. "Good luck."

We were the first match of the night, and the burgeoning crowd showed that the fight was soon to begin. Students, teachers, and tourists all came to watch amateur boxers – mostly college students save for my opponent – pound on each other for three, two-minute rounds in the season-ending exhibition of the Harvard Boxing Club.

My opponent and I had fought once or twice before that night at the YMCA in Central Square, where the club held its Saturday practices. In our last practice fight, our coach and constant match referee, Doug Yoffe, stopped us early. It was my second fight of the day, but we had only been a minute into the first round. After pushing us apart, Coach said in his thick Boston accent, "Let's save that for the people. They'll want to see that." Then as I started to leave the ring on the opposite side from my opponent, Coach stopped me and implored quietly with his fists raised to his chin, "Keep your hands up."

Years after his fighting days, Coach Yoffe was still built like a heavyweight boxer, standing about 6ft tall with a barrel of a chest and bulging biceps. He looked like he had never lost a step from when he was a title-holding amateur fighter himself. He also always seemed to have his hands in fists, bouncing at least at chest height, as if he was ready to spar at any moment. From a distance, this figure would have made him seem imposing, if he was not always the happiest person in the room. His thick Boston accent, rare to hear in the dignified halls of Harvard, also seemed to induce smiles during even mundane conversation. After I survived a body shot sparring session against him in one of my initial practices, Coach gave me what remains one of the highest compliments I have ever received: "You got heart, kid." I was hooked from that moment.

The yearly exhibition was dedicated to Kenneth Moskow, a former Harvard boxer and CIA undercover agent who had died unexpectedly two years after he left the CIA. One of Ken's brothers was there in tribute to him that night. With my headgear and gloves on, I was standing next to the ring right before Coach was going to call Ken's brother up. I had not met him, but I told him thanks and said, "Your brother's really an inspiration to me." He made a face like he was sick to his stomach, and I wondered what I had said. He then jumped up in the ring, introduced the fight, and my walk-on music – "All of the Lights" by Kanye West – started playing. My opponent walked on to a recording of his son playing cello. Even in that intense moment, I remember thinking, "This guy is a pretty badass dad."

Squash teammates and friends were chanting variations of "Blood! Blood! Blood!," "Let's go, Jay!," and "We hate Expos!" as the fight began. That excitement turned into me catching a clean left hook seconds into the fight and tripping over as I tried to catch myself. I popped up, and Coach stared in my eyes to check to see if I was OK. I knew what he was thinking and pulled my hands up. I slowed down for the rest of the first round and landed a few punches. I then knocked down my opponent once in the second round and once in the third. We did not actually keep score, but I counted that as a win.

The semester ended a few weeks after the fight, and I returned home to Baltimore. I was resting and preparing for Marine Corps Officer Candidate School in Quantico, Virginia. I prioritized working out, seeing close friends, and learning how to make a bed with hospital corners from my mom in the days leading up to leaving. On one of my last nights, my dad told me he had an old childhood friend who was coming over to visit. I remembered the name Toby Finney as my dad's friend who had served in Vietnam, but I had only met him as a child. Coming home after seeing one of my friends for dinner, I walked down into the basement where Toby and my dad were catching up. Toby jumped up from the couch to shake my hand when I walked in.

"Here's the boxer and soon-to-be Marine! You'll need boxing in the Marines. I had to have my head on a swivel in the Army. And mostly because of other Americans."

Toby and my dad grew up a few houses down from each other in Roland Park on the north side of Baltimore City in the late 1950s and 1960s. They balanced their time racing make-shift go-karts through alleyways and joyriding in borrowed cars down to Washington DC, mostly for the lower drinking age.

Toby was two years older than my dad and not a classmate. He spurned the private-school tradition of his family and most of the neighborhood kids to attend City, a public school, in east Baltimore. When he graduated from City with no desire to attend college in 1968, he had much different decision than my college-bound father would two years later.

Toby decided to enlist for a three-year tour of duty rather than wait to be drafted and consequently followed a different family tradition into military service. His dad had been a Marine who served in the Pacific theater during the Second World War. While Judge Tucker was leading his armored reconnaissance battalions across France into Germany, Toby's dad was fighting island-to-island against the Japanese from the Philippines to Japan. That island-hopping campaign forced Toby's dad to face horrors similar to what Judge Tucker experienced in Europe. The deaths in the Pacific theater in single battles spanning months like Iwo Jima (6,140) and Okinawa (12,520) surpass the entire US death total from the eight-year Iraq War (4,505).

Toby's dad never spoke about the war or much at all of his time in the military. After Toby's own experience in Vietnam, he would think the ones who had it the worst at war never spoke about it. Still, Toby was joining a proud line of Finney men who had served their country in the military, including his father, a grandfather who served in the First World War, and an older cousin Reddy Finney who served in the Korean War in the precursor to the Navy SEALs.

In spring 1968, Toby's decision to serve was more nuanced than the decisions of his relatives. The anti-war movement was strengthening around the country. The draft was increasing once again and pulling more young men into forced service. Violent resistance to the civil rights movement was revealing the worst aspects of racism in the US, and Martin Luther King, Jr's assassination in April two months before Toby's high-school graduation made any real progress seem overly optimistic.

Anti-Vietnam fervor was understandable. For the first time in a major US conflict, US media could broadcast images and videos from the front line that showed the horrors of war to the average American. Film could be developed in Japan and flown within days to the US. Photographer Larry Burrows shot and published, in the same month, his famous, emotive photographs of Marines wounded and killed in battle in *LIFE Magazine* in October 1966. Images like these and accompanying stories filled the nightly news. By 1968, media reporting of the war also turned largely pessimistic. Never before had an ongoing war been seen so clearly by a US public in nearly real time.

US politicians also struggled to communicate how we ended up at war in Vietnam and why it needed to continue. The Vietnam War was a complex consequence of foreign-policy decisions that started with the bifurcation of Berlin, the borders Judge Tucker had to defend from the Soviets. The Cold War began in earnest in those final days of the Second World War, as the US and Soviet Union squared off as competing superpowers in the post-war world order. Like Berlin, the world divided into west and east, capitalism and socialism, competing world views that drove competition and conflict.

The greatest threat to world stability in the post-war years was direct conflict between the US and the Soviet Union. Stanley Kubrick's *Dr. Strangelove: Or How I Stopped Worrying and Learned to Love the Bomb* depicts the world in 1964 on the brink of nuclear disaster, mocking the trivial advantages the two world powers seek over the other that push them to mutual destruction. That palpable societal fear of nuclear war is familiar in 2022. The potential use of tactical nuclear weapons by Russia in its ongoing invasion and occupation of Ukraine, while unlikely, represents a global existential threat. Nuclear war over Taiwan with China remains a more distant threat, yet further escalations in summer and fall of 2022 portend the continued need to maintain dialogue and encourage diplomatic over military solutions to conflict. The hope is that these fears will remain only fears as well.

Indirect conflicts between the US and the Soviet Union, like the Vietnam War, would represent the most active and damaging manifestations of the Cold War. These confrontations were born from the policy of "containment" meant to stymie Soviet expansionism through focused encouragement of fellow capitalist governments. However, the father of the "containment" policy, career diplomat George Kennan, did not call specifically for bellicose action in his writing of "The Long Telegram," the document that first introduced the ideas which would become known as "containment" to US government leaders.

Kennan was the Chief of Mission, or Chargé d'Affaires, in Moscow when he sent his superiors in the State Department his vision for countering the burgeoning Soviet influence after the Second World War. It was February 1946, only a month after Judge Tucker received his discharge papers returning home from Europe. If the US did not lead with a stable, secure, and prosperous vision for world governments to follow, Kennan warns the Soviet Union would, which would challenge the global standing of capitalism overall. Kennan concludes, though, "to solve internal problems of our own society" would be a "diplomatic victory" greater than any foreign-policy achievement. Kennan knew war abroad would not prevent or solve persistent problems at home.

In spring 1950, Paul Nitze, President Truman's Director of Policy Planning at the State Department, cautiously theorized when the "containment" policy could justify warfare. Nitze wrote National Security Council Paper 68 (NSC-68) to communicate a clear vision of the country's national security policy in the face of Soviet expansionism. President Truman accepted Nitze's vision as the official government policy, even though at the time it was classified as top secret. On possibility of war with the Soviet Union or other socialist states, Nitze writes, "The resort to force … is therefore a difficult and dangerous act for a free society, which is warranted only in the face of even greater dangers. The necessity of the act must be clear and compelling."

The first "clear and compelling" case for the use of force in the Cold War came later that summer in June 1950, when communist North Korea invaded South Korea. In defeat after the Second World War, the Japanese Empire had withdrawn and ended thirty-five years of occupation of the Korean Peninsula. Soviet and US forces quickly divided the peninsula at the 38th parallel into two states: the north supported by the Soviet Union and the south supported by the US. The previously unified peninsula lasted only four years divided before North Korea attempted its re-unification.

President Truman led an effort through the United Nations to respond with force to repel the North Korean invasion. Over the 3-year war, over 1.5 million US men were drafted into the military, and 54,246 would lose their lives. In July 1953, the war ended under the leadership of former Allied Commander President Eisenhower, and the 38th parallel between North and South Korea was re-instated. "Containment" had maintained the global status quo at a costly price.

The intervening years between Korea and Vietnam were the years of childhood and adolescence for Toby and my dad. The draft continued in peacetime, but being drafted into military service did not seem like too much more than a short delay on the way to a normal life. When Toby and my dad became teenagers, that vision of normal life felt more likely to be disrupted.

In 1964, US leaders decided there was another "clear and compelling" case for war, this time in the South China Sea. France had lost its war in Indochina in 1954, and the former colony split into North and South

Vietnam on the 17th parallel. The US supported South Vietnam, the democratic, capitalist state thought to buffer communism's advance from China and the Soviet Union through Southeast Asia. On an intelligence mission supporting South Vietnam in the Gulf of Tonkin in August 1964, the USS *Maddox* was attacked by North-Vietnamese torpedo boats. There were no US casualties from the attack. President Johnson, less than a year removed from President Kennedy's assassination and three months away from facing election, would then galvanize support to bring the US into another war.

That war brought Toby into boot camp or basic training in the summer of 1968. The war was at a turning point. A surprise attack by the North Vietnamese during Tet, the Vietnamese new year in January and February of 1968, made victory seem both more costly and less likely than originally imagined. The Soviet Union had been increasing its economic and military support for North Vietnam and aimed to make the war as costly and damaging for the US as possible. For Toby though, all he knew was that he was going, in one way or another.

Toby's primary focus was training, both physically and with a rifle. He and his fellow recruits held on to the mantra, "The more you sweat in training, the less you bleed in war." Toby would credit his training from his instructors in basic training, hardened combat veterans themselves, with saving his life in Vietnam.

Physical training in basic training often took the form of hand-to-hand fighting, and the pugilistic art Toby would enjoy the most: boxing. Toby's only experience with boxing had been sparring with his father as a teenager, mostly for their casual entertainment. In the first boxing tournament of basic training, Toby's drill instructor chose him to represent his training platoon. More than 200 recruits and instructors circled around the ring for the event, hoping to see their platoon take home the victory. Toby's drill instructor gave him the short, motivational speech of "Don't lose or I will kill you" before pushing him into the ring.

Toby did not lose. The crowd's cheers when the referee waved off the match and moved to protect Toby's staggering opponent stayed with him for the rest of his life. The elation he felt both for himself and his platoon brought about a deep admiration for boxing. Boxing also started to build a sense of self-confidence he would rely on throughout his time in the military and beyond.

A natural teammate, Toby melded effortlessly into the team atmosphere of initial military training. He helped build up his fellow recruits when they were struggling and made friends who would follow him through the Army. The best friend he made was Danny, who enlisted not too far away from Toby in western Maryland. Danny and Toby's friendship would evolve and grow through many hours standing post and patrolling together in Vietnam more than a year later.

His success as a teammate also precipitated his success as an individual. Proficiency in the boxing ring helped him score well on the physical aspects of training, like running, hiking, and obstacle courses. Toby also developed specific skill for marksmanship on the M14 rifle and weapons handling overall.

Scoring well at basic training gave Toby different paths he could follow for his next two-and-a-half years in the Army. His instructors showed pride in the growth they had seen in him in the few short months of training and wanted to guide him into a good career, or at very least a good enlistment. Toby knew the decision he made would define his time in the Army and in Vietnam. To Toby, the decision felt like the first he faced with life-and-death consequences.

Self-Awareness Exercise – "Ticket to Ranger School": PV2 Toby Finney had two primary options leaving basic training: attempt the Army's elite Army Ranger School in Ft Benning, Georgia, or attend a heavy equipment operators' course through the Army Corps of Engineers in Ft Belvoir, Virginia. Toby's instructors pressured him to attempt Ranger School, both for the honor and the growth that would come in earning that qualification. Toby was clear-eyed about his future though and thought he did not want to make a career in the Army. The choice he knew would define his job in the Army and his potential role in Vietnam. How would you analyze the situation?

Toby analyzed the situation pragmatically and was not overly fatalistic. He knew much of the path that could lead him to Vietnam and combat was out of his control, regardless of the job he chose. Toby focused on what was most important to him – and that was his life and career beyond the Army. Toby chose to attend the heavy equipment operators' course because he thought it could help him find a job in construction or engineering once he returned home.

Toby knew he let down his instructors with his decision, and soon after he began his next course, he realized he let himself down too. When deciding, Toby had had difficulty knowing how much he should listen to the guidance of more experienced mentors, his instructors at basic training, over his own instincts to plan for his future after the Army. He realized his instructors had seen a drive in him that he had not seen in himself; his gut instinct had been wrong because he had not been able to see himself clearly. Toby chose the easier path and regretted his missed opportunity for further growth.

That regret followed Toby to Germany where he put his heavy equipment certification to work in the distinguished role of a trash and ammunition hauler. Every day, Toby loaded cargo, drove around tractor trailers, and wondered what he would have learned patrolling in the woods and jumping out of airplanes near Ft Benning, Georgia. Luckily, Toby found more time for boxing, which kept him in shape and away from some of the dangerous distractions of heavy drinking and drugs that were prevalent among soldiers on base.

Only a few months into his time in Germany, Toby learned his orders changed: he was assigned as a year-long augment to Vietnam and would depart in less than a month. Toby relished the opportunity to leave his stagnant role in Germany. He knew he would make the best of whatever challenges were ahead for him in Vietnam. After a short leave with family and friends back home in Baltimore, Toby boarded a plane and started a long journey to Quy Nhon in South Vietnam in October 1969.

Toby's first ride on a Chinook helicopter up the coast of South Vietnam on the way to Quy Nhon did not give him much of an idea of the landscape, but he had seen enough pictures of the Vietnamese jungle to know what was ahead of him. Camp Granite, a large, built-up Army base about 300 miles south of the border between North and South Vietnam, was going to be Toby's new home. Upon arrival, he started adjusting to its heat, humidity, and pervasive smell of decomposing trash.

The morning after his arrival, he learned he was assigned to a new role once again: an 11-Bravo or basic infantryman. Part of this job entailed manning guard posts on the perimeter of the base, sitting as targets in the night for any enemy attack. The more active role required him to conduct patrols in the jungle to gain intelligence on enemy positions and prevent the enemy from staging any larger attacks on the base. When Toby learned of his new job, the regret of not taking on the more advanced training of Ranger School hit him one more time. The sight of a body bag off-loaded from a helicopter in those initial days at Camp Granite added gravity to that regret.

In South Vietnam, the enemy was an insurgent force known as the Viet Cong, or VC. The VC generally staged small-scale, hit-and-run attacks aiming to wound or kill as many Americans and troops as possible without having to face US firepower directly. Toby spent his nights on post scanning through the dark for a VC surprise attack and his days on patrol looking for any indicators of VC attack staging areas.

Toby experienced his first major VC attack after only a few weeks of settling into his post and patrolling routine. The attack started just after sunset. Toby had been in between guard shifts and was in a makeshift latrine when the first mortars started blowing up around him. He immediately sprinted to the nearest bunker before an explosion lifted him into the air and sent him flying headfirst towards the bunker. He came to in the bunker with another bunker inhabitant politely telling him to pull up his pants. The attack then ended as quickly as it had started. Toby was injured by shrapnel and his headfirst dive across gravel into the bunker, but he spent the night helping rebuild the base defenses and tending to the wounded. In the morning after all the more serious casualties were treated, a medic pulled wood and metal shards out of Toby's side.

In subsequent weeks, patrols pushed farther away from base to disrupt potential VC staging areas. On one of these patrols, Toby and his small team came across a hamlet in a small clearing hidden in the dense jungle. Some women and children milled about between the group of several huts, ignoring the patrol's approach. The absence of young men served as a warning sign for potential support for the VC. Intelligence reporting also told them hamlets in this area were used to stage for attacks like the one that wounded Toby's side. The patrol moved to surround the village and begin a detailed search. Toby would remember the scene as idyllic if it had not been for the rifles and gear he and his fellow soldiers were carrying.

As they approached the hamlet, Toby heard screaming coming from one of the huts. He and another soldier moved forward cautiously to investigate. Inside, they saw a woman giving birth and another woman tending to her. The juxtaposition of life and death in a war zone made the idyllic scene in the clearing feel even more bizarre. After a brief, inconclusive search of the hamlet, Toby's patrol left the scene largely as they had found it.

Not every patrol was as innocuous for Toby in those first few months. Sometimes, they were tasked to search hamlets more thoroughly, which caused more disruption to civilian life. Toby felt demoralized when he would have to rummage through sacks of rice and personal possessions for weapons, find nothing, and then look in the eyes of the Vietnamese whose lives he upended.

Returning from these more disruptive patrols also made them a target for hasty VC attacks. One such time, Toby's patrol got hit in an ambush near a suspected VC supply line. After returning fire and dissipating the attack, Toby's patrol started to tend to their own wounded. They only had one serious casualty – a man from Alabama who had often ranted to anyone who would listen about how great the segregationist policies were in the American South. A Black medic from Texas stabilized him and prepared him for casualty evacuation. Toby wondered if the Alabama man would see the world differently when he got home.

After two months as an 11-Bravo, Toby received orders that shifted him back to a role as a heavy equipment operator. He was tasked to help set up austere fire bases out in the jungle for other units, whether US, South Korean, or South Vietnamese. Toby's work with bulldozers and other heavy machinery would allow them to create firing platforms for artillery.

A smaller, more austere base meant less amenities, more guard duty, and more patrols. However, this type of working environment generally required the troops to be more professional, which was a welcome change for Toby. Toby created meaningful relationships with like-minded people away from the petty crime, drugs, and meaningless fights that were common on the built-up bases.

Toby quickly learned to appreciate the dedication and intensity of the South Korean soldiers, known as the "ROKs" for Republic of Korea, that he worked with on an ascetic firebase closer to the border between North and South Vietnam. The ROKs had a work ethic that the average US soldier did not come close to matching. From the ROKs, Toby also learned a new fighting style to complement his boxing: hapkido, a Korean martial art. A ROK friend described to Toby how the hapkido principles of awareness and decisiveness force opponents into unfavorable decisions. Toby learned how these principles also applied in combat by observing, orienting, deciding, and acting faster than the enemy. Toby started to feel steadier on patrol and in combat with this new training from the ROKs. Although built from different origins, John Boyd's Observe-Orient-Decide-Act (OODA) Loop became standard military doctrine in the years following Vietnam with the same goal: to make US troops calmer and more decisive under fire.

The professionalism of the ROKs was evident in all facets of warfare. After a sporadic attack on the firebase from the VC, the ROKs tended to their wounded and began to search the firebase's perimeter. In their search, they found three wounded enemy soldiers. Toby saw one as he was brought on base and knew he could not be more than 15 years old. The ROK commander ensured that all three received proper medical treatment before being transferred off their firebase to higher headquarters.

Toby's firebase with the ROKs had been positioned specifically to interdict the North Vietnamese Army, or NVA, who were thought to use nearby passage lines to travel deeper into South Vietnam. The NVA were "regulars" and fought with better equipment longer and harder than the VC insurgents Toby faced back at Camp Granite. This tangible NVA threat attracted more intelligence-collection assets and specially trained troops to the firebase, including one sniper Toby came to know well named Vance.

Vance was both the most easygoing and impressive soldier Toby ever met. He was never in uniform, spoke Vietnamese fluently, and had already dedicated almost three years of his life to the war in Vietnam. His constant humility, despite his obvious proficiency, knowledge, and accolades, was the lasting quality Toby remembered above anything else.

Toby and Vance's relationship would be tested and strengthened under fire. One night, Toby and Vance were sitting with some ROK counterparts when the firebase was attacked with heavy and steady volleys of rocket-propelled grenades (RPGs). Vance grabbed Toby immediately and led him to cover near the perimeter where they could safely return fire. Vance attached a night scope onto his sniper rifle and began scanning the jungle. He took several shots and then instructed Toby to fire at a specific patch of trees in the dark. Toby trusted his orders and began firing. Vance then took several more well-aimed shots just to the right of where Toby fired. The attack then dissipated, and quiet returned in the night. In the morning, they searched the perimeter and found several dead enemy soldiers where Vance had taken his shots. Vance's leadership and Toby's trust in him under pressure were critical in defense of the firebase.

Toby continued his work constructing and fortifying austere firebases throughout spring and into early summer 1970. He would return only briefly for days at a time to the built-up bases outside of Quy Nhon in between missions. Then in late summer with only two months left in Vietnam, Toby was surprised to learn he was changing roles once again. Promoted to sergeant, Toby was ordered to lead safer duties in camp logistics. Outside of short security patrols, he would not leave the base. While disappointed at first, Toby was happy he would spend more time with Danny, who was on base with him finishing out a year-long tour as well.

Danny and Toby jived well as natural friends. They balanced professional and jovial natures, both committed to fixing cultural problems they saw on base and enjoying the humorous moments they could make out of the bizarre world they lived in. The day Toby was leaving to start the journey back home, Danny surprised him by saying he had signed on for another tour.

Self-Awareness Exercise – "The Door Gunner": As Toby prepared to leave Vietnam, Toby's close friend Danny told him he had decided to sign up for six additional months as a door gunner. His new role, taken mostly for the extra money, would start in the weeks after Toby left. Toby was shocked his friend would put himself in such danger. He only had moments with his friend before he would leave Vietnam. Toby wanted to communicate to Danny all of the competing emotions he felt about his decision, but he did not know how his friend would respond. How would you analyze the situation?

Toby could not hold back his initial anger at Danny. Danny only responded by getting defensive and angry himself. Toby realized quickly that he would not change his friend's mind. Danny only wanted Toby to respect his decision, even if Toby would not approve. During their goodbye, Toby gave him that respect. Toby boarded the helicopter out of base, sick to his stomach that he was leaving his friend behind.

Toby returned home in October 1970 to a country that had become wholly negative to the war. The atrocities committed by US soldiers during the My Lai Massacre in spring 1968 had become public knowledge by fall 1969. Four students had been killed during an anti-war protest at Kent State in May 1970. Neil Young's song "Ohio" was released a month later that June and memorializes the four dead and sings that the war "should have been done long ago."

President Nixon slowly acquiesced to the anti-war movement. The draft reached its final minor peak in 1968 and would continue to decline until the last 646 men were drafted in 1973. The last US troops left Vietnam that spring. The South Vietnamese capital Saigon would fall to the NVA a year later in 1974. "Containment" had failed at a costly price.

Toby spent his last five months in the military away from the war and its politics. He joined the Army's top boxing team while stationed in El Paso and won fights against some of the best boxers in the country, including one who had been on the direct path to the 1972 Olympic Trials. Toby received his honorable discharge and began a slow transition away from the military and the war that had come to define his adult life.

Shortly after arriving back to his parents' house in Baltimore, he received a letter from Danny's parents. He had been killed in action, providing supporting fire for his fellow soldiers from his post as a door gunner. Toby spent the first of many long nights alone thinking about his friend and the moment he left him behind in Vietnam.

Toby would take on several different jobs in Baltimore over the next two decades. His experience behind bulldozers and trucks did help him with brief stints in construction jobs, but he searched for more meaningful employment. He found work as a farmhand on a horse farm out in Baltimore County that seemed to fit his love for the outdoors and his diligent work ethic. Toby passed many meaningful years of his life with large, beautiful animals that did not judge him for his past or where he had been.

Eventually, Toby would marry, move to Florida, and raise a family. His sons became the pride of his life, a pride embodied by the thought if he could be anything in life, at least he would be a good dad. With his sons starting college, he made excuses to travel and found his way back to Baltimore. On a free night in May, Toby called my dad and asked him if he had any time to catch up.

In the basement that night, Toby, my dad, and I talked together in front of a blank television screen that was never turned on. I sat in a chair on the corner of the L-shaped blue basement couch across from Toby and faced him directly as he talked about his experience in the Army and at war. My dad sat in between us, mostly listening and laughing whenever the exploits of their childhood came up.

Toby talked more about boxing and only spoke briefly about what he did in Vietnam. He said that he was just another 11-Bravo and "hippy on a bulldozer" for one long year. He spoke wistfully about being in "the boonies" away from the built-up bases and the stunning sight of the west coast of the US out the window of the plane on his way home. He was more focused on me and my future in the Marines than he was on himself. After I told him enough of where I was headed, Toby said, "At least you won't be a door gunner."

I did not know what he meant at the time, but my dad seemed to. Toby had not spoken that night about losing Danny. I just pictured the crazy door gunner in *Full Metal Jacket* and laughed. "Definitely not. Luckily."

Toby did not respond, and I felt as if I had missed the point he was making. I waited for him to say more. "My dad, the Marine," he gestured towards me. "He once told me that people change but not that much. I think that's utter bullshit. If you can come to terms with yourself and what you've done, change will happen. That's what I've been trying to do, all these years later."

My dad, Toby, and I then sat in silence for what felt like minutes. I got up to leave and thanked Toby for sharing some of his experience with me. Toby stood up to shake my hand then too. My dad smiled at his son and his childhood friend from the couch.

"Takes heart to want to join in the middle of the war," Toby said as we shook hands.

"Well, I think the war is easier these days than it was in your time."

Toby shook his head, looked away, and then stared back at me.

"We'll see."

"You Got Heart, Kid" Summary and Discussion Questions

Clear and Compelling

The decisions to go to war in Korea and Vietnam are often compared as related attempts to stymie Soviet expansionism. Still, both Kennan and Nitze argued the best defense against Soviet expansionism was a strong, vibrant, and prosperous society at home. War should have remained a last resort.

1. When did the US have a "clear and compelling" reason for foreign intervention in the twentieth century or the early twenty-first century and decide not to intervene?
2. When does a foreign-policy issue become more pressing than a domestic problem at home?
3. Nitze writes in NSC-68, "[War] is also an act which cannot definitively end the fundamental conflict in the realm of ideas." Societies in the post-war years had a choice between liberty and authoritarianism, unsteady democracy and promised stability, similar to the choice governments face today. If war cannot end the conflict between these ideas, what can?

Ticket to Ranger School

After excelling in basic training, Toby had the choice to attempt the elite Army Ranger School or attend a heavy equipment operators' course with the Army Corps of Engineers. Toby chose the easier path – heavy equipment operators' course – because he thought it would help him get a job in construction or engineering after the Army. He would regret not seeking the challenge and growth of Ranger School.

1. How do you balance following gut instincts and taking advice from people you trust?
2. As a mentor, when is it permissible to be forceful with advice when you see someone taking a path you do not agree with?
3. John Wooden, renowned UCLA basketball coach, once said, "Things turn out best for the people who make the best of the way things turn out." How did Toby move past his regret and make the best of the way things turned out?

The Door Gunner

The day Toby was leaving Vietnam, his close friend from basic training, Danny, surprised him with news that he had signed on for an additional tour as a door gunner. Toby was overcome by emotion at the thought of his friend putting himself at such unnecessary risk and wanted to change his mind. He realized quickly that all his friend wanted was for him to respect his decision. Danny was killed in action several months later, leaving Toby only with memories of their time together and this difficult last goodbye.

1. As a friend, when is it permissible to be forceful with advice when you see someone taking a path you do not agree with?
2. What are effective methods to change a friend's mind (or a boss's or a subordinate's)?
3. What are effective methods to grieve a lost friend or loved one?

Chapter 3

IT'S YOUR TURN NOW, FUCKER

I remember staring awestruck at the air-traffic control tower at Kuwait City International Airport. It was September 2016, and I had just landed on my first deployment, knowing that Kuwait was a stopover for my ultimate destination in Western Iraq. The War Against ISIS, starting in earnest in 2014, was at a turning point with some of the most intense fighting ahead in Northern and Western Iraq. As I stood with my fellow Marines in the dark, something about the tower's seemingly alien shape made me pause and wonder about the new world I was about to enter.

It was there waiting in the outdoor hangar for the bus to a military airfield that I saw the words scribbled on the door of a port-a-john, "Ha Ha, it's your turn now, fucker." I smiled and laughed and snapped a photo with my cell phone. I guess it is my turn, I thought. But I guessed my turn would be somewhat different.

The path that led me to my turn in the Middle East felt like it winded more for me than for others. A good story would say I knew I needed to be in the military as I grew up in the shadow of 9/11. A better story would say I knew I needed to be in the military when my usually reticent granddad gave me some Australian coins he collected during the Second World War. He had opened up in a rare moment that day to tell me how much his service meant to him. A worse story would say I just wanted to be like some of my friends from high school, who were applying to military academies. All these stories are true.

Once I started exploring the path through Reserve Officer Training Corps in college, it quickly became a need, not a want. A want I could turn away from, I could forget, I could ignore. A need bit at me, gnawed at me, and turned the most banal sounds and moments into deep pain, regret, and what ifs. Like the sound of the 1 Bus arriving in Harvard Square, disturbing my sleep in the darkest part of the night, as if asking, "Why aren't you getting up and heading back to ROTC?"

Truth is I was scared. I woke in the middle of the night and heard that bus slam to a stop and wondered and questioned and felt my stomach move horizontally to my feet. Night after night, I stared at the ceiling and mulled my decision – to apply for Army medical school and drop ROTC – paralyzed by fear and doubt.

I was scared I did not actually want to be a doctor. I was scared I would ditch Army med school like I dropped ROTC. But what I was really scared of was failing, failing at Marine Corps Officer Candidate School, the only uncertain path ahead. Once I realized that was my main fear, I had to go. I owed it to my parents and my sisters not to be afraid.

But that's not a good story. And that still left me to question what I was looking for. When I got to Quantico for Officer Candidate School, that search became simpler: at one memorable point, all I was looking for was a rifle.

"Good morning, Staff Sergeant. Candidate Brooks requests permission to speak to Sergeant Instructor Staff Sergeant Martin, good morning, Staff Sergeant!"

"WHAT!!"

"This candidate can't find his rifle."

"WELL, FIND IT!!"

I ran back downstairs in the barracks to search where we had been organizing gear after a training event out in the woods. No rifle. I saw where I had placed it and then turned my back. No rifle.

"Good morning, Staff Sergeant. Candidate Brooks requests …"

"WHAT!!"

"This candidate still can't find his rifle."

"You mean, THIS ONE??"

Staff Sergeant Martin pulled the rifle from behind his back and dangled it in front of my face, one fist closed around the barrel of the weapon, the other placed menacingly at his side. The 6ft 5in, well-built Marine stared at me and laughed with a maniacal smile, as I reached to grab my weapon from him.

"ESSAY! Weapon accountability!"

Relieved, I took the rifle and accepted my essay punishment, as if my acceptance meant anything. Essays were the typical punishment for more serious offenses at Officer Candidate School. Offending candidates had to write 300-word essays in perfect naval letter format, a format which made more sense for a typewriter. To ensure the essay had 300 words exactly, every word over three letters was underlined and numbered from 1 to 300. The format encouraged creative use of articles and prepositions in closing sentences.

I wrote an essay about the Iceman, found in the Alps, who lost his bow and arrow and was shot in the back. Another story which is only a story. I closed with a lesson in history – that the Germans destroyed the British in the First World War because they had "weapon accountability" over their superior machine guns, a historical fact I would have trouble finding sources for.

A week later, as we stepped off on our culminating hike of the first half of Officer Candidate School, I heard Staff Sergeant Martin yelling in the back. I was in the front, about to lead the hike as platoon guide. "WHERE'S BROOKS AT?"

"Here, Staff Sergeant."

"You wrote the essay about the weapons? That was a good read. Not like the rest of you jokers. With your trash essays."

I smiled in the dark, a rare action in the previous five weeks, and turned to my platoon mate Antonio who was shaking his head and smiling back at me. I would continue to train with Antonio for the following three years, and we would have many more hours together hiking, patrolling, and rope-climbing as we attempted to earn our role as Marine infantry officers. He would become one of my closest friends. We did not know that then though. We started to hike back into the woods and humidity. So went my only moment of not failing at my first run of OCS, a strange concept for someone who feared failure from the start.

I returned the next summer and failed only slightly less. At the end of that six weeks, a burly Marine Gunnery Sergeant pressed an Eagle, Globe, and Anchor into my palm. The winding path then took a point, like a compass, and seemed to turn with all its energy to the east to the wars of my generation. My turn seemed inevitable, and I sought it, with everything I had.

Yet, the truth of the question remained: I did not know what I was searching for. I knew war only from Hollywood, and Hollywood paints a different picture of war than reality, the reality Judge Tucker hoped to warn me of. With friends not too long after receiving my EGA, I watched *Lone Survivor* in theaters, the story of four Navy SEALs compromised during a reconnaissance mission and their fight against the Taliban to escape. LT Mike Murphy, the leader of the element, is killed calling for extract for his men, sacrificing himself so that he could save them, a true story for which he received the Medal of Honor, the military's highest award for valor. Hollywood depicts this tragic moment with moving music, idyllic views over a valley in Afghanistan, and the motivating last words from Mike Murphy to his teammate Marcus Luttrell: "Marcus, you're never out of the fight."

Months before the movie's release, Marcus Luttrell, the only Navy SEAL to survive that mission, sat down with Anderson Cooper on *60 Minutes* and described the moment when his best friend Mike Murphy died:

> [Murphy] started to crawl left. And I was out in the open, waving my hands. I was like just come down to me. That's all I wanted him to do, was just come down to me. And, uh, I heard his gun go off, and a lot of gunfire in his area. I was trying with everything I had to get to him. And he, uh, he started screaming my name. He was like, "Marcus, man, you gotta help me. I need help, Marcus." And it got so intense that I actually put my weapon down and covered my ears, 'cause I couldn't stand to hear him die. All I wanted him to do was stop screaming my name. And, uh, they killed him. And I put my weapon down in a gunfight, while my best friend was getting killed, so that pretty much makes me a coward.

I found that interview only as I taught and tried to communicate to my class a clear, unadorned picture of war and trauma. I wanted to show them something different than Hollywood. I wanted to show them the true pain, loss, and suffering that is omnipresent in war. A younger version of myself probably could have used that same reinforcement before heading into the command center in Iraq.

War isn't moving music; although when I sat with my radio operator and spontaneously broke out into "Teenage Dirtbag," we felt more moved than we had in weeks. War isn't idyllic views; although the desert sunsets from the roof of the medical center and minarets in town squares I saw only via drone feed might stay with me as some of the most beautiful things I'll ever see. War isn't motivating words; although I might have gotten lucky every now and then, I was more likely to stumble telling a Marine we should be proud to be in Iraq during Christmas and have him look at me and say, "You alright, Sir?" "Thanks for asking."

At its most fundamental level, war is death, and every death is tragedy, young or old, rich or poor, guilty or innocent. It took me time to admit that seeing that tragedy through my experiences in the video game of modern war had affected me. The moment I should have known I could not hide any more was when my heart beat out of my chest in a classroom in San Antonio, Texas. The topic of discussion was civilian casualties, and I was thrust back to deployment two years prior with its turbulency, confusion, and pain in full color.

Slowly more open to what I experienced, I realized that feeling pain from observing death and trauma is not an experience saved only for those who went to war. A great friend and mentor, Marcus Williams, who is the focus of Chapter 13, said to me once, "Coming home from war, you might have experienced the same level of trauma as someone who was in a bad car accident."

Michael McNamara, founder of the concept "Post-Traumatic Winning," takes that concept even further, writing that, "We're not unique because we've lived through a traumatic event. Most people do at some point in their lives. . . . Trauma is Trauma is Trauma. The source of trauma ultimately doesn't matter."

Observing harm to others can manifest as moral injury, a related but distinct concept from Post-Traumatic Stress Disorder (PTSD). Experiencing physical trauma, at war, in a car crash, or due to assault, is commonly thought of as the cause of fear, flashbacks, numbness, and anxiety associated with PTSD. However, observing trauma, without experiencing physical harm or danger personally, can provoke feelings of guilt and blame that result in similar symptoms.

The list of questions in the table below, taken from the Department of Veterans Affairs National Center for PTSD, is the primary screening tool to diagnose PTSD. A score of three or higher defines "probable" PTSD. "In the last month, have you …":

1.	Had nightmares about the event(s) or thought about the event(s) when you did not want to?	YES	NO
2.	Tried hard not to think about the event(s) or went out of your way to avoid situations that reminded you of the event(s)?	YES	NO
3.	Been constantly on guard, watchful, or easily startled?	YES	NO
4.	Felt numb or detached from people, activities, or your surroundings?	YES	NO
5.	Felt guilty or unable to stop blaming yourself or others for the event(s) or any problems the event(s) may have caused?	YES	NO
	Total score is sum of YES responses in items 1–5	**TOTAL SCORE**	

Notably, this screening tool does not differentiate between physical and moral injury. Such differentiation may only be necessary to determine proper treatment and therapy. The lasting symptoms of experiencing physical trauma can persist too due to moral injury, scars of regret and guilt for the physical trauma experienced. Moral injury may be missed in this screening, but it also may be indistinguishable from PTSD.

The concept of moral injury still improves understanding of experiences of trauma. Volunteers of America, through its Shay Moral Injury Center founded in 2017, has led at the forefront to promote resources for healing moral wounds. One of the therapies the Center suggests is to write a poem or story about the experience. If I had known that or been more self-aware, I would have started writing immediately after I returned from Iraq in 2017. In some ways like many others, I learned the hard way, not understanding or appreciating the effects of my experiences.

Learning the "hard way," without properly healing from PTSD or moral injury, can cause trauma to surface at the worst times: in the midst of changes in a serious relationship, during stressful events at work, or at a family crossroads. The ability to ensure troubling past experiences do not hinder growth at these critical moments represents resilience and strong mental health. Michael McNamara's and Volunteers of America's efforts to normalize experiences with trauma and struggles with mental health build resources for a society where these issues are prevalent.

How prevalent mental-health issues are is often shocking. However even in our personal lives, it is difficult to imagine that many of the people we admire the most have struggled and regressed in their own life journeys. They have made mistakes, battled with maintaining their own mental health, and dealt with unfortunate circumstances. That common realization is a metaphor for appreciating that US society overall has significant difficulties with mental health. A study of a diverse cohort of nearly 10,000 Americans in 2005 provided researchers with the estimate that almost half of Americans will experience a mental health disorder at some point in their lives. A mental-health disorder, while vaguely defined by medical literature, can be succinctly understood as a "significant behavioral or psychological syndrome or pattern ... associated with present distress or disability or with ... an important loss of freedom" that is not "culturally sanctioned" such as in grieving a loved one.

Conversely, the World Health Organization (WHO) defines mental health as, "a state of well-being in which every individual realizes his or her own potential, can cope with the normal stresses of life, can work productively and fruitfully, and is able to make a contribution to her or his community." Reading that definition precisely should suggest the difficulty or even potential rarity of attaining optimal mental health. Developing resilience, finding meaning, and achieving purpose in life are difficult and often ephemeral feats – we succeed at times and fail at others. An often-quoted report to the US Surgeon General in 1999 estimated that only 17 percent of US adults meet the WHO's criteria for optimal mental health.

An example of a family of five can explain this data more understandably than considering the percentages alone. At any given time in a five-person family, only one person would be experiencing optimum mental health. Over the course of a lifetime, two of these five would suffer from a mental-health disorder. Perhaps this example explains why family relationships can be so difficult.

However, this data does not have to be thought of pessimistically. Psychiatrist Thomas Szasz began arguing in the mid-twentieth century that the majority of mental illness is more of "an explanation for problems in living" than true diseases or disorders. That same example of a five-person family might seem a little less shocking if described through Szasz's concept of mental illness. At any given time in this five-person family, only one person would not be dealing with significant life challenges. Over the course of a lifetime, two of the five would face life challenges significant enough to seek help. While this wording still highlights the difficulty of family, Szasz's concept of mental illness importantly normalizes struggles with mental health as natural parts of life. We all face trauma and challenges at different times and in different ways; asking for help and seeking help should be as natural as the fact that we face difficulties in life overall.

With these thoughts in mind, I attempted to normalize the discussion of mental health, moral injury, and trauma within my class. I wanted to provide them with a scenario they might experience or might have experienced already in high school. Yet, I wanted the scenario to be less than what they would expect in an exercise with the explicit goal to understand mental health and trauma. I then reached back to an enduring memory from my junior year of high school to invent the scenario.

On an otherwise forgettable weekend, I stopped by an unsanctioned high-school party at a friend's house. I had been grounded for drinking at his house a year prior, but I was responsible and not drinking at that point in my life, a level of responsibility I should have returned to after both coming home from deployments and transitioning from the military. I saw a casual friend named Frank at the party. He seemed drunker than usual. We "dapped up," and I said, "You're not driving home, right?"

"Nah, man. Nah."

I left the party and went home to do chemistry homework. I thought I was probably the only one who did homework that night. The next morning, I started getting texts as I was sitting at my desk, "Did you hear about Frank?"

Frank had flipped his car on his way home. He survived and walked away. I knew I could have been his sober driver, and I always wondered how I would have felt if Frank had died or if Frank had killed someone else. Blending truth and reality, I created an exercise from the experience.

Communicating and Receiving Trauma Exercise: You (call yourself John) are catching up with a friend (Paul) from lower school who went to a different high school from you. You were close in lower school but have moved apart a little. You know something is bothering Paul from what happened over the weekend. All you know is it involved a party and another mutual friend, Frank, from lower school who went to the same high school as Paul.

Scenario (known only to "Paul"): You (Paul) went to a party with your close friend Frank. Frank was driving, but you both agreed to leave the car at the party and take a taxi home. You left earlier than Frank because you were tired but confirmed Frank would not drive home. You woke up the next morning and learned Frank had gotten in a car accident. Frank was OK and did not hurt anyone else. But you're upset and stewing on how Frank lied to you and put himself and others at risk.

In class, I told the scenario only to one student, who was playing "Paul" who left the party early. Another student, who did not know the scenario, acted as "John," the one who wanted to help his friend who seemed off. I started the exercise as if they were seeing each other on the street, and they began the conversation. The rest of the class judged how well the two communicated and received the story of trauma.

While early in the semester, this exercise showed me that many seniors in high school are already adept at communicating and receiving trauma. "John" knew the key was to listen and be supportive, not to dig. "Paul" felt that support and then opened up by asking "John" if he could talk about something that was troubling him. "John" focused on listening actively and accepted his friend's story. "John" did not give unsolicited advice and knew "Paul" probably just wanted to hear, "That sucks. I'm really sorry Frank did that."

While an effort in acting, practicing the communication and receipt of trauma is something that helps us understand the right ways to vent and the right ways to console. Moments sharing trauma serve as flashpoints in any relationship, crossroads that could either strengthen or weaken a bond more than we can foresee. Acknowledgment of the importance of these moments compels us to contemplate how to improve our actions during them.

You rarely get to choose to experience a traumatic event; those experiences are still not guaranteed when you sign up to go to war. Still, war and trauma are inherently linked, and some wars are unavoidable, the War Against ISIS being one and Judge Tucker's more clearly another. Trauma itself is an unavoidable facet of human life: trauma, loss, and suffering serve as unifying elements across all professions, races, and genders. We can learn to communicate and tell stories of the difficulties of what we experience until it as natural and effortless as breathing. Then too, each of us can learn to listen to another's experience with trauma more compassionately. Together, it might just make all of us that much closer and more resilient as a society.

"It's Your Turn Now, Fucker" Summary and Discussion Questions

Calling to Service

I struggled for two years with my calling to serve in the military and in war. I dropped in and out of Army ROTC from 2010–11 as I tried to find my path, the initial path that would define the rest of my life. Indecision was a critical element of the journey that eventually taught me the strength, courage, and confidence I relied on in difficult points in my service.

1. How have you found or how will you find your own calling?
2. What are the marks of success or failure that define your path?
3. Who are the people that serve as guides along your path?

Hollywood's Depiction of War

Marcus Luttrell's interview with Anderson Cooper paints a stark picture of war compared with *Lone Survivor*. Both versions serve a purpose. The engaging and inspiring Hollywood movie brought in thousands to see the experience of some US troops in Afghanistan; the interview communicates the real and lasting effects of trauma and conflict.

1. Why do more stark depictions of war trauma like Luttrell's not make it into Hollywood movies?
2. How do most Hollywood war movies contrast with Tim O'Brien's description of a "true war story"?
3. What are some unintended effects of romanticizing war?

Communicating and Receiving Trauma

Experiencing trauma is a natural part of the human experience. Becoming more natural in understanding, communicating, and receiving trauma improves resilience – an admirable trait that confers strength under pressure. Moral injury, or the weight of responsibility for personal or second-hand experiences with trauma, is an important concept related to PTSD. Both moral injury and PTSD are necessary to understand as natural responses to experiences with trauma.

1. How can you practice communicating and receiving stories and experiences of trauma and moral injury?
2. How can society "normalize" experiences with trauma and moral injury to encourage and support survivors?
3. What are the best ways to support those who have experienced trauma or moral injury? What are the best ways to support yourself?

Chapter 4

BIRD DOWN

"I'm talking with my platoon commander."

Jon Kubala, a broad-shouldered, completely bald Marine sergeant, said over his shoulder to another Marine without breaking eye contact. We were on a transient base in Kuwait, on the way home from my first deployment in April 2017. It was the first time Kubala and I had seen each other since leaving 29 Palms seven months prior. I felt a strange, undeserved pride in that moment hearing him say those words, a pride built from leading a platoon with Marines like Kubala who was then my second-in-command.

Being a scout sniper platoon commander was the job everyone wanted but knew nothing about. The title alone attracted Marines to the position, and I was not immune. One night soon after getting the job, I regrettably told a girl in a bar in Las Vegas that I was a scout sniper platoon commander. She stared back at me with no sense of recognition or interest; it did not take me much longer to realize titles do not really mean anything.

The truth was that the scout sniper platoon commander was not a trained scout sniper. The platoon commander is put in charge of graduates of one of the best sniper schools in the US military, who know much more about and are far more proficient at their craft than the platoon commander could ever dream of being. It is a leadership challenge from Day 1, a challenge that requires a proper balance of humility and confidence. Since Day 1 usually involves giving a speech to the platoon that the platoon commander has imagined for years and the Marines could not care less about, it is an uphill climb immediately.

The scout sniper platoon commander is also usually sitting in a command center, a life that was somewhat familiar for me by the time I got on deployment to lead one. Receiving and analyzing what the sniper teams see on the battlefield, planning resupply, and coordinating the teams' insert and extract are the main roles of the platoon commander. To young, idealistic Marines seeking the challenges of combat, the real job is not as alluring as being an actual sniper, the role most probably imagine.

While not to that detail, I had a somewhat more complete vision for why I wanted to be a scout sniper platoon commander and what the role would entail. The job was the pinnacle of a ground intelligence officer; ground intelligence mixed the most intense physical and leadership experiences of infantry – the running, hiking, and shooting often imagined when thinking of the military – with the most intricate and challenging analysis of intelligence. Marcus Williams, the first Marine officer I ever met, was a ground intelligence officer; he was a dedicated, passionate, and selfless leader, who had faced two combat deployments to Afghanistan. I did not need to look any further for other role models to seek to emulate.

The only problem was I was terrible at shooting. My only real experience with guns came from brief stays at my uncle's farm out in Virginia. Once, after failing to hit anything during skeet shooting and missing my share of shots at a target sheet with a pistol, my uncle looked at me and said, "Wouldn't want to be in a foxhole with you, Jay."

I laughed and could not blame him. My skills did not improve when I joined the military either. I failed my first time shooting on the rifle range, which meant I wore the dreaded "pizza boxes" on my dress uniform, the symbol of a marksman, the lowest qualification for shooting. While a platoon commander in real combat would not shoot in most scenarios, due to the responsibility of command and control, and certainly never shoot a sniper rifle, appearances in uniform still mattered. Even two-and-half years later, when I shot again after returning from deployment, my luck was not much better. Kubala looked at me revolted as I came off the range as a sharpshooter, the qualification one below expert that most Marines attain. The pride I felt by him simply calling me his platoon commander paled in comparison with the embarrassment I felt then. I admitted, "I don't know what to tell you, man. I suck."

I luckily had more mentors who pushed me along into ground intelligence. My first platoon commander at OCS was another ground intelligence officer and role model who drove me to follow in his footsteps. Katey van Dam, my platoon commander at The Basic School, the initial Marine officer schooling at the start of active duty, seemed to look past my poor shooting record too. She was one of the best attack helicopter pilots in the Marines and knew several ground intelligence officers from her generation. Her biggest compliment to me was that

I reminded her of some of them. Looking through my record near the end of training, she paused at my shooting score, "Is this right?"

"Yes, Ma'am."

"OK. Doesn't matter."

Taking over the platoon in May 2016, I learned quickly to rely on my senior enlisted, then Staff Sergeant Brian Henexson, who looked so much like a Marine that he had spent his first tour posing for commercials at the Marine Barracks at 8th and I in Washington DC. He was a proficient scout sniper and a practical leader. My team leaders, one step below Henexson, were also capable scout snipers and had some deployment experience in Iraq and Afghanistan. Team leaders were usually non-commissioned officers in their early twenties who had graduated from the Marine scout sniper school. They led four-to-six-man teams that would insert and infiltrate into a hide site and observe and report from that position for days on end. For Henexson and me, the success of our platoon hinged on them.

The biggest threat we faced as a nation in 2016 was not ISIS: it was North Korea, at least in the eyes of the US military. While Henexson and I knew we were only months away from taking the platoon to the Middle East, the large-scale evaluations and training exercises we had to complete before deployment set us against a fake enemy that resembled this threat. As the scout sniper platoon was the forward eyes for the infantry battalion in an assault, our first tests would be observing and reporting in advance of hundred-man or more attacks on North Korean-style defensive positions.

The puzzle of employing scout sniper teams was a complex chain of decisions that were usually made well ahead of an actual engagement. My team leaders and I planned insert points, where a helicopter or vehicle would drop them off, infiltration routes, the path they would take from the insert to the hide site, actions on objective, what they would observe and report upon in that hide site, exfiltration routes, the path they would take to their extract point, and finally the extract point, where they would get picked up and taken back to the command center for debrief, rest, and refit. On top of that basic mission planning, we planned how we would talk to each other, how we would resupply the team, and what we would do if the team got compromised. Every mission in training was its own decision-making exercise that we knew we might have to do one day against a real enemy.

Deliberate planning, in the weeks and days leading up to an exercise, took patience and competence, not only in the tactics of sniper employment but also in dealing with others. Often, we spent time trying to influence our superiors or support agencies like pilots that the plan we wanted would be the most effective. For our superiors, we had to prove that our plan gave us the best observation point on the enemy with the least likelihood for compromise. For pilots, we focused on the insert and extract points, arguing the locations would be safe for the pilots and allow us to move undetected into and out of the hide site.

Hasty planning, in the middle of an active mission, tested dexterity and battlefield awareness. Like Judge Tucker all those years prior, to be successful, we had to understand the capabilities of our platoon, our supporting agencies, our adjacent units, and our enemy. Those decisions represented the best tests we had to be ready to face a real enemy. My first tests came quickly in June 2016, only a month after taking over the platoon.

Under a thin layer of netting that seemed to block a marginal amount of the desert summer sun's heat, I rested with one knee on the ground and my forearm across the other. I stared at my team leader, Sergeant Anthony Dattilo, the type of guy who never stopped smiling and also just happened to be an extremely proficient scout sniper. We wore helmets, sunglasses, gloves, and flak jackets and had rifles draped in front of us. The black tablets in our hands, loaded with maps and imagery of the Mojave Desert, were the focus of our attention. It was Day 2 of a battalion or thousand-man assault up a barren mountain pass. Our first missions, planned in the days prior to the assault, had been successful to get the battalion up to this pass. We received orders to put another team forward to continue the assault, and Dattilo's team was ready for another challenge.

Self-Awareness Exercise – "Day Insert": Sergeant Dattilo's scout sniper team had to insert and infiltrate to a position north in the mountain pass ahead of the infantry battalion to provide information on the enemy's position for an upcoming battalion-level assault. Due to the artificial time constraints of the exercise, the insert and infiltration had to happen during the day, which would have been too big of a risk to take in most real-world situations. Sergeant Dattilo had two amphibious assault vehicles on stand-by, ready to drive up the pass as his insert platform. They were big, loud, clunky vehicles not known for stealth, but the staging area and route towards the insert point were blocked from the main enemy's direct line of sight thanks to an intervening hill that sloped down from the west. The enemy had the capability to observe, however, through their own scouts and small drones. Sergeant Dattilo could attempt to insert completely via stealth or ask for the battalion to create a diversion that could distract the enemy. He could also tell his commander that the mission was impossible and not worth the risk. How would you analyze the situation?

This problem was one of the first tactical situations I faced as a platoon commander. I had served as the officer in charge for the insert, the role of a platoon commander in some cases to support the teams on their way in. After we returned, I hopped off the amphibious assault vehicle and returned to the thin layer of netting I had learned to appreciate. I kneeled back down and grabbed a small pouch of peanut butter out of my pocket. Almost immediately, the radio then started buzzing, and I realized quickly Dattilo's insert did not go as planned.

I had influenced Dattilo to pick the diversion option, as I thought the enemy was certain to see the large amphibious assault vehicles heading up the pass. I decided we could make it look like the vehicles were going forward only to fix obstacles that had been emplaced earlier that day by engineers in the same vehicles. As Dattilo's team was inserted with one of the vehicles on the far side of the pass, another Marine and I jumped out of the second vehicle in the center of the pass and moved around some of the obstacle stakes, acting as if we were making some quick adjustments. Dattilo's insert and our quick attempt at tactical deception took only a few minutes. We linked back up with the other vehicle and headed south down the pass to our staging area.

The enemy role-players had seen my vehicle moving around stakes, as intended, but then they had searched the area more broadly with a small drone and found the other vehicle on its way out from inserting Dattilo and his team. While impossible to know whether the enemy role-players would have seen the vehicles if we tried for a simpler stealth insert, I took this moment as a lesson in the problem of trying to do too much. I might have overestimated how much the enemy was actually watching. For a high-risk insert, I also could have been with the team at their insert point and waited as quick-reaction force in case they had been immediately compromised.

The third choice, saying it was impossible, was probably not the right answer either. While the risk was high to Dattilo and his six-man team, the information Dattilo and his team could have reported back might have saved the lives of hundreds of Marines in an assault. Understanding cost benefit in raw numbers is one of the more piercing but important utilitarian lessons from the military. All in all, the simpler choice, the stealth insert, was likely the better one.

The quick reaction force on standby was a platoon of Humvees fitted with anti-tank weapons led by my friend Kyle Kavanagh. He immediately got his Marines ready and started moving to his trucks to rescue my team. Over his shoulder as he jumped in as vehicle commander for one of his trucks, he calmly said, "I don't have space for you, Jay." That was his nice way of telling me I was an idiot and should go back to my maps and intelligence reporting. Kyle picked up Dattilo and his team and quickly returned them to the staging area. Dattilo's actions to report that his team was compromised immediately when he noticed a small drone overhead could have saved his men's lives in a real-world scenario. If he had not noticed the drone overhead, his team would have had to face a group of role-players who had just started preparations to attack their position. That quick decision, similar to Judge Tucker's the first night after he landed on Omaha Beach, took strong battlefield awareness and humility.

Later that night under the cover of darkness, Kyle's platoon served as security to insert Dattilo's team back to a position on the hill where they could observe the enemy ahead of the battalion assault. I was vehicle commander in the passenger seat for a Humvee driven by an intelligence analyst that carried Dattilo's team. Right after we dropped off the team and started driving back, the intelligence analyst, not helped in the slightest by his vehicle commander who could barely see through his night-vision googles, turned into a ditch. Kyle and his Marines immediately sprang into action to pull us and the truck out. Gratefully, Kyle didn't say anything to me then.

The next day, I faced another decision that mixed leadership and tactics. Kris Ko, one of my most proficient scout sniper team leaders, was inserted the evening prior into a hide site farther north on the west side of the pass. His mission was to watch a possible enemy reinforcement avenue of approach above the attack position that Dattilo and his team were observing. They had had a grueling hike through the night up to their hide site and were observing the pass through the mountains. However, even though his insert and hide sight were part of the deliberate planning everyone in our battalion should have been aware of, not everything went to plan. I was in the command center with my second-in-command Staff Sergeant Henexson, when we started to realize we were facing a serious issue.

Self-Awareness Exercise – "Team on the Hill": Sergeant Ko was in position observing a mountain pass to the northwest of the enemy's main element. His observation post was critical as the mountain pass could be used to reinforce the enemy defense during or after the battalion's attack. However, the 81mm mortars platoon had set up farther west than they were supposed to, and his position was now too close to the gun-target line, which put him and his Marines at risk. I was told Sergeant Ko would have to move positions. I had to decide if I could argue against that order. If I couldn't, I needed to figure out how to deliver the news to a tired scout sniper team that did not have a lot of water to spare. How would you analyze the situation?

Arguing for Sergeant Ko to stay and asking the mortars to move was not going to work, even though I did try. The same cold, utilitarian argument won out: the mortar platoon was larger, carried heavier equipment, and took longer to set up. They were not moving. My main decision then became how to deliver the news. I spoke plainly over the radio and told Sergeant Ko: "Sierra 4, this is Sierra Actual … 81s set up too far to the west … You need to move your hide sight 500 meters west … Stand by for updated grid for 81s and new hide site."

Sergeant Ko dutifully copied down the new locations I gave him and started doing his terrain analysis. Almost immediately, I heard his heated voice come back over the radio to me. "Sierra Actual, this is Sierra 4 … Movement not feasible … Tell 81s to set up where they planned to."

I looked at Henexson, who was shaking his head and staring at the rocks at our feet. I had to turn the table and empower my team leader, which is what I should have done from the beginning. I reiterated the issue, told him the mortars were not moving, and asked him where he thought he could move and what he needed to move. Sergeant Ko picked a new location, not far from where I suggested, and asked for a resupply of water. Henexson and I quickly agreed.

After dark, I got in a Humvee and drove down to the mortar platoon, which was close enough for a resupply link-up with Ko's team. He left his assistant team leader with two other Marines to start breaking down the hide site and planned to meet me there with two more from his team. They would then link back up with their other element and start hiking to the new hide site. When I arrived, I saw the mortar platoon commander Kyle Daly running up to me. He was a wrecking ball of a human and never stopped talking, but he was an extremely loyal friend. "Tell Ko to move his ass, Brooksy! We're laid in here for good!"

I shook my head and sighed. I asked Daly to make sure he would continue to resupply Ko's team if they needed water in a few more days. Ko showed up soon after, hiking in from the west covered by the hills. I gave him and his team some water, and he vented about the mortar platoon and having to move, saying directly he did not want to listen to someone who was not a sniper. I listened, agreed with him, and told him to call me if he needed anything and that we would have his back. I left him by telling him I knew his team was going to perform well.

When Ko, tired, angry, and covered in dirt from head to toe, stared me down that day at the mortar position, I was forced to contemplate how I was perceived by my Marines. I should have been able to see from Ko's perspective that when I gave him a new position, I was taking away his own agency and initiative, rather than helping, as I naïvely thought. I even made him look powerless in front of the team he was leading. By asking Ko what he would do from the beginning, I could have steered and influenced him to the same solution and skipped an event that almost broke the critical trust between platoon commander and team leader.

These driving moments and difficult decisions did end up building the foundations for the mutual trust we needed in the platoon. By that point in training, we had already spent weeks together in the desert, away from cell phones and the distractions of the modern world, focusing only on each other and the mission we all took seriously. When Henexson and I ran our own training, we focused on sniping and urban warfare. Urban warfare, the most difficult mission we could get tasked with on deployment, was still as dangerous and challenging as when Judge Tucker faced it in Butzbach. Urban warfare called for high-intensity live-fire exercises, as our Marines would move through buildings and shoot at different targets as they appeared. We built trust quickly under designed stress in close quarters, shooting targets side-by-side.

That trust started to show when we had time out of the desert and were back in the office too. During a standard, one-on-one performance evaluation, I asked a proud, strong, young Marine named Drake, who sat across from me, how his younger sister back in Texas was doing. He talked of his sister often: I knew how proud Drake was of her, and I knew how much his younger sister looked up to Drake. He started crying, talking about how he thought his sister was hanging out with the wrong people. He paused, and then told me his sister was pregnant, and he knew her boyfriend was a "druggie" and not ready to support her or a child. I told him he was the light as an example in his sister's life and that he would continue to be that light. We shook hands, and I wondered what I had done to earn Drake's trust in that moment. I knew that I needed to be more aware of the struggles my Marines could be having back home. I also needed to break down any barriers I had set up between me and the others.

The sense of responsibility for my platoon and my Marines' entire well-being was a weight, described often as the burden of command. The gifts were the small moments across a table from a Marine who opened up to me. The difficulties were the bigger moments when a Marine told me he did not trust me. The pain was the thought of losing any of them, in training or combat.

I continued to support my teams from expedient command centers in the Mojave Desert that summer during our culminating large-scale exercise. Our platoon continued to perform well, even if we had some growing pains. One night, I was focused on the next insert conducted by an impressive team leader named Wes Aparicio. Aparicio had briefed the mission perfectly 3 days prior to the commanding officer of the regiment, the unit above our battalion that controlled more than 5,000 Marines. The only problem was that Aparicio had a black eye from the night prior when he got in a fight with Drake. There were murmurs around the room when he stood up to brief. I leaned over to the senior enlisted of the regiment, a dedicated and firm Marine who was also a scout sniper.

"We're still growing up."

I was waiting to hear from the pilots that Aparicio and his team had taken off. I was sitting near a radio outside the command center when I saw Aparicio leaning out of a Huey flying almost directly overhead to the northern mountain pass where his position would be. I went back into the tent that represented our command center and told my radio operator that I was pretty sure they took off.

Three days later, the time was ticking closer to extract. Aparicio and his team had performed well and radioed us that they were waiting at the extract point for the Hueys to arrive. The same point of the mission then hit us, the radio silence between when we thought they would get picked up and when it would actually happen. I was in the command center sitting across from the military's version of an air-traffic controller, a pilot himself, called the air officer. I watched him take off his headset, put it on the table between us, and stare straight ahead. Then over the radio in the corner, I heard the muffled call, "Bird down."

I stood up from my chair and jolted towards the corner of the command center to the radio. Any composure I had was lost, and I blurted out, "We lost them." Exercise controllers burst into the command center and yelled that the exercise was paused, without giving details of what happened. We all stood in disbelief. I imagined writing letters to Aparicio's parents and the parents of every single member of his team, apologizing for not preventing the loss of their sons.

Aparicio's voice then came through on the radio. He said a fighter jet went down as it was making a bombing run as part of the exercise. His team was OK, and they were about to board the Hueys to leave.

I walked back to my chair and made eye contact with the air officer across from me. He had not said a word and was sitting rigid in his chair. And then I started smiling. I could not help it. It felt maniacal, bizarre, evil, a smile I could not hold back. I said I was sorry and tried to hide my face. I felt so much relief that it was not my guys who were dead that I could not show compassion when it was someone else who had died.

I met Aparicio after he returned to the command center. He described to me the scene from the hill of watching the plane disintegrate during the bombing run in what would turn out to be a mechanical failure. The pilot was 35 and had a family. I was left to wonder who wrote to his wife.

Leading the platoon brought more difficult decisions as we approached deployment. The stress and tempo of the training led some to cut corners, an unacceptable breach for a sniper platoon built on the trust that they will do the right thing when miles away from the command. As I finished running a standard annually required military fitness test with the platoon, I turned to Kubala and asked him if everyone had completed the test. He told me they had. I then let the guys go shower up before a day of office work and classroom training.

> Self-Awareness Exercise – "Cheating on the Test": Rumors began to reach me that some of my platoon "cheated" on the fitness test and reported scores on a certain portion, a timed run with several small events that took about two minutes, without actually running it. I was shocked and disappointed. I could do a quick investigation myself and try to figure out what happened, but my boss, the Weapons Company Commander, might need to know about a breach of this magnitude immediately. How would you analyze the situation?

I sought counsel from older officers in my unit of my same rank and asked them what they thought I should do. They said I should keep our boss out of it and discipline the guys myself. I agreed and felt that was a fair plan. Marines had certainly done worse and gotten away with it.

However, in that short time, the rumors had trickled up the chain to my boss. He came to me and asked why I had not said anything. Luckily, he believed me when I told him I was planning to tell him, but I had just wanted to figure out more details and have a plan for the discipline we should take. For someone who is bad at lying, I took that as a lucky win, but I knew afterwards that getting caught in that lie could have made the situation even worse.

The rest of the day was then a blur of interviews with each of my Marines. My boss, Henexson, and other key staff were all present and asked questions to determine who had cheated and why. We played good cop, bad cop. At one point, one of my Marines, who had not cheated, a former professional surfer whose hair was probably too long, forgot where he was and saluted my boss indoors. Since Marines do not salute indoors, everyone stared at him like he had lost his mind, which he had.

We learned painfully that Kubala had lied himself and had not run the test. Both Ko and Drake had not run it either. That night in the dark, the entire platoon re-ran it, start to finish. As we came off the last event, I pulled them into a circle.

"Earlier, one of you asked why we did not keep this at the platoon level."

"Sir, if I could explain," Kubala jumped in, the one who had blurted out in our platoon meeting earlier that day that the cheating should never have gotten to my boss.

"Just stop. Stop … If you have been watching me and you call what you as team leaders did today leadership, I've failed you, and I am a failure… Staff Sergeant, you got anything to add?"

I did not lead Henexson well into that talk, and I do not remember what he said. I walked off into the dark and wondered what deployment, then days away, would hold for my platoon.

Discipline for the breach varied. Kubala was supposed to take his team to an important and interesting mission in Baghdad. Instead, his team sat in Kuwait, and Aparicio's team took his place. With the negative attention on the platoon, Dattilo was left to be trusted with a high-visibility mission that involved training the Jordanian Army in Amman. He had been hoping to take his team to a more active role in Iraq and was clearly disappointed. Kubala was still the best and most likely to take second-in-command, since Henexson was changing jobs and not deploying with us.

A few weeks into deployment, Dattilo called me on a secure line with exciting news: his team was selected to work with Army special forces and open a small base on the tri-border area of Syria, Iraq, and Jordan. Dattilo told me, "You were right. This was the place to be, Sir! Thank you!" I hung up the phone and thanked God for my luck and prayed at the same time he and his team would be OK.

After Dattilo and his team moved, Kubala and I had sniper teams with him at the tri-border area of Syria, Iraq, and Jordan; outside Mosul during the beginning of its clearance by Iraqi Security Forces; on Al Taqaddum Airbase not far from where I was at Al Asad in Western Iraq; in Baghdad; and in Kuwait. Slowly, Kubala and I rebuilt trust as we supported our teams remotely. I talked to Kubala on a secure line from my command center a few nights a week.

As deployment wore on, our teams were doing well independently without much support from us. Our main effort became to plan every detail of the most important event for the platoon once home: the screener, the recruitment for young Marines to join the scout sniper platoon and replace those Marines getting out of the military or moving on to different jobs. Our long hours planning and developing the screener helped us stand face-to-face in Kuwait again trusting each other and looking forward to the challenges ahead.

When the screener finally arrived, we pushed the new platoon candidates physically and mentally. My team leaders and I arrived early to the morning events and sat listening to Steve Holy's "Love Don't Run," at least the first few seconds where he sings, "This is gonna hurt. This is gonna hurt like hell. This is gonna damn near kill me." The screener brought one more difficult moment, a crossroads that all my training in leadership did not prepare me for.

> Self-Awareness Exercise – "I Quit … I mean I'm Hurt": Our scout sniper screener was going well. The main issue though was that not enough Marines had tried out, and the platoon would likely still be too small. On the last timed run of the screener before we would transition to field operations, one of the Marines fell out. He had been leading throughout the week and had even been through some initial scout sniper training. I thought he was injured, which would not guarantee he had to fail the screener, but apparently he said as he pulled up, "I DOR [drop on request]. I quit." The Marine immediately regretted saying the words and stated he was injured and just could not do the run. Injuries were natural and forgivable; quitting was not. How would you analyze the situation?

When we all returned from the run, Kubala came over to me with some of the other leaders of the screener. I said if he's injured, we are not dropping him. Kubala, much bigger, stronger, and physically impressive than the scrawny quasi-athlete I was, almost jumped at my throat. With the candidates and the rest of the platoon in front of us, we glared and half yelled at each other under our breaths. I dismissed the platoon, and Kubala, the other leaders, and I went into a barracks room. I said we could leave rank at the door and talk like men.

I wanted to keep the Marine who said he quit, but no one was on my side. "I quit" was an unforgivable phrase. My lesson was that we should have made that red line clear from the beginning, making sure everyone trying out for the platoon understood it. I left the barracks room, knowing we had lost a good Marine for the platoon, but also aware that I needed to keep the trust of Kubala and the others if the rest of the screener was going to be a success. I made peace that we were not going to get enough Marines from the screener, so in a way, I accepted failure.

The second half of the screener led us to the greener pastures of Camp Pendleton on the Pacific for a week of patroling. On our last night, I stood up on a hill with the other leaders, who had all deployed with us and come home. We watched the sun set over the ocean, a view we never got on our desert bases. The moment was coming for me to say something, and unlike on Day 1, they might actually listen.

"It was the pride of my life to lead you. A pride I will hold forever, but in a quiet way, as it is one I don't think I deserve. You will forever be my Marine Corps."

My proudest moment though was a week or so later, when the award I wrote for Kubala came through. The battalion gave him his award one of his last days before getting out of the military. After the ceremony, we hugged, and he said, "You got me, Sir."

"You made me better. I couldn't have done it without you."

"Bird Down" Summary and Discussion Questions

Day Insert

My scout sniper team leader and I had a difficult choice to make in a training exercise when forced to insert his team in the middle of the day. I probably "overthought" and "overanalyzed" the role-playing enemy when I created and executed a clunky diversion plan. The diversion ended up calling attention to the insert rather than distracting from it.

1. What are good tactics to avoid "overthinking" and "overanalyzing" a situation?
2. What are common traits of effective plans or courses of action?

Team on the Hill

I had to tell my team leader to move his team's hide site because another element in our unit had set up in the wrong place. My team leader felt he and his team were being punished for someone else's mistakes. I failed to empower him with choice and initiative when I chose a new location for him; I should have first asked for his opinion and then asked how I could support him.

1. Why can trying to help someone appear to take away their own agency?
2. Why do perception and intent matter in communication?

Bird Down

I failed to relay compassion after I learned Aparicio's sniper team was safe and another aircraft had crashed. The moment remains a lesson for me in the importance of emotional control.

1. How could I have prepared better for moments like "Bird Down"?
2. What are the best ways to regain composure and recover trust after losing emotional control?

Cheating on the Test

Days away from deployment, critical members of my platoon cheated on a largely ceremonial fitness test. I had to decide how I would discipline them and when I would tell my boss about it. My boss ended up finding out and took the discipline process out of my control.

1. When should you wait to relay "bad news" to a boss, superior, or colleague?
2. How do you reestablish trust with people who have broken your trust?

I Quit ... I mean I'm Hurt

An impressive Marine had performed well during our scout sniper screener but was nursing an injury by the end of the first week. At the top of a hill on our last run, he said, "I quit," but then later said he was just hurt. The words "I quit" were unforgivable, even if an injury would have been forgivable.

1. When does a breach, lapse in judgment, or mistake become unforgivable?
2. When is ignorance an acceptable justification for forgiveness?

Chapter 5

NO ONE IS BUILT FOR CAPTIVITY

The morale, wellness, and recreation (MWR) center at Al Asad Airbase in Western Iraq was just a few plywood walls and desks. It was on the near side of a big hangar that you passed on the way into the gym. The Wi-Fi was free but certainly hacked by a foreign entity: any credit-card information you used likely ended up in a database in Russia. Care packages from across the country adorned nearly every surface with notes from children and teachers thanking you for your service. I wrote back once, saying thank you to them.

There was a ping-pong table where Louie used to crush me but not as badly as he did in the gym. On Christmas, a few of us got together at 5 a.m. to watch *It's A Wonderful Life* since Lance and Kitter would be off shift then. The beanbag chairs we all sat on looked the same when I came back a year or so later. The same too were the phones I used to call home, when I used to hear about friends' drinking misadventures and when I used to talk to my grandfather. A Navy veteran and fellow Harvard grad, he could tell in one of those conversations I was struggling with something , even if I tried to hide it. I remembered the chair I sat in when he told me:

"Sometimes, Jay, you have to learn to lose."

When I was back in that room about to start the long trip home for the second time, I used those phones to talk to my boss who was in Kuwait. He had some news: once home, I was moving and taking on a new job on the east coast. I would be working in information operations, the military's term for counterpropaganda and social engineering. I did not know at all what that entailed, but I knew there were no deserts on the east coast.

The winding path eventually led me to a cafeteria in a government building, where a man named Noah broke out into John Legend in the middle of the quiet lunch we were sharing. I smiled and tried not to break eye contact. The anti-social people around us seemed horrified to have their comfortable routine broken up by song.

"Give your all to me, I'll give my all to you … Loyalty is my biggest vulnerability, Jay. We do this, we do it all the way. You're in or you're out."

"I'm in, brother."

"Cause I give you alllll …"

"I get it."

Noah's path to that cafeteria was more circuitous than mine. Growing up in Jamaica Plain in Boston, on the west side of Green Street Station, he walked the half mile or so to one of the oldest public high schools in the country. He was a star basketball player for the Boston English Eagles but did not get many looks from college recruits.

Noah graduated from Boston English in 2001, undistinguished but close enough to the top of his class for his parents to be proud. He was still playing pick-up and working small jobs when 9/11 hit. He thought of the bronze plaques on the wall in the lobby of his school he passed every day after going through the metal detectors. The plaques listed the names of the graduates who died fighting in the Second World War. He knew a Marine general went to his high school too, so he enlisted in the Marine Corps.

Noah became an 0311, infantry Marine, and excelled immediately in military life. He was selected for scout snipers and trained with his battalion's sniper platoon. His leadership would eventually give him a slot at sniper school, where he could earn the respected title Marine scout sniper with its colloquial tag "hog" for "hunter of gunmen." The school was physically and mentally demanding, with tests in precision shooting at various distances under time pressure, reconnaissance infiltration called stalking lanes that had instructors actively looking to compromise the students, radio communication across different frequencies and equipment, and patrolling evaluations through the hills of southern California. When Noah graduated, a lead instructor and senior enlisted with the rank of gunnery sergeant came up to him and shook his hand.

"I didn't think you were going to make it."

"Why is that, Gunny?"

"That shine. We all thought we'd see your Black forehead glisten in stalking lane."

"I made it, Gunny."

"I guess you did."

Noah returned to his platoon and began to teach the skills he mastered at sniper school. His passion, though, became radios, and he was quickly known as one of the best radio operators in his unit. In 2004, he deployed to Western Iraq and served in a combined machine-gun sniper team through the Battle of Fallujah, a city ten times the size of Butzbach. He decided soon after that battle he did not want to go back to combat. He met an intelligence analyst on his way home in the same plywood MWR at Al Asad I grew to love, who had heard of some of his team's work and gave him a business card. The card listed a unit he could try out for back home. The analyst wrote his number on the card and told Noah to give him a call.

The next year, Noah was struggling with the decision of whether or not to re-enlist. He called the number on the business card and said he was ready to try something new. He left the military and joined a secretive military unit as a civilian, where he would apply his passion for radios and communication. He would go back to Iraq, but he would not have to see direct combat. His focus instead was hostage rescue, and he created the communications infrastructure to track captors and support special forces during rescue efforts. This line of work took Noah to eastern Ethiopia at the end of 2011. Al Shabbab, a Somali terrorist organization with historic ties to Al Qaeda, had just captured two humanitarian workers: one American and one Dane.

> Self-Awareness Exercise – "Sensor Emplacement": Noah's unit provided him with special sensors that tracked movement in hard-to-reach places for hostage rescue missions. Noah generally had to get approval from his command in the US to emplace sensors, but exceptions could be made in time-sensitive scenarios. Noah had just arrived in Ethiopia but had worked closely with the Ethiopian Army before, who knew him as "Workneh." An Ethiopian partner invited Noah on a patrol of some of the desert near Somalia, exactly where he wanted to emplace sensors. His leadership likely would want him to wait for approval, but the opportunity was hard to pass up. How would you analyze the situation?

The "easier to ask for forgiveness" mantra was probably with Noah in this situation, the same way it was for Judge Tucker when using the P-47s. However, Noah did not have the full battlefield picture when he decided to emplace the sensors. The sensors required planes to fly over and receive data periodically at a noticeably low altitude. Right before one of these fly-overs, a local Somali with potential information about the hostages had planned to meet with a US intelligence officer at a nearby location in the desert. The Somali was spooked by the plane and called off the meeting.

While Noah was struck by some particularly bad luck, his command still chastised him. He had broken protocol when emplacing the sensors and had not properly coordinated the fly-overs. Noah took the criticism in stride. He knew he had made a mistake, but he conserved his energy to focus on the next step, confident his work would facilitate the hostages coming home. A month or so later, his communication infrastructure helped support the SEAL team that rescued both the American and the Dane.

By this point in Noah's career, he had been supporting hostage rescue missions for more than half a decade. The work had taken him all across the globe, usually on several month rotations away from home. Sometimes, he would be the lone representation on a mission or operation for the US government. Early in his career that gave pause to some people abroad, who gave him looks as a Black man that seemed to say, "You are leading this?" "Yes, motherfucker, I am."

As he got older, the time away started to wear on him and his family more. He had gotten married, soon after joining the military, and had a young son and daughter. He worked to be present in their lives as much as possible when he was home and to make sure he did not miss important life events while he was away. His command once let him fly back from Ethiopia in 2016 to see his son start in his first varsity basketball game as a freshman at Georgetown Prep outside of Washington DC. He had to ask, of course, for that to happen, but he knew how much it would mean to his son for him to be there.

Transitioning to and from high-intensity, high-stakes missions so often could be jarring on its own. Noah learned the best way for him to transition was to volunteer in the country before leaving, even if it meant delaying seeing his family by one or two weeks. That's how Noah got the nickname "Workneh" – "you are gold" – from his Ethiopian counterparts. One of the soldiers he had gotten to know happened to pass him working in a soup kitchen in Addis Ababa after he was supposed to have left the country. The soldier, passing through the poorer part of town only to drop off clothes for a relative, decided to come back and volunteer with "Workneh" for the day too. Noah could not generally volunteer in active war zones like Iraq and Afghanistan. He still spent enough time in Africa and South America that he got to serve many local cultures in entirely different capacities before heading home.

Noah's last deployment would take him to Northern Syria in 2017 as the tide turned against ISIS at key strongholds on their western and eastern flanks: Raqqah in Syria and Mosul in Iraq. Noah had to smile when he saw 11th Marine Expeditionary Unit, several hundred

Marines from an infantry battalion and a few cannons from an artillery battalion, arrive to support the battle outside Ayn Issa. Most of them had never been in a combat zone before. Noah only told a few of them he was a Marine, and none that he had fought in Fallujah.

Noah, while he watched the war closely, was not in Syria to support the Kurdish Army's fight against ISIS. His mission remained hostage rescue; his focus this time was another Marine, who had been captured years before outside Damascus.

Austin Tice followed Noah to Fallujah several months after Noah had returned home in 2005. They did not know each other in service, but their paths overlapped and intersected, both from the post-9/11 generation to join and serve in war. Tice was a veteran and freelance journalist on his way home to Washington DC when he was kidnapped and disappeared in Syria in 2012. Noah would then be the one to follow him, arriving in Syria soon after, the first of several trips in attempt to rescue a fellow Marine. By early spring 2017, Noah was certain there was a breakthrough. He felt they were weeks away from getting Tice home, thanks to interlocutors within President Bashar al-Assad's Syrian government. Then a hundred miles to Noah's west, President Assad's fighter jets dropped sarin gas on rebel forces holding out in the protracted Syrian Civil War.

Self-Awareness Exercise – "Marine in Captivity": The Syrian Regime under President Assad was historically at odds with the US due to its use of chemical weapons, which are banned under the "limit unnecessary suffering" tenet of the law of armed conflict. President Obama called the use of chemical weapons a "red line" which could not be crossed and would warrant international intervention in the Syrian Civil War. When President Assad crossed that red line in 2013, attacking civilians and rebels just east of Damascus, President Obama demurred and avoided intervention. In 2017 with the impending defeat of ISIS, the Syrian Civil War was approaching a tri-state stalemate, with the Kurds controlling Northeast Syria, Syrian rebel forces controlling Northwest Syria, and President Assad controlling the remainder of Southern and Central Syria. The Euphrates River held as the main dividing line between these three states. President Assad then took a risk to break that stalemate against the Syrian rebels through the use of chemical weapons. Recently inaugurated President Trump, aware of President Obama's red line and the ongoing discussions with the Syrian Regime to rescue Austin Tice, had to decide how he would respond. The global community would likely want a strong response. Those close to Austin Tice would perhaps want something more measured. How would you analyze the situation?

I was a few days from leaving Western Iraq when my base was put on high alert. The news did not hide many secrets, so I had a decent idea of why. I remember thinking it was probably an overreaction, to worry of an attack on a base in Western Iraq because of our attack in Syria, but I was about to leave and would have sat in a bunker all day if told to. Noah, outside of Raqqah, was also put on high alert. He knew much more than I did though and realized his chance to rescue Austin Tice was likely lost. President Trump had ordered a strike on the airbase used to launch the chemical-weapons attack. Fifty-nine cruise missiles later, the communications channel Noah had through the Syrian Regime was closed.

Noah understood the bigger picture of the battlefield behind this decision: he knew the military strategy, the US obligation to prevent unnecessary suffering and indiscriminate attacks against civilians, and the political strategy, the desire of a newly inaugurated president to look stronger than his predecessor. The painful reality for the family and friends of Austin Tice is that the utilitarian argument won out again. President Trump had to make a difficult decision that balanced the outcomes of thousands against the still uncertain outcome of one veteran Marine, held in captivity.

Noah returned from that deployment and wanted to commit more to family life. He took a stable job outside of Washington DC that would not make him deploy again. He shifted his focus to counterterrorism, rather than hostage rescue, and somehow ended up across the table from me. He wanted to create a project to defeat a particularly potent aspect of ISIS propaganda. I followed his lead all the way to the end of my career.

On my last day in that cafeteria, we got one more lunch together. I had already started teaching, and he was drinking coffee proudly out of a mug my school had bought for him as an esteemed guest speaker. He knew all of my path forward, and I told him about the stress I felt leaving the military and leaving counterterrorism after so many years as the focus of my life.

He smiled at me. I was worried he was going to start singing. But I thought he was thinking about something else entirely, perhaps his own journey, back and forth from war zone after war zone for almost two decades.

"Go be a doctor, brother. Nothing would make me happier. And if I ever see you back in this building, I'll punch you in the face."

"No One is Built for Captivity" Summary and Discussion Questions

Race in the Military

Noah battled racism in the military, both at home and abroad. In 2021, the military continued to grapple with structural barriers that promoted inequity within its ranks.

1. What are some of the structural barriers in the military that prevent equitable outcomes for people of color?
2. What can organizational leaders and individuals do to remove these barriers?

Sensor Emplacement

Noah encountered a similar moment to Judge Tucker where he could "ask for forgiveness rather than ask for permission" in "Sensor Emplacement." When Noah decided to take that risk, he did not have a full picture of the battlefield and faced consequences for his mistake.

1. How was the situation Noah encountered different from "P-47s On Station"? How were the two situations similar?
2. What are some of the character traits Noah relied on to recover from his bad luck?

Marine in Captivity

President Trump may or may not have faced this decision directly when he decided to strike Syria in 2017. As a thought experiment, the decision tackles the concept of utilitarianism – how decision-makers in war must weigh the costs and benefits to many over the costs and benefits to a few.

1. When in war is saving an individual more important than saving many?
2. Every death is a tragedy, rich or poor, young or old, guilty or innocent. Do you agree or disagree?

PART II

DECISION-MAKING

The skill to translate complex information into proper action

Be comfortable with the gray

"And right action is freedom / from past and future also."

T.S. Eliot

"In the end, the decision you make makes you."

John Wooden

Chapter 6

WHEN INACTION BECOMES A DECISION

Darrell Curley stood halfway up Drake Avenue in Marin City, his back turned towards the public housing complex he called home. He was 17 years old, tall, broad-shouldered, and strong. Punching the heavy bag at the local community center gave him enough physical stature to make people think twice before messing with him. It also helped him cope with growing up poor, part of a Black community that seemed to be forgotten.

Darrell and his father lived in the shadow of the Golden Gate Bridge, only miles from some of the wealthiest parts of San Francisco. His granddad had worked in a shipyard nearby that built cargo ships for the war in the Pacific. He remembered his granddad's stories, the pride his granddad felt from the hard, meaningful work supporting his country, even if his country did not support him after the war.

Even more than forty years after the end of the Second World War, segregation and redlining had kept the Curleys below the poverty line. An only child, Darrell had been the focus of his parents' lives before his mom left when he was in high school. Darrell's dad got pulled into the wave of a new drug that was terrorizing the community, so his mom moved in with relatives in Oakland. She used to ask him every night if he had done his homework and would walk him to school at Tam elementary to make sure he got there safely. Darrell decided to stay with his dad, thinking his dad would just come looking for him anyway. His mom would call sometimes, but she would hang up if his dad picked up the phone.

He stared at the Baptist church up the street on the corner. He had not been to church or school in weeks. The community center where he boxed was on his left, but he could not bring himself to walk in.

He had just found two of his best friends smoking crack in his living room. They had broken into his dad's stash. Darrell had walked out and never wanted to come back.

He hopped on a bus across the Golden Gate Bridge into San Francisco, not really sure where he was headed. He ended up walking along the bay towards the bridge to Oakland, thinking that he could catch another bus and go find his mom. Right on the water before the bridge, he saw a small US Army Recruiting Center. He paused, thought of his granddad, and then went in.

An Army sergeant named Barry Chase greeted him as he walked through the door. Sergeant Chase was wearing his full-dress uniform and stood up to shake Darrell's hand. "What can I do for you?"

"I need to get out of here quick."

Sergeant Chase laughed. "Should I be running too?"

"No, I just need to get out of here quick."

Sergeant Chase smiled at Darrell. He told him to sit down, and they could talk out options. Darrell told him that he had not been to school in a while but had not dropped out yet. Sergeant Chase handed Darrell his business card and told him to go back to school. "Once you get your diploma, give me a call."

He spent more time hitting the heavy bag and kept away from his dad and friends as much as he could. A year and a half later, he finished his degree at Tamalpais High School. The day after graduation, he took the bus back across the Golden Gate Bridge to go see Sergeant Chase. Sergeant Chase greeted him with a smile and said, "I knew you'd be back." Darrell would recite Sergeant Chase's number from memory whenever he told his story of joining the Army.

Darrell took orders as far away from Marin City as he could get and ended up in Japan on the other side of the Pacific. He became an infantryman and earned his role in a machine-gun squad. Darrell's platoon sergeant was a hardened Vietnam vet named Brent, who claimed he carried ears from Viet Cong prisoners of war in his breast pocket. Brent pushed Darrell hard as a young private and put him under the watch of another young soldier from California named Manny, who was three ranks above him as a specialist.

Darrell quickly learned to run with a 27lb M240 medium machine gun on his shoulders. He then learned to crawl under barbed wire while Brent shot live rounds overhead in infiltration lanes that would have looked familiar to Judge Tucker. Darrell enjoyed the toughness and mentorship of the Army and adapted well to his new life. However, Darrell joined the Army to get away from Marin City. He never thought he would go to war.

Darrell entered the military at a time when war seemed altogether unlikely. The four-decade Cold War was finally ending. President Ronald Reagan had delivered his famous speech at the Berlin Wall imploring Soviet Union leader General Secretary Mikhail Gorbachev to "tear down this wall" in June 1987. Seconds after that memorable line, President Reagan had echoed the theme of "containment" again, saying "to be sure, we in the West must resist Soviet expansion." Two years later when the Berlin Wall fell in November 1989, victory for Kennan's "containment" became certain. East and West Germany would begin a year-long process of reunification. The "Iron Curtain" and communism fell in Europe, as liberalism, free markets, and democracy took hold.

The Iraqi dictator Saddam Hussein's invasion of Kuwait in August 1990 would shatter the peaceful image of this new world order and bring Darrell and a generation of Americans to war. Hussein had massed troops in Southern Iraq under the guise of a military operation before crossing the border into Kuwait and seizing strategic oil fields.

Darrell deployed almost immediately after Hussein's invasion to Operation DESERT SHIELD, the reinforcement of the border between Iraq and Saudi Arabia and the US's first involvement in the Gulf War. The Saudi Arabian King Fahd had requested international forces to guard the border and prevent Saddam Hussein from invading his country. Watching from Afghanistan, Osama bin Laden, the terrorist mastermind of Al Qaeda and a Saudi himself, was appalled that foreign, non-Muslim militaries were invited to the kingdom that holds Islam's holiest sites: Mecca and Medina. Osama bin Laden had thought his guerrilla army of holy warriors, or mujahideen, should have been the forces requested by King Fahd. This perceived betrayal would help make the US Al Qaeda's primary target in the years following the Gulf War.

Darrell waited and rehearsed in the deserts of Saudi Arabia during fall 1990, while his leaders conceived and designed the liberation of Kuwait. Their plan included one of the most successful uses of military deception in modern war. Misdirecting the Iraqi Army, at the time the fourth largest in the world, reduced the casualties of the US and its allies and precipitated the defeat and withdrawal of Hussein's army from Kuwait.

Decision-Making Exercise – "Manipulating the Press": The plan to liberate Kuwait, which became known as Operation DESERT STORM, was maintained with the strictest amount of security. Very few military planners and leaders were read-in to the exact details of the operation. Some high-level public-affairs officers were though, as they prepared media releases and statements for the different phases of the conflict. A contact at a media organization asked one of those public-affairs officers, off the record, what he should be looking for. "I just need a story, don't need to know anything, just point me where it matters." The attack was days away. The public-affairs officer could point to the ground attack or the amphibious attack, the former real, the latter deception. He could also say nothing. What would you do?

In the days leading up to the ground assault in February 1991, thousands of Marines prepared for what they thought would be the battle of their lives. They conducted rehearsal after rehearsal of amphibious assaults into Kuwait. Media reporters happened to be on ship with the Marines and broadcasted their preparations for the world to see. Iraqi soldiers lined the beaches of Kuwait with heavy fortifications, expecting an attack. Darrell and Marines and soldiers then pushed through the deserts of Saudi Arabia and Iraq and attacked the weak flank of the Iraqi defense.

The military never directly misled the media or any news organization. The wrong and illegal decision for the public-affairs officer would have been to point towards the amphibious assault. The best decision would have been to say nothing. However, the military does not have an obligation to correct news media if they make the wrong assumption when they see Marines conducting rehearsals in the Persian Gulf. General Norman Schwarzkopf, the commander of all forces for DESERT STORM, stated the misplaced media coverage was likely helpful but not something they planned or tried to influence. General Schwarzkopf maintained in 1995, "I will swear on a stack of Bibles that we never, ever deliberately manipulated the press."

The US has significant laws in place that prevent the military from manipulating the media or public opinion. These laws serve as the important distinction between state-sponsored propaganda and state-sponsored information. Strategic truth is the US's strength; it builds allies' trust and forces adversaries to respect stated intentions. The military might have to mislead its enemies from time to time to create specific advantages, but the US's overall goal and purpose should never be in doubt.

Still, the US has failed to live up to this standard at different points in its history. Notably, the public deception in the weeks following the friendly fire incident that killed US Army Ranger and professional football player Pat Tillman in Afghanistan is a scar on the US's commitment to championing the truth, as Jon Krakauer describes in Tillman's biography *Where Men Win Glory: The Odyssey of Pat Tillman*. The fact that this deception occurred in May 2004 in the lead-up to the re-election for President George W. Bush's second term seems to remove any doubt from its disingenuousness. At the beginning of the Iraq War, Krakauer describes a related public-relations strategy to paint the rescue of US Army Private Jessica Lynch in an overly heroic light to distract the US public from early difficulties in the war. These failures should be exceptions that prove the rule in terms of the US government's commitment to the truth; however, a free and independent press and the continued encouragement of broad public discourse are required to keep the government honest.

On day two of the ground assault, Darrell and his machine-gun squad halted at a small outpost of buildings. While the Iraqi defense had been lighter than expected, they had still been in several firefights and taken a few casualties. Darrell and his squad had to clear Iraqi bunkers filled with booby traps and found endless pages of propaganda that showed de-humanized caricatures of President George H.W. Bush. The cartoons proclaimed all the lies that embodied the US to the Iraqi soldiers.

Darrell had driven one of their squad's vehicles through the night, including through minefields laid by the Iraqi forces. It was midday when they paused, but it was dark, and the sun was blocked out entirely. Hussein had given orders to set fire to the Kuwaiti oil wells and created an environmental catastrophe. Breathing the densely polluted air is thought to have given rise in part to "Gulf War Syndrome," the strange and unexplained health issues Gulf War veterans have experienced even decades later.

Darrell and his platoon's hasty assault across Iraq into Kuwait caused them to encounter many Iraqi soldiers who had already surrendered. By the time they stopped at what was formerly an Iraqi command center, they had too many prisoners of war assigned to them in their care. Brent gave Darrell and his squad the duty to guard twenty Iraqi soldiers. Brent put Darrell's immediate supervisor, Specialist Manny, in charge and left for other platoon duties. Darrell would then be faced with a decision that would stay with him all his life.

Decision-Making Exercise – "Moment of Surrender": During the second day of the ground war of DESERT STORM, Private Darrell Curley and his machine-gun squad were responsible for almost twenty Iraqi prisoners of war that they were supposed to guard and feed. The Iraqi soldiers were at their most vulnerable: they were hungry, tired, and dirty, as they had been in the desert for weeks without logistical support. Specialist Manny received boxes of Meals Ready-to-Eat, or MREs, to provide to the Iraqi prisoners. The boxes contained different meals: some vegetarian, some chicken, some pork. Specialist Manny ordered Private Curley to separate all of the pork MREs into one box and provide that box to the Iraqis. The famished Iraqi soldiers, almost all Muslims, would not be able to eat the pork MREs, due to their religion. Private Curley had to decide if he would call out Specialist Manny for this obvious wrongdoing. What would you do?

As Darrell finished collecting all of the unopened pork MREs from the Iraqis, a dark-skinned officer approached Manny. He inspected the food that they had given the Iraqi prisoners and immediately recognized what they had done.

"Who did this and who is in charge?" the officer said, firmly and forcefully.

Darrell was silent and stared at the wall behind the officer. Manny spoke up and said they had received the box just the way it was – "with only pork MREs." Darrell then turned his back to the officer and slammed his eyes shut. He heard the officer order Manny to get new cases of MREs; he would supervise as they provided more food to the Iraqis. Darrell would learn that he was an intelligence officer who spoke fluent Arabic, and his job was to interrogate the Iraqi prisoners. Darrell never forgot his mercy and care for the Iraqis, the same Iraqis who just a few hours prior would have shot at any of them.

Only 20 years old at the time, Darrell felt powerless. He had faced a test of moral courage, and he had failed. At the time, Darrell thought speaking up to Manny would only get him yelled at and probably would not have stopped Manny from doing what he wanted to do anyway. What he did not realize then was how much guilt he would feel for failing the test. Darrell had violated what he valued and his own moral code, and he would not get a second shot to redeem himself.

The war would end only days later, and Darrell would return to Japan for several more years of service. He immediately requested reassignment away from combat and became an administrative specialist. Through the 1990s, pushing papers in a comfortable job in a military at peace, Darrell started to listen to a rapper who had moved into Darrell's old public-housing project in Marin City just after he had left. Tupac Shakur was killed while Darrell was still in Japan, but he read Shakur's *The Rose that Grew from Concrete* after his death and decided he had to head home.

After more than ten years in the military, Darrell returned to halfway up Drake Avenue and walked straight into the community center. He passed the boxing ring where he had spent so much time as a young adult and found a career counselor. Darrell pictured the injured soldiers he saw abroad, both Americans and Iraqis, when he told the counselor he wanted to be a trauma nurse for the local community. He used the GI Bill to go to nursing school, and he sought to help and treat the young people like him from Marin City in their most vulnerable moments.

Darrell excelled in the high-intensity flow of the emergency department of Marin General Hospital, just up the street from where he went to high school. People would ask him how he stayed so calm and on an even keel in difficult moments, and he would laugh that nursing was easier than driving through a minefield. After a few years, Darrell reconnected with his mom. She had moved to Baltimore to be with extended family, so he followed her east to help take care of her as she got older.

Darrell found a new community in Baltimore that needed just as much help as Marin City. One quieter night on shift in the emergency department, he saw me, a visitor who looked out of place. Darrell walked right up to me, introduced himself, and started talking. He had a US Army lanyard on, so I asked him about his time in the military and told him I had just recently gotten out. We quickly learned we had both spent time in Iraq. His eyes lit up, and he looked at me with a smile. "We're brothers then. Both in the shot-at-and-shot-back club." It did not seem to matter to him that all of my "shooting" had been from a command center. Darrell would mention later how disappointed he had been that veterans from wars previous to him had not fully welcomed him home, because his war experiences were different in intensity and length.

I spent several more nights that spring shadowing doctors in the emergency department and luckily overlapped often with Darrell. He told me the difficulty he had returning from war, partially because of how one-sided the war had been and the jarring number of Iraqis they had killed. He laughed that he did not even try to date for years after he got back to Japan. He said he had had some things to work out and could not think of letting another person in when he was only partially there. I wondered when I truly got back from the war: after my first deployment, my second, or when I left my last job fighting the remote war from home.

I stood with Darrell one night when a man walked into the emergency department and complained of mild chest pains. Darrell got the man into a hospital bed, and I followed along as he began testing and treating the man in one of the spots in the hallway closed in by curtains. He always tried to calm patients by making conversation, so Darrell asked the man where he was from. The man said Iraq. I saw Darrell pause, and he said quietly that he had been in Iraq once. The man, who had been nervous and uncomfortable, seemed excited. Darrell tried to shift focus to his treatment, but the man pressed for details. Quickly, they figured out that they were on opposite sides of the war during DESERT STORM: Darrell a US soldier and the man an Iraqi soldier. The man told Darrell, "I escaped from Iraq, came to this country, and have the life I can now." The man then smiled at Darrell and said thank you. Darrell finished the initial exam and was ready to talk to the rest of his care team. He knew the man was going to be fine. I did not hear what Darrell said to the man, but he shook his hand and started walking away.

Darrell felt more distant than usual as we headed back to the front. I stayed by his side and wondered what I could say. Darrell then stopped, turned to me, and put his hand on my shoulder.

"I just thank God we all made it home. You, me, him."

"When Inaction becomes a Decision" Summary and Discussion Questions

History of Inequity

Marin City's history provides a striking example of how institutional racism inhibited equitable outcomes and stifled wealth generation for people of color in the second half of the twentieth century. Many veterans did not have access to housing loans, available to many through the GI Bill, solely due to the color of their skin. The community that worked in the shipyard also did not have adequate employment opportunities at the end of the war.

1. How should these historical inequities be rectified today?
2. What sectors of society could benefit from more manpower as part of post-war jobs programs?

Manipulating the Press

The planning and execution of military deception during the Gulf War offers a thought experiment on one of the most critical aspects of US democracy: a free and fair press. "Free and fair" means the government cannot knowingly lie to or manipulate the media, even to protect the lives of US servicemembers.

1. Countries like Russia and China can use their state-run medias as instruments of national power in war or steady state competition. Should the US laws have exceptions for war? What if the US is at war with Russia or China?
2. What precautions should media companies take when they are covering active military operations?

Moment of Surrender

When providing security for Iraqi prisoners of war, Darrell faced a moral dilemma that would stay with him in memory for more than thirty years. Darrell was not in a position of authority and did not think he could speak up to make any difference in what was happening.

1. The Iraqi prisoners of war received food they could eat soon after they returned the pork MREs, and they were treated much better than they had been for weeks in the desert. Why would Darrell still feel like he had made such a mistake?
2. What are the best ways to speak up when you are not in a position of power and recognize something you do not agree with?
3. How can organizations enable people at all levels to speak up when they recognize injustice?

Chapter 7

I CAN HEAR YOU

In summer 1997, US journalists Peter Arnett and Peter Bergen waited for several days for a once-in-a-lifetime meeting in Northeast Afghanistan. Through months of effort, they had planned and coordinated an interview with Osama bin Laden, the reclusive terrorist leader and financier. Bin Laden's media advisor eventually arrived at their initial meeting place to take them into the mountains of Tora Bora. There, they would become the first Western journalists to interview the Saudi multi-millionaire for television.

Bin Laden had recently issued a religious decree, or fatwa, he titled "Declaration of War against the Americans Occupying the Land of the Two Holy Places." His declaration of jihad, or holy war, decried US failures in Lebanon in 1983 and in Somalia in 1993 – both examples of US withdrawals from Arab nations after successful attacks by less powerful foes. Through Arnett, bin Laden had a conduit to communicate this fatwa to the world. As translated by CNN, bin Laden described to Arnett why he had proclaimed his jihad against the United States:

> The US government has committed acts that are extremely unjust, hideous, and criminal through its support of the Israeli occupation of Palestine, and we believe the US is directly responsible for those killed in Palestine, Lebanon, and Iraq. Due to its subordination to the Jews, the arrogance of the United States regime has reached the point that they occupied Arabia, the holiest place of the Muslims, who are more than a billion people in the world today. For this and other acts of injustice, we have directed jihad against the US.

Bin Laden spoke these words calmly without any visible emotion on his face. Arnett then pressed him on whom he would target in this new war. Bin Laden responded echoing his written fatwa that US troops in the Middle East, especially in Saudi Arabia, were his primary targets. His stated objective was clear: to force another US withdrawal from the Middle East.

Arnett concluded the interview with a simple question: "What are your future plans?" Bin Laden paused only briefly and then responded, not breaking eye contact with Arnett. "You'll see them and hear about them in the media. God-willing."

Bin Laden rose to prominence through another jihad in Afghanistan in the 1980s. The Soviet Union invaded Afghanistan in late 1979 to support an unpopular and secular communist government that was struggling to hold on to power. Pro-Islamic factions, known as the mujahideen or those who engage in jihad, galvanized popular support and led an insurgency against the Soviet-backed government. Osama bin Laden left his comfortable life as an heir to a profitable construction company in Saudi Arabia to join and lead the mujahideen in their war.

Compared often to the American War in Vietnam, the Soviet War in Afghanistan was a battle of "containment" much closer to home for them. The Soviet Union bordered Afghanistan directly to its north through modern-day Turkmenistan, Uzbekistan, and Tajikistan. The US took advantage of this opportunity and aimed to make this war as costly and damaging for the Soviets as Vietnam had been for the US. Through the CIA, the US funneled weapons and other material support to the mujahideen. One of the most critical weapons Americans provided was the FIM-92 Stinger man-portable air-defense system, a shoulder-fired, surface-to-air missile launcher that could shoot down Soviet helicopters with only minimal user training necessary.

Ten years later in 1989, the Soviets withdrew from Afghanistan and left the fledgling communist government to support itself. The Soviet Union had failed to generate more popular support among Afghans for the communist government, and the costs of war had become insurmountable. More than 15,000 Soviet soldiers had been killed. The impending fall of the "Iron Curtain" in Eastern Europe and collapse of the Soviet Union precipitated their withdrawal, as Moscow had more pressing issues to handle.

The Taliban, or students, a fundamentalist Islamic group, would take over Afghanistan in 1993. A regional group, the Taliban focused only on ruling Afghanistan through a strict implementation of Sharia Islam. Women were forbidden from education or any meaningful roles in public. Local leaders were chosen and installed by an Islamic council. Islamic judges held court and levied punishments like stoning for adultery and cutting off hands for thieves. The once cosmopolitan city of Kabul, Afghanistan's capital that grew and modernized in the 1960s, regressed into a period of darkness.

Osama bin Laden, having gained notoriety for his financial and military leadership within the mujahideen, had global visions for continuing jihad after the Soviet withdrawal. Bin Laden founded his militant terrorist group Al Qaeda, or the base, and sought to expand the regional success of mujahideen in Afghanistan into a worldwide movement. Bin Laden relied on a similarly harsh interpretation of Islam to the Taliban. Al Qaeda drew on Salafist Islamic teachings, a largely ostracized minority within the Sunni sect of Islam, to attempt to justify his attacks on the US and their allies.

By bin Laden's declaration of war in 1996, he had already attacked US troops in Saudi Arabia twice, once in Riyadh and once in Khobar. Those attacks resulted in five and nineteen Americans dead respectively. Sitting with Arnett in Tora Bora, bin Laden had already set in motion his next moves in the war when he warned Arnett that the rest of the world would soon see and hear more of Al Qaeda.

At the turn of the twenty-first century, Al Qaeda expanded its efforts outside of Saudi Arabia. Bin Laden also further revealed his willingness to attack non-military targets. Bin Laden released a new fatwa in 1998, signed with other terrorist leaders including his long-time deputy, Ayman al-Zawahiri, that called on killing "the Americans and their allies – civilians and military."

Only months later, on the same day in August 1998, two truck bombers conducted near simultaneous bombings of the US embassies in Tanzania and Kenya, located over 300 miles away from each other. The bombing in Nairobi was the deadliest and resulted in more than 200 of the 224 total killed in both attacks, although almost all of these dead were local civilian Kenyan embassy employees. Bin Laden likely aimed for another Beirut, the bombing of the Marine barracks in 1983 he glorified in his 1996 declaration of war for killing more than 200 Marines, but he killed almost entirely Kenyans from a civilian work force. Two years later in October 2000, Al Qaeda militants used a small boat to conduct a suicide attack on the USS *Cole* that was refueling in the port of Aden in Yemen. The bombing killed seventeen US sailors but failed to sink the ship due to the heroic efforts of the crew.

Even with these more sophisticated attacks, Al Qaeda and bin Laden remained somewhat obscure, known well only in US, British, and allied law-enforcement and intelligence communities. Bin Laden met with more journalists after Arnett, hoping to raise his profile and attract more followers to his cause.

The attacks on September 11, 2001 would elevate bin Laden and Al Qaeda more than he could have ever hoped. At the World Trade Centers in New York City, the Pentagon in Washington DC, and the crash site in Shanksville, Pennsylvania, 2,977 people lost their lives. Like Darrell Curley in 1990, a generation of Americans then felt their next war was coming.

Three days after 9/11, President George W. Bush stood on the rubble of the World Trade Centers with his left arm around the shoulder of a New York City firefighter. He was surrounded by a crowd of first responders and held a bullhorn in his right hand to address them. As he began to speak saying how all Americans were in support of them, their efforts, and everyone lost in the attack, a man from the crowd yelled, "George, we can't hear you!" President Bush turned in the direction of the man and responded, in a way that came to define the entire country's response to 9/11. "I can hear you. I can hear you. The rest of the world hears you. And the people, the people who knocked these buildings down, will hear all of us soon."

Roars and chants of "U-S-A" forced President Bush to pause for a full twenty seconds before he could continue his speech. When he finished, he shook the firefighter's hand and then waved a small US flag back and forth in front of the crowd. The roars and chants continued. President Bush's "bullhorn speech" remains not only a moment of unmistakable patriotism but also a harbinger of the war that was to come.

Addressing a joint session of Congress on September 20, President Bush presented the first outline of the War Against Al Qaeda and what would become the Global War on Terrorism. President Bush described the enemy: Al Qaeda and its larger network of terror. Importantly, he defined them as a "fringe form of Islamic extremism" that was wholly separate from the millions who practice Islam peacefully.

> I also want to speak tonight directly to Muslims throughout the world. We respect your faith. It's practiced freely by many millions of Americans and by millions more in countries that America counts as friends. Its teachings are good and peaceful, and those who commit evil in the name of Allah blaspheme the name of Allah.
>
> The terrorists are traitors to their own faith, trying, in effect, to hijack Islam itself.
>
> The enemy of America is not our many Muslim friends. It is not our many Arab friends. Our enemy is a radical network of terrorists and every government that supports them.

After President Bush's address to Congress, the Taliban continued to refuse to hand over bin Laden. Three weeks later in early October, fighter jets from the US and United Kingdom began a bombing campaign on Taliban and Al Qaeda targets in Afghanistan. What would become a twenty-year war in Afghanistan had begun.

And all of this might never have happened. While many decisions and mistakes allowed for Al Qaeda's and bin Laden's success on 9/11, one decision by another US president stands out as an important thought experiment.

Decision-Making Exercise – "A Little Town Called Kandahar": In an interview taken the day before 9/11, President Clinton spoke publicly about the chance he had to "get" Osama bin Laden in the late 1990s. While the complete truth of the scenario is unknown, President Clinton stated that he would have had to kill "three hundred innocent women and children" to kill bin Laden in what is likely to have been a Tomahawk cruise-missile strike. Bin Laden had been tracked to Kandahar, the spiritual home of the Taliban, and US intelligence agencies had reported a rare, real-time location for the terrorist mastermind. President Clinton weighed the decision: the probable death of an evil man against the lives of many innocents. What would you do?

President Clinton decided if he went through with the missile strike, he "would have been no better than [bin Laden]." The strike was called off. Bin Laden lived to continue leading and planning 9/11, which by then was already in motion.

In the War Against ISIS, the US military adopted the "non-combatant casualty cutoff value," or NCV, to aid decision-making in moments like the one faced by President Clinton. The laws of war prohibit the targeting of non-combatants; however, collateral damage is a tragic and painful aspect of war that is not always a war crime. Military leaders assigned numerical NCVs to targets, like a house ISIS fighters maintained as a command center or vehicle ISIS fighters used to transfer weapons. The numerical NCV forced the question – "would this target still be a military necessity if X civilians died in collateral damage?" Responsible leaders, often generals with thirty years or more experience, would have to be able to answer yes. President Clinton thought killing the then largely unknown bin Laden was not a military necessity if 300 civilians were to die as well.

Collateral damage directly inhibits success in war, at least from the perspective of the US and its allies. Insurgent groups like ISIS understand the laws and measures of the US to avoid civilian casualties and hide among the population to protect themselves and make collateral damage more likely. Even in these scenarios, any civilian casualties in any strike would prompt an immediate investigation. These investigations forced responsible leaders to take accountability for the strike procedures that allowed for such a tragic and damaging mistake. If an investigation then showed the approved NCV was broken, responsible leaders faced even more scrutiny.

The use of NCV was an effective way to ensure that the possibility of civilian casualties was considered and minimized in every engagement. Due to careful measures in targeting, like the ones my command center practiced from 2016–17, civilian casualties and collateral damage were tragic, exceptional events in the war, rather than constant elements of it.

The US, the United Kingdom, and their allies quickly defeated the Taliban and Al Qaeda within the three months after 9/11. In the Battle of Tora Bora, one of the final large-scale military engagements in December 2001, US and British special forces with allied Afghans fought to corner the remaining Al Qaeda elements in the mountains of Northeast Afghanistan. Bin Laden himself was thought to be hiding in the cave complexes in a location close to where he met Arnett four years before. However, US troops were undermanned on the ground during the battle, and bin Laden escaped to Pakistan.

The War in Afghanistan transitioned to nation-building, and Al Qaeda re-built itself as an insurgent threat to that effort. Al Qaeda still conducted attacks around the world, including high-profile bombings of public transportation in Madrid and London in 2004 and 2005 that killed 191 and 56 people, respectively. However, the US and its allies in the Global War on Terrorism increased pressure on Al Qaeda through surveillance and targeted strikes to limit their ability to conduct operations outside of the Middle East.

The invasion of Iraq in 2003 gave Al Qaeda more opportunities to train and attack Americans and their allies from another battleground. Abu Musab al-Zarqawi, a Jordanian who had fought with the mujahideen in Afghanistan in the 1980s, intensified the Iraq War through his leadership of Al Qaeda in Iraq (AQI). Zarqawi took advantage of the chaos and disorganization from the initial re-building effort in Iraq to precipitate some of the worst conflict in the Iraq War.

Zarqawi's tactics provoked a broader intra-Islam conflict. Zarqawi deliberately targeted Shia Muslims, the second largest sect of Islam behind Sunni and the majority of the Muslims in Iraq and Iran. By targeting Shia sites of worship such as the Imam Ali Mosque in Najaf, Iraq, in August 2003, Zarqawi precipitated increased conflict between Sunni and Shia to raise more Sunni support for his insurgents in AQI. Zarqawi expertly manipulated media to amplify and highlight persistent intra-Islam grievances and his divisive messages by staging and documenting brutal beheadings for fixated worldwide consumption.

Years of collaboration between the US and Jordan eventually led to an airstrike that killed Zarqawi in 2006. Zarqawi's tactics of divisiveness began to fail, and the US and its allies shifted tactics to focus on empowering local leaders. Sunni Iraqis, key elements of this new strategy, began to ostracize and defeat extremism from within their own communities in what became known as the "Sunni Awakening" in 2007. Iraq unified again as a diverse country of Sunni in the west, Shia in the east and south, and Kurds in the north. The US's role in the Iraq War slowly came to an end in 2011.

The seeds of a different awakening began to sprout across the Arab world as the Iraq War was ending. Arabs of all backgrounds would take to the streets to protest against authoritarian governments. Protests started first in Tunisia and spread across North Africa to Egypt and to Syria in the Middle East. The first act of the "Arab Spring" in Tunisia began simply with a frustrated fruit-seller.

Decision-Making Exercise – "The Fruit Seller": Mohamed Bouazizi was a 26-year-old street vendor in Tunisia. He had been harassed for years by corrupt local officials, who siphoned away his earnings through bribes. In December 2010, he was harassed to a breaking point when his fruit scales were stolen by a corrupt official. He thought he could not continue to make a living and wanted to send a message of his frustration to his government leaders. What would you do?

Bouazizi first went to the local government office to protest his injustice. When his complaints were not heard, he grabbed a can of gasoline and set himself on fire. His self-immolation precipitated larger protests against the corrupt and authoritarian Tunisian government. Soon after his death, Tunisian President Ben Ali relinquished power after more than two decades. Tunisia reformed its government as a democracy.

The "Arab Spring" spread to Egypt and Syria with less conclusive results. Protests in Tahrir Square in Egypt would force dictator Hosni Mubarak to give up power; however, democracy remained unstable, and protesters would return to the streets again unhappy with their newly elected president Mohamed Morsi. The Syrian revolution became a civil war with no end in sight with three main warring factions: the Syrian Regime in the east and south, Syrian Kurds in the northeast, and Syrian Sunnis in the south and northwest.

The years after Bouazizi still brought some hope. Osama bin Laden was killed the following spring by US special forces. The Iraq War ended, and the War in Afghanistan was de-intensifying. Widespread protests clamoring for democracy in the Middle East seemed like they would turn into meaningful change.

In spring 2013, I had dinner with one of my teachers at my favorite spot in Harvard Square, a dive bar called Charlie's Kitchen. He was a young philosophy Ph.D. and taught a section of a class simply titled "Liberty" that examined the history, philosophy, and implementation of liberty in government. He knew my planned future in the Marines, and the conversation drew towards the wars in the Middle East and the "Arab Spring." When the conversation stalled, I remembered him looking away, like he was about to say something controversial.

"You know we'll wonder when we look back at the Arab Spring years from now what started it all. Before Bouazizi."

"What do you think started it?" I asked him, smiling.

"Well. Maybe the Iraq War. The first toppling of a Middle Eastern authoritarian government in this century. Thirty, forty years from now, if Iraq, Tunisia, Egypt, and Syria and all these countries have prosperous democracies, we might even say the Iraq War was a good thing."

A year later, even fewer would make this optimistic argument. Former Al Qaeda in Iraq leader Abu Bakr al-Baghdadi introduced his new terrorist group, the Islamic State of Iraq and al-Sham, or ISIS, to the world. Baghdadi had carefully recruited and strengthened an army out of the lawlessness and power vacuum of the Syrian Civil War. Disadvantaged Sunnis in Northern Syria and Iraq joined Baghdadi's ranks to fight perceived religious and economic injustice.

When Baghdadi's army swept into Iraq in 2014, a new chapter of the Iraq War would begin. The question of why the US started that war in 2003 gained new scrutiny, as it became clear US troops would have to return to Iraq. The supposed objective of bin Laden's jihad – to remove US troops from the Middle East – was set back once more.

"I Can Hear You" Summary and Discussion Questions

Declarations of War

Osama bin Laden first communicated his declaration of jihad to the world in 1996. His goals and targets were stated clearly. Bin Laden wanted the US to stop supporting Israel and withdraw from Saudi Arabia. All active military in the Middle East and especially in Saudi Arabia were his targets. In 1998, he released a second fatwa to expand his target list to include "Americans and their allies – civilians and military."

1. The majority of US troops left Saudi Arabia in 2003 at the beginning of the Iraq War, leaving only a small training force behind in Riyadh. Was Osama bin Laden successful?
2. Some argue that bin Laden was more manipulative than his stated intentions: although bin Laden publicly stated his goal was to remove the US from Saudi Arabia and the Middle East, some argue he actually sought to draw the Americans into long, protracted wars that would result in the overall denigration of US society. By 2022, Al Qaeda was largely powerless due to relentless pursuit from the US, United Kingdom, and their critical allies. Democracy though, in the US and around the world, seemed to be at a critical flashpoint. Who won? What might Kennan and Nitze argue?

A Little Town Called Kandahar

President Bill Clinton said in an interview that he once had a chance to kill Osama bin Laden in the late 1990s. Although different details have been postulated for his actual decision, President Clinton stated there would have been some level of collateral damage, including women and children killed in any US attack on bin Laden. President Clinton thought "then I would have been no better than him. And so I didn't do it."

1. How many deaths in collateral damage are acceptable to kill a terrorist mastermind like Osama bin Laden? What about a serial killer?
2. Every military operation includes a level of uncertainty. In this case, bin Laden could have left his location while the missiles were in flight. How likely would success need to be in a strike to kill bin Laden with known collateral damage? 80 percent? 90 percent?

The Fruit Seller

Mohamed Bouazizi's self-immolation brought about the "Arab Spring" in 2011, in which Arabs from North Africa to the Middle East took to the streets to protest against authoritarian governments. Tunisia, where Bouazizi started the revolution, successfully implemented democracy for ten years before President Saied dismantled parliament in July 2021. Changes elsewhere have also not been straightforward: Syria continues to struggle in a decade-long civil war, and another authoritarian government quickly replaced Egypt's Morsi.

1. The science fiction movie *Bladerunner 2049* posits "Dying for the right cause. It's the most human thing we can do." Is there a cause you think is worth dying for?
2. Bouazizi could not have foreseen the movement he would start. The success of the "Arab Spring" is also inconclusive. Does lack of certainty change what's worth dying for?

Chapter 8

PUNCHING YOUR PLAN IN THE FACE

Bright flashes of light wobbled and streaked thousands of feet into the night sky over our heads. The sound crashed through the silence of the desert, as rocket after rocket disappeared among the stars. I stood with a British officer named Steve Pengilly on the roof of our base medical center, as we watched our unit fire rockets at ISIS positions miles away. Steve was a decade older than I was and led the company of US Marines and British and Danish soldiers in charge of base security. Steve and I had been leaving the command center when the order had finally come through to fire, and I had asked Steve if he wanted to watch from the roof. He had given me a funny look but agreed. When the strike was ending, Steve turned to me and said simply, "Thanks for the heads up, Brooksy."

During the shoot, I had stood transfixed, thinking I was watching the scene I would recognize in a Hollywood movie. As we left the roof, I realized Steve had seen that movie many times before. Still, I thought that moment would make it hard for me to leave the military, a sight so bizarre and meaningful and shared with an ally and mentor I respected. I walked back in the dark to the hangar where I slept wondering what moments had kept Steve in the Army.

Steve graduated from Sandhurst, the UK's military academy, in 2001. He had grown up with family stories of four generations of war veterans. When he was old enough, he had known he would follow their example into service. Steve's great-grandfather fought in the First World War in some of its most iconic battles in Flanders Fields in Belgium. Steve's grandfather Fred Pengilly was a paratrooper and jumped into Normandy behind German lines the night before D-Day in June 1944. The paratroopers helped prepare the battlefield for the invasion and the arrival of Judge Tucker and his men days later.

Fred Pengilly was wounded by a German sniper while he fought his way back to his battalion before D-Day. Fred still made a second jump later that spring in March 1945 in Operation Varsity, a battle that secured a strategic crossing for Allied forces across the Rhine River into Northern Germany. Steve's father fought against communist-backed rebels in the counterinsurgency war in Dhofar, Oman, in the early 1970s.

Though for Steve in 2001, he thought he might not have the opportunity to continue the family legacy of fighting in war. He had a recent picture of military service from an older family friend, Tom, who was part of an Army unit based in the center of London. Tom told Steve stories that made serving in the military sound more like being part of a gentlemen's club. Morning physical training consisted of riding horses through Trafalgar Square. Training exercises required Tom to spend two weeks in the Alps skiing yearly. An orderly helped Tom dress for his nightly, mandatory black-tie dinners in London when he wasn't "training."

Steve imagined a similar Army lifestyle for him. Steve was in his office at an infantry battalion when 9/11 shattered that image and directed his path to the Middle East. Tom had just left the Army to take a comfortable job in finance, and Steve would never let him live that down.

To their chagrin, Steve's unit watched the initial invasion of Afghanistan from the North of England. They would be among the first though to begin preparations for another war in the Persian Gulf. Weapons of mass destruction had become common parlance, and all wondered if Saddam Hussein, the US's adversary from the Gulf War twelve years prior, was hiding anything in Iraq. Steve and his platoon of thirty soldiers did not listen to every speech as US leaders asserted Hussein's danger to world order, because they already felt war was inevitable. They trained with determined intensity until they arrived in Kuwait in spring 2003 and prepared for the push north to Baghdad.

Preparation took the form of extensive planning and rehearsals in airfields that dotted the Kuwaiti desert. Since Iraqi intelligence spied on them closely, they could not appear too busy or hurried, lest they give up their plans to invade north. Steve's unit relied on nightly wargames in a secluded part of an aircraft hangar to rehearse the invasion.

Wargames were a critical part of the planning process. Like a board game, leaders from each military element in the unit made moves on a map, while a "red team" of fake adversaries played the enemy's response, challenged assumptions, and incorporated elements of chance. The turns played out and taught them what they could expect to see on the battlefield and how their plan could fail.

The last wargame before the invasion made Steve uneasy. His platoon had been decimated by an enemy force that was larger and better equipped than expected at a key set of houses on the outskirts of the Iraqi city Basra. The houses were along Steve's platoon's assigned lane, a form of control measure that made friendly fire between adjacent units less likely. He had stopped by the small hooch of the intelligence shop and requested surveillance of that location before his platoon would arrive.

Steve still felt like he was walking his men into a trap and found himself unable to sleep. He spent the night scanning a blank map he had saved which showed the terrain around Basra and studying a card deck provided by their US military partners. The cards had the faces and names of high-value targets in the Iraqi government and military, the men most important to the success of the defense of Iraq. Steve kept the eight of clubs at the top of his deck, which featured the name of the governor of Basra.

Decision-Making Exercise – "Seizing the Initiative": British Army Lieutenant Steve Pengilly and his platoon pushed north with their infantry battalion into Southern Iraq in March 2003. As his platoon pulled into the urban sprawl south of Basra, an Iraqi T-72 tank began firing on his platoon. Steve's armored fighting vehicles were no match for the firepower of the tank. There was a US fighter jet overhead nearby that had just released its last bombs and was out of further ammunition. Steve had an adjacent unit with anti-tank weapons on his eastern flank and knew more airpower would be available within fifteen minutes. What would you do?

Upon seeing the tank ahead, Steve immediately reversed his platoon and ordered his vehicles to keep a building in between them and the tank. The tank had forced Steve's platoon into a hasty defense, and Steve knew he had to take an action to force the tank to react to them. Steve requested the unloaded US jet to conduct a "show of force" or a flight directly overhead the tank at a low altitude. The tank commander seeing the fighter jet would then have to decide if he would stay in range of the fighter jet or seek cover himself. The "show of force" would buy Steve's platoon time to hold in their defense until the additional aircraft could arrive overhead and strike the Iraqi position.

The Iraqi tank commander, sitting in a slightly exposed defensive position, made the decision to seek better overhead cover after the US fighter jet flew only 300ft above him. Steve observed the tank moving from its position, but he still held his platoon back until the additional aircraft could weaken the Iraqi defenses. He did not request support from the adjacent anti-tank unit, due to the risk of friendly fire when crossing between the assigned platoon lanes and the time it would take to coordinate. Once the fully loaded aircraft arrived on station and weakened the Iraqi defense, Steve pushed his platoon forward and seized the Iraqi defensive position before the Iraqis could regroup and attack them.

Steve consolidated his forces in a new defensive position and oriented on the Iraqis retreating north. The tank had delayed Steve's platoon's approach, so he and his soldiers were some of the last to set into a defensive posture after the morning's attack. He observed the new position from the turret of his armored fighting vehicle and made sure he was aligned with his adjacent platoons. From the turret, Steve heard the approach of another vehicle to his rear. The senior enlisted of the entire infantry regiment, several echelons above Steve's platoon, shouted out to him, "Sir, you are required at the battalion operations tent straight away."

Steve was the last officer to arrive at the battalion operations tent, which was more than ten blocks to the south of Steve's platoon's new line. The commander, holding a 2½m stick and standing over a terrain model of part of southern Basra, greeted Steve and told him to sit down. "Gentlemen, these are orders for an attack that will take place at 1115h this morning." Steve looked down at his watch; it was 1030h.

The commander proceeded to walk through the orders for the attack on some of the last strongholds in southern Basra and then left the tent to allow the officers below him to work out the details. Steve turned to his fellow platoon commanders and began an expedited wargame. Steve studied the several buildings that he was assigned to attack and forecasted where the Iraqis would defend and attack him from once he got there.

Generally, they would have more time to deconflict and prepare their soldiers for an attack that carried significant risk. The risk was not only from the still-determined enemy, but also from friendly fire in the ever-present confusion of urban combat. As Steve and the other platoon commanders considered the plan and the Iraqis' reaction, they created new control measures in addition to their assigned platoon lanes in the form of restrictive fire lines, in this case streets they would not shoot across.

Steve raced back to his platoon to deliver the orders of the attack. They pushed forward almost immediately several city blocks and attacked the Iraqis, who were still scrambling to set into a fortified defensive position.

When Steve's platoon began to seize their objective, the restrictive fire line of the north–south running street proved critical. The platoon commander to Steve's east told him after the battle his soldiers would have shot into Steve's building, because it appeared they were taking fire from the west and the smoke obscured who was actually inside.

Steve's battalion would remain in Basra as Baghdad fell in April, three weeks after the start of the invasion. Steve and his soldiers began to set up patrol bases over several city blocks to expand their presence and quell remaining pockets of resistance. Later in April at the battalion operations tent, Steve heard in a briefing that the Basra governor had surrendered. He went back to his patrol base, took the eight of clubs out of his deck, and threw it in the burn pit.

With Basra under British control, Steve and his battalion found themselves keeping the peace in a city that they had just invaded and seized. Steve's platoon dealt with small protests and riots, mostly over the cost of gasoline and rising unemployment. On his way back to England that summer, Steve worried about these riots, led by unemployed soldiers from the disbanded Iraqi military, and wondered how soon it would be before he and his battalion were back in Iraq.

Steve would serve as a company commander in Iraq less than a year later. Then a captain responsible for more than 200 men, Steve saw firsthand how the war began to change. Riots and protests became an insurgency, and the insurgency took the Iraq War into a challenging chapter with ambiguous measures of success. Steve and his soldiers saw significant combat with Shia Militia Groups, aligned with and supported covertly by Iran.

On a third tour in Iraq, Steve found himself in another wargame, this time in an established base outside of Basra in summer 2005. Their battalion of armored fighting vehicles and tanks was tasked with augmenting any unit expected to get into significant combat with insurgents in and around Basra. Steve's role was the operations officer, responsible for facilitating that overall mission of over 1,000 men.

The wargame centered around the movement of nearly forty-five tanks and other vehicles from one base north of Basra to another south of Basra. Moving that many vehicles drew a lot of unwelcome attention from the established insurgency. Due to the city's proximity to Iran, Basra was an even more dangerous place for explosively formed projectiles, funded by Iran and implemented by Shia Militia Groups on the ground. The wargame specifically was meant to help prepare Steve's unit for what would happen if they encountered an ambush at specific points along the route. With all the key leaders and staff in the battalion operations tent for the wargame, the executive officer

Dan, a superior officer to Steve, started off by saying, "I want to ensure that we get out of our own base in the right order and right movement. Let's assume all of our tanks are on the road, come to the exit of the base, instead of turning left to Basra, the lead turns right."

Steve immediately started laughing. "What's so funny, Steve?"

"That will never happen, Dan."

"It could."

"No, it could not. Let's fast forward to the bridge where we could get ambushed."

Dan looked annoyed. "OK. To the bridge."

Two days later as Steve sat in the turret of his armored fighting vehicle preparing to leave the base, he watched in horror as the lead vehicle took a right rather than a left towards Basra. The next vehicle devotedly followed the lead, as did the next and the next and several others before the column could be stopped. After an hour of turning around the column of tanks, the mission was cancelled and moved to another day.

Steve realized immediately he had discounted a possible mistake, and while unlikely, a mistake that they could have and should have prepared for. Only by incorporating all possible events, from likely to unlikely, does wargaming truly prepare for execution. Dan found Steve later and said, "I told you it could bloody well happen." Steve could only shake his head and apologize, but he gained an appreciation for the requirement to prepare for rare events.

Steve would serve another tour in Iraq, for the fourth time outside of Basra in 2009. Lasting damage from the invasion and tensions between the two main sects of Islam, Sunni and Shia, continued to fuel unrest in country. As Steve watched the war close in 2011, he still wondered when he would be back. The rise of ISIS in 2014 made that return all the more likely, and in 2016, he led a contingent of British soldiers to Al Asad Airbase in Western Iraq.

A few weeks after the night with Steve on the roof, I was on shift in the command center when calls started to flow in. First, a security post had reported that they saw a fire on the east side of base. The phones seemed to ring constantly after that with others reporting what they were seeing. We realized our quiet night had quickly turned serious. My senior enlisted for the command center, a tall, lanky West Virginian who survived only on Mountain Dew and cigarettes, shifted a base surveillance camera to where the security post had reported the fire. "Nothing there, Sir. Oh wait." He shifted the camera again as it was focused on the wrong area. The room had a moment of collective gasp as we then saw what was a massive fire take up the small surveillance screen. Based on the location and what we could see, we presumed a barracks housing US and allied troops had caught fire.

Steve and his company of British soldiers had just rotated back to the UK. A new British company commander and his soldiers now faced this test within their first few days on the job. When the post had reported the fire, Steve's replacement gave his orders and then headed up to our command center. He walked through the door and took a spot in the corner to supervise, a position Steve often held himself during critical moments of base security. The base commander and all other leadership flowed into the command center soon after. Immediate questions needed to be answered: Was anyone injured? Was the fire spreading? How much did we lose? Was the base still safe?

The command center reverberated with intensity as we sought to answer those questions and provide support to the troops on the ground. I heard Kyle and Daly on the radio, in charge of the mobile security elements, mobilize immediately. Kyle's platoon served as security for the designated firefighting element, and they got on scene close to the fire. Kyle reported that the few people in the barracks when it caught fire had escaped and everyone was accounted for. Kyle's platoon was evacuating some who had minor injuries to the base medical center. The fire seemed to be contained, but there were also weapons and ammunition stored in the barracks that was on fire. Daly's platoon took up reinforcing positions at some of the weaker positions on base, in case ISIS or another enemy was somehow using this moment of confusion to attack.

Kyle called in that the fire was getting so hot ammunition and weapons started exploding and shooting inside the barracks. Kyle evacuated everyone else in the area and fell back with the firefighting element to a safe distance. The base commander ordered the entire base into lockdown. Lockdown would only be lifted once the fire was dead and no more ammunition could explode.

The firefighters had to let the fire die out on its own since they could not get close due to the risk posed by the live ammunition. We would learn a misplaced electrical plug in the barracks had sparked the fire. Weapons and ammunition also should not have been stored in the wooden barracks.

As the base lockdown lifted and the command center returned to a calmer state, I looked back at Steve's replacement in the corner. He had his arms folded and was staring past me to the front of the room, where the screens still showed surveilled ISIS locations far off in the desert. When Kyle and Daly called in that they were standing down, he started walking towards the door. He hit me on the shoulder and said, "Good job, Brooksy."

I smiled but immediately thought of Steve, then back home in the UK. The event, even with its stress and uncertainty, had almost seemed routine, since before Steve had left, he pulled me, Kyle, Daly, and other officers from the unit into a wargame for this exact scenario. We had stood over a table with an enlarged map of our base and played out what would happen and what we would do if a fire broke out. Daly had rolled his eyes behind Steve's back when we started. There is not much to burn in the desert on a largely fireproof base, so most of us were counting the minutes until we could leave the room. Still, Steve had forced us to prepare for an unlikely event, and when it happened, we responded just like the pieces we had moved on the map that day.

Facing danger and confusion, the Marines and soldiers on base security had performed well; they had moved several casualties quickly to the medical center and evacuated others from the vicinity of the fire, while ensuring no enemy could take advantage of the situation. That night, Steve's replacement met Kyle, Daly, and their platoons as they returned. He told them how well they did and then left them to debrief, relax, and decompress on their own.

Steve had to laugh when he learned of the base fire, but he held back from saying "I told you it could bloody well happen." He was proud of the Marines he had led and the replacements he had prepared for that moment. Though back in the UK, Steve had already shifted his focus elsewhere, as he had received new orders to deploy again only weeks after returning from Iraq to serve as an advisor in Kabul. Though he would miss his family, he knew he had to take on the mission and calling to lead more men under fire. Despite all of his sacrifices to train, prepare, and lead his troops, he always downplayed his role, saying any success belonged to his men, never to him. All he held onto was a quiet pride in the men he led. That was what kept him in the Army.

"Punching Your Plan in the Face" Summary and Discussion Questions

Seizing the Initiative

During one battle in the invasion of Iraq in 2003, British officer Steve Pengilly's platoon encountered an Iraqi T-72 battle tank that posed a significant threat to him and his troops. Steve employed Colonel John Boyd's concept of the Observe-Orient-Decide-Act (OODA) Loop to plan and take decisive action: through creative use of airpower, he seized the initiative, forced the Iraqi tank commander to react to him, and took control of key terrain in the battle.

1. What character traits did Steve rely on to seize the initiative in this moment?
2. How can Colonel John Boyd's concept of the OODA Loop be used outside of military or fighting contexts?

Wargaming the Wrong Turn

By Steve's third tour in Iraq, he had already seen the significant benefits of wargaming to test a plan. These wargames allowed Steve to predict enemy outcomes, incorporate elements of chance, and rehearse key friendly actions. However, during a wargame in his third tour, his friend posed him with an immediate friendly action he thought impossible: a wrong turn at the start of a convoy. When the wrong turn actually happened, Steve learned that he should not have overlooked that unlikely but challenging possibility.

1. How do you balance preparing for unlikely outcomes without spending too much time on them?
2. What are the best ways to incorporate chance and probability into planning?

The Base Fire

Steve prepared us well for the unlikely event of a fire on a largely fireproof desert base. Following Steve's example and the plan he had set in place to respond to a base fire, Steve's replacement took up position in our command center where he could supervise and empower his subordinates, Kyle and Daly, to take control of the situation. Training Kyle, Daly, and the rest of the men on security for this moment, Steve was responsible for our flexible and timely response to a dangerous situation.

1. Good leaders place themselves at the "point of friction," the place where the most could go wrong, during critical events. Steve often supervised from our command center during heightened moments of base security, in the same way his replacement did during the base fire. What are the positives and negatives of a leader supervising from a command center versus supervising on the ground, in this case perhaps with Kyle near the barracks on fire? What are examples of the "point of friction" for leadership outside of military contexts?
2. What leadership qualities made Steve such an effective leader?

Chapter 9

THE TALE OF TWO PASSENGER JETS, MISTAKENLY SHOT DOWN

I was driving home from squash practice in my junior year of high school when my friend gave me a call. He asked me where I was.

"Tonight is our first practice. You were supposed to be here already."

I realized I had completely forgotten. I had agreed to help him coach his younger brother's middle-school basketball team. I pretended I remembered agreeing to that very significant time commitment and told him I would be early for the next practice.

Just over twelve years later in January 2020, I was sitting with the team at a sports bar for a long overdue reunion. They were young men, college graduates, far from the middle-school boys I met at their second practice. I was proud to see them grow in the two years I coached them; I was shocked just how much they had grown by then.

Midway through dinner, I made the mistake of checking my phone. I had a host of notifications from a social-media tracking application and some texts from friends. Iran had shot six ballistic missiles at Al Asad Airbase in Western Iraq. I spent the rest of dinner smiling with the team, but I thought I would remember the moment as one of my last before my next war started. Though thinking that war was coming, against Iran, the country stuck between Iraq and Afghanistan, was a feeling shared by many veterans of the wars in the Middle East.

Why that feeling was so common could derive from the actions of a grandson of President Theodore Roosevelt. Kermit Roosevelt, Jr lived the life of James Bond without the flashy girlfriends. He was an intelligence officer with the Office of Strategic Services, the precursor to the Central Intelligence Agency. In the early 1950s, Roosevelt thought the US, as the emerging world power, could build strong relationships in the Middle East. This worldview propelled him to cross into Iran using a fake name, hide under a blanket in the backseat of a car traveling into the Iranian palace, and make friends with the Iranian king called the Shah. Together, they planned to overthrow the democratically elected Prime Minister Mohammad Mosaddegh.

Decision-Making Exercise – "Diplomacy Hidden in the Backseat": In summer 1953, Roosevelt presented his plan to overthrow Prime Minister Mosaddegh and install a compliant Iranian general, Fazlollah Zahedi, in his place. Shah Reza Pahlavi would maintain full power over Iran and ensure the country remained a close ally of the West. Prime Minister Mosaddegh had planned to nationalize Iranian oil, removing the influence of British Petroleum and other Western investors. Nationalization was also thought to be a step closer in worldview to Iran's neighbor to its northeast, the Soviet Union. Roosevelt's leaders must decide whether or not to approve the plan. What would you do?

The approval of Operation AJAX, the code name for Roosevelt's *coup d'état,* left a scar on the Middle East. Shah Pahlavi's crimes against his own people and the Iranian Revolution solidified its problematic legacy. However, the thought of the Iron Curtain expanding through the Middle East was enough to drive at least some of Roosevelt's leaders towards approval. That approval did not come without significant dissent: diplomat George Kennan, the father of the Cold War policy "containment" that outlined efforts to stymie the expansion of the Soviet Union, and Paul Nitze, the author of National Security Council Report-68 (NSC-68) which implemented "containment" into official government policy, were adamantly opposed to intervention. Nevertheless, ensuring the Shah's continued power was a choice of regime stability and stood in contrast to the US's purported image as a bulwark for democracy.

Since 1953, the US has faced similar questions on the benefits and dangers of the regime change. The failure of the Iraq invasion fifty years after Operation AJAX exemplified the dangers of removing a strong leader, even an unpopular one. The continued disintegration of Libya after the death of Muammar Gaddafi served as another example less than ten years after Iraq.

The US policy on which leaders the country supports and why cannot be drawn on clear lines, even the lines the US would like to espouse the most: pro-democracy or pro-human rights. After Libya, the US has avoided publicly stating a goal for regime change for almost all countries, even stated adversaries. President Trump's support for Venezuela's Juan Guaidó stands out as the primary exception.

Roosevelt's plan was successful, and the Shah reigned for more than two decades. Iran was one of the strongest US allies in the Middle East and had a large arsenal of US military equipment. The Shah, though, faced charges that he expanded the military only to use it to quell internal dissent. The Iranian people, facing poverty and poor institutions for education, perceived that the Shah's riches grew while they suffered. Operation AJAX's critical mistake of taking democracy away from the Iranian people sowed the seeds of revolution that had taken hold by the end of 1978. In early 1979, the Shah ceded power and left his country, aging and in dire need of cancer treatment.

Decision-Making Exercise – "Treating the Shah": Shah Reza Pahlavi left Iran in exile. He had few supporters left, as his regime in Iran was accused of corruption, mass murder, and the disenfranchisement of minorities. The progression of his cancer advanced rapidly, and he requested treatment in the US. President Carter had to make the decision of whether or not to admit the Shah for cancer treatment in New York City. President Carter's Secretary of State Henry Kissinger was adamant the US should admit the Shah. Not admitting him was tantamount to allowing him to die; admitting him could embolden critics already frustrated by the stalwart US support of the Shah. What would you do?

President Carter's humanitarian decision to admit the Shah for treatment precipitated another scarring event for US and Iranian relations: the 1979 Iranian Hostage Crisis. Iranian protestors stormed the US embassy in Tehran only days after the Shah was admitted to New York City and held fifty-two hostages until the start of President Reagan's term in 1981.

Society likely would see this decision differently today than it did fifty years ago. Refusing medical treatment, even for a criminal, might seem like the less informed decision. On the other hand, an exiled, disgraced leader might not deserve medical treatment. The US could have absolved responsibility: not every cancer patient has the right to treatment in New York City. This line has not been tested again.

The anger of the Iranian people at the time was palpable and apparent to President Carter's administration. With hindsight, admitting the Shah should have come with an increase in security at US diplomatic missions in the Middle East. The example of Al Asad

Airbase in Western Iraq going on high alert for the US strike on Syria in April 2017 might show the US government has learned this lesson.

Iran shifted from a monarchy to a theocracy. The Iranian Ayatollah, the spiritual leader of Shia Islam in Iran, would quickly install a government and hold on to power. The Ayatollah supervised elections and controlled all aspects of the government and the military. Saddam Hussein observed as Iran's neighbor to the west in Iraq and saw this Shia revival as a threat, considering the disenfranchised Shia majority he ruled in his country. In the midst of the revolution in 1980, he would attack Iran and start a devastating eight-year war.

The Iran-Iraq War, which Saddam Hussein named "Qadisiyah" in reference to the ancient Arab-Persian battle shortly after the foundation of Islam, would bring unimaginable suffering to the people and militaries of Iran and Iraq. Soldiers faced extensive use of chemical weapons and died by the hundreds of thousands as their countries warred over control of the Shatt al-Arab, the confluence of the Tigris and Euphrates rivers on the border between Iran and Iraq.

During the war, the US supported Saddam Hussein and Iraq, in partnership against the mutual enemy of a freshly hostile Iran. Most of the US's support came through combatting the Iranian Navy in the Persian Gulf. In July 1988, that support would engender another lasting wound in US-Iran relations. The USS *Vincennes*, tasked on a combat mission in the Persian Gulf, misidentified an Iranian passenger jet and shot it down with a surface-to-air missile, resulting in the deaths of 290 civilians.

The war ended just over a month later. Both sides would declare victory, although no borders would change. In Iraq, Hussein built the Hands of Victory in Baghdad, massive crossed swords at the entrances to the Great Celebrations Square just north of the Tigris. Hussein also named the man-made lake north of the Haditha Dam Lake Qadisiyah, a lake I would stare at in awe of its beauty through drone feeds on my first deployment. On the other side in Iran's capital Tehran, the Ayatollah raised the Holy Defense Museum, in tribute to the conflict and the Iranians who died fighting.

Saddam Hussein would quickly turn from convenient ally to adversary less than three years later, as he and the Iraqi military invaded Kuwait in an attempt to annex lucrative oil fields. The US would respond in decisive fashion and liberate Kuwait in what would be known as the Gulf War or Operation DESERT STORM.

While the Cold War had ended, Roosevelt's vision for the Middle East remained incomplete. Iran and Iraq stood out as persistent adversaries, halting the expansion of US influence and priorities for the region. President George W. Bush's State of the Union address in

2002, months after 9/11, reiterated this thought and labeled Iran and Iraq as two key nodes of the "Axis of Evil." North Korea, the adversary my infantry battalion prepared to fight the most in training from 2015–18, was the third.

This line of thinking drove the US invasion of Iraq in 2003. While officially on the sideline of the war, Iran supported Shia Militia Groups fighting against US and allied forces. Explosively formed projectiles, advanced IEDs that could pierce armor, arrived in the Iraq War thanks to Iran. US and allied deaths from explosively formed projectiles serve as lasting evidence of the expertise and material Iran shared with those fighting the US.

As the Iraq War ended in 2011, President Obama sought the easing of tensions with Iran. This major foreign-policy breakthrough could have re-shaped the Middle East in ways that Roosevelt first intended. In 2014, the Joint Comprehensive Plan of Action was signed, colloquially known as the Iran Nuclear Deal. The agreement lifted economic sanctions on Iran in exchange for assurances Iran would not seek nuclear weapons.

I was in Kuwait leading a small intelligence section in May 2018 when President Trump announced the US was leaving the Iran Nuclear Deal. Over the previous four years, Iran had used some of the economic relief from the lifted sanctions to fund a more expansive foreign policy. Iran, through its Iranian Revolutionary Guard Corps, supported militant groups waging war across the Middle East from the Houthis in Yemen, to Hezbollah in Lebanon, and Shia Militia Groups in Iraq and Syria. These actions, destabilizing the Middle East from the visions of Roosevelt, President Obama, and President Trump, were the key trigger for the US to leave the deal. I remember turning to one of my intelligence analysts across our small room jammed with computers and plywood desks and announcing the news. He responded: "Wow, Sir, you think we are going to war?"

I said I hope not. He nodded and turned his standard playlist of break-up music back on. The news was not unexpected, but we did know that the region we studied so carefully was changing. As the War Against ISIS waned, part of our focus turned towards the potential war with Iran.

Less than two years later in 2019, the embers from the long-standing US-Iran conflict began to enflame. The immediate chain of events that led to the missile attack on Al Asad Airbase started with a rocket attack Iran supported on a different US and Iraqi Army base north of Baghdad in December 2019. An Iraqi-American interpreter, Nawres Hamid, had been killed in that attack.

I learned from two of my interpreters from my first deployment, Louie and Saif, that the interpreter community is small. Sitting with them at dinner at a Greek restaurant months after the attack, I asked Louie and Saif, in a moment of inattentiveness, if they had known Hamid. They both stared at me. Saif then pushed his phone across the table and showed me a picture of him kneeling with a fist on a coffin draped in an American flag. I did not need to ask who the coffin belonged to.

With the death of Hamid, President Trump ordered airstrikes on Iranian-supported Shia Militia Groups in Western Iraq. These airstrikes then prompted significant protests at the US embassy in Baghdad, some that turned violent and seemed to have hints of a more coordinated attack to come. The US government thought Qassem Soleimani, the leader of the Iranian Revolutionary Guard Corps, was preparing a significant attack on the US embassy.

President Trump's next move brought the US and Iran to the brink of war. The US military killed Qassem Soleimani in a drone strike after he landed on the military portion of Baghdad International Airport. The news of this strike shocked many, even those closely watching the conflict. As Iran prepared to respond, we waited, wondering when the all-out war would begin.

As I sat with my old players at a sports bar during Iran's ballistic-missile attack, we learned there were luckily no US casualties. Early warning from intelligence sources allowed troops to seek cover and prepare for the missile attack. Fifty-one aircraft were moved off base in the hours prior. Evacuated air maintenance, dining, living, and gym facilities were all destroyed in the attack, but no US, allied, or Iraqi troops were killed. The early warning was a critical success in saving US lives and preventing all-out war between the US and Iran. Though moments after the attack, history began to rhyme in a tragic way.

Decision-Making Exercise – "Incoming! Incoming! Incoming!": An Iranian radar technician, a member of the Iranian Revolutionary Guard Corps, was monitoring key base defense signals just after Iran's ballistic-missile attack on Al Asad Airbase in Western Iraq. The room's energy was heightened, as the Iranian military believed all-out war was inevitable like many from the US military did. The radar technician began to receive signals that seemed to show someone had returned fire: a missile was heading towards them. The technician did not have many options. He could start the process to destroy the incoming missile or wait and check his work with a peer or supervisor. What would you do?

A quick decision by members of the Iranian Revolutionary Guard Corps repeated the painful mistake of the USS *Vincennes*. Without enough time to analyze radar readings, the Iranian Revolutionary Guard chose to take an offensive posture and shoot a surface-to-air missile at what they thought was an incoming threat, rather than wait, confirm the radar inputs, and risk their own destruction. After initially denying involvement, Iran admitted that the Iranian Revolutionary Guard Corps had shot down a Ukrainian passenger plane leaving Tehran's airport and killed 176 people, including 57 Canadians. While there were no US or allied deaths from the missile attack in Iraq that night, the true casualty total would include those 176 deaths.

President Trump, perceiving Iran's failed and costly ballistic-missile attack as another victory, thought the US was in a strong position to negotiate a peace more suitable to US interests. Seeking to outline this plan for peace and prevent further Iranian attacks, President Trump addressed the world soon after the attack in a speech and closed with: "Finally, to the people and leaders of Iran: We want you to have a future and a great future – one that you deserve, one of prosperity at home, and harmony with the nations of the world. The United States is ready to embrace peace with all who seek it."

In summer and fall 2021, key members of President Biden's administration began negotiating a re-entry into the Iranian Nuclear Deal. Whether or not the US or Iran should return to the 2014 deal in light of the intervening seven years remains a question; Iran's continued support for militant groups across the Middle East and the US's inconsistency between administrations cloud the answer.

The only certainty is that war between the two countries must be avoided. All of us who thought the war was coming must continue to be wrong.

"The Tale of Two Passenger Jets, Mistakenly Shot Down" Summary and Discussion Questions

Diplomacy Hidden in the Backseat

Kermit Roosevelt, Jr, a grandson of President Theodore Roosevelt, created a *coup d'état* to overthrow the democratically elected Prime Minister Mohammad Mosaddegh of Iran in 1953. In the early days of the Cold War, Operation AJAX seemed like a necessary action to defend US and Western interests in the Middle East from Soviet expansion. By the Iranian Revolution in 1979, it was clear Operation AJAX left a scar on the Middle East and had lasting unintended consequences.

1. When would creating or facilitating a *coup d'état* be necessary?
2. How have US policies for foreign intervention ebbed and flowed since 1953?
3. When will be the next time the US intervenes militarily in a foreign country? Does providing weapons, as in Ukraine in 2022, count as intervention in war?

Treating the Shah

President Carter's decision to treat the dying Shah took the opposite approach from utilitarianism and focused solely on doing the "right thing" for an individual. The decision triggered the Iranian Hostage Crisis, where fifty-two Americans were held in captivity for more than year.

1. When does an individual lose the right to medical treatment?
2. What are some methods to balance firmness and compassion when holding someone accountable?

Incoming! Incoming! Incoming!

The passenger jets shot down in 1988 and 2020 were both tragic mistakes, the first by the US and the second by Iran. This thought experiment shows the difficulty of understanding and acting on complex information under time pressure and emotional stress.

1. How can you prepare for rapid decision-making in scenarios where failure is not acceptable?
2. What organizational structures can improve individual rapid decision-making?

With my jacked interpreter Louie at the end of my first deployment, Al Asad Airbase, Iraq, April 2017.

Judge Tucker (seated, centered) on Omaha Beach with several officers from 83rd Recon, June 1944.

When I received the enduring advice "Don't Go to War" from Judge Tucker, Richmond, Virginia, November 2014.

Toby Finney in Vietnam, 1969.

Landing a jab but still letting my right hand drop during an exhibition, May 2012.

The note I saw written on my way into Iraq, September 2016.

An MV-22 Osprey preparing for takeoff at night, Kuwait, 2018. I spent a significant amount of time in transit between bases during my second deployment, either on Ospreys or C-130s. When I traveled to Afghanistan to work with my close friend Kevin Zimmerman in 2018, I quickly provided some unsolicited advice. Kevin looked at me and said, "I don't come to Kuwait and tell you how to do your job." (*Photo Credit: Gabino Perez*)

Training in the 29 Palms desert during Infantry Officer Course with fellow ground intelligence officer Will Boudreau, September 2015.

With my platoon sergeant Brian Henexson before I left for deployment, 29 Palms, California, September 2016.

Planning details of our scout sniper screener with one of my Marines, Camp Pendleton, California, August 2017.

Kyle Kavanagh overlooking 29 Palms, California, July 2017.

My scout sniper platoon after returning from our deployment and completing our screener on First Sergeant's Hill in Camp Pendleton, California, August 2017.

British Army officer Steve Pengilly in Iraq, 2016.

Steve's father in the Falklands after the war, 1982–3.

USMC birthday celebration with Steve and Daly at Al Asad Airbase, Iraq, November 2016.

An illustration of the moment that opens Chapter 8, Al Asad Airbase, Iraq, 2016. That night, I watched HIMARS shoot at an ISIS target far from our base and felt like I was watching something out of a film. When I stepped down from the roof, I remember thinking it would be hard to leave the military. (*Illustration Credit: madhuwantighosh from Fiverr*)

Marcus patrolling with his Marines before the "bridge," Helmand Province, Afghanistan, 2009.

An illustration of Marcus crossing "the bridge" last, Helmand Province, Afghanistan, 2009. (*Illustration Credit: madhuwantighosh from Fiverr*)

An illustration of the four-nation lunch I had with my partners, Al Asad Airbase, Iraq, August 2018. (*Illustration Credit: madhuwantighosh from Fiverr*)

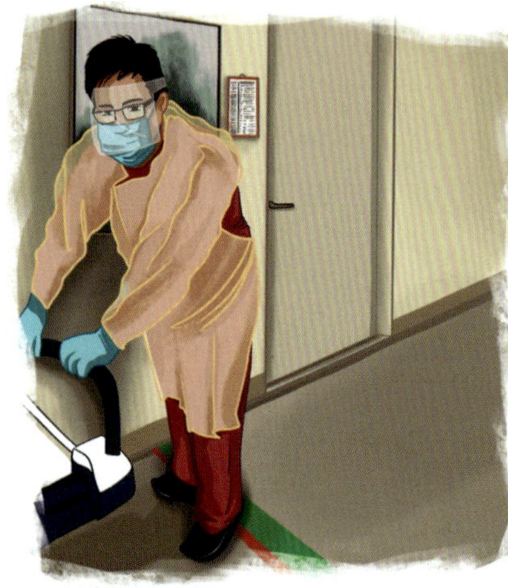

An illustration of Homer working in a New York City hospital during the COVID-19 pandemic, March 2020. (*Illustration Credit: madhuwantighosh from Fiverr*)

Observing a quadcopter training flight at Al Asad Airbase, Iraq, August 2018. (*Photo Credit: Carlos Lopez*)

A Marine recovering a quadcopter during a patrol outside of Camp Manion, Al Taqaddum Airbase, Iraq, August 2018. We called this the "Jesus photo," which demonstrated the infrared (IR) flood light as part of the quadcopter's capabilities. This patrol gave rise to the "Drone Overhead" decision-making exercise included in the appendices. (*Photo Credit: Gabino Perez*)

A night partnered patrol with Iraqi Army soldiers outside of Camp Manion, Al Taqaddum Airbase, Iraq, August 2018. My role when I traveled to different bases in 2018 was mainly to observe training and usage of quadcopters and other small unmanned aerial systems. However, I also worked with patrols to gain a better picture of the security posture of the bases. Some of the nights not patrolling in TQ ended playing chess with the company gunnery sergeant in charge of base security, a former scout sniper himself who had helped with the training of my platoon. We would argue whether our overall mission was important. His only concession came in partner patrols. "Joining the Iraqis? That is important I'll give you that." (*Photo Credit: Gabino Perez*)

Two Kurdish soldiers near the front line along the Euphrates River, Eastern Syria, 2018. As the Iraqis declared victory against ISIS in December 2017, the Kurds were our most critical partners to ensure the defeat of ISIS in Syria. (*Photo Credit: Gabino Perez*)

My Tribe that sent me off on my first deployment, September 2016.

My Tribe that welcomed me home after my first deployment, May 2017.

A final welcome home party after my second deployment, January 2019.

Two grandfathers and one of their grandsons. Left to right: James Smith, USN, 1951–5; Frank Brooks, USN, 1942–5; James Brooks, USMC, 2014–21.

With Sully on my last day in the Marines, Quantico, Virginia, March 2021.

My reflection in the Global War on Terrorism Memorial in Ft Benning, Georgia, January 2021.

A photograph of Lieutenant Abdullah that features on a memorial at Al Asad Airbase, Iraq. He dropped out of medical school in 2014 right before graduating to join the Iraqi Army and fight ISIS. He would lead an explosive ordnance disposal (EOD) platoon, because he felt it fit the skills he had been developing in surgery. Talking about his military service, he said, "The best thing for me is the pride of being a solider. I do it for my father, my children and my family. I do it for my country. When it comes down to it, I have saved many more lives by being an EOD solider than I would have as a doctor." He was killed in spring 2016. Our paths never crossed, but they are symmetrical: Abdullah went from medicine to the military, I from the military to medicine.

Receiving the 2020 Marine Corps Association & Foundation Operations in the Information Environment Officer of the Year Award from the commander of US Cyber Command and director of the National Security Agency General Paul Nakasone, September 2021.

Performing at an open mic in New York City with Josh, April 2022. I'll be playing for you forever now, brother.

Chapter 10

YOU'RE ALWAYS DEALING WITH PROBABILITIES

In a largely empty cafeteria in Kuwait, I sat across from James Jin, the "gunner" or chief weapons officer in my battalion. We had just spontaneously and inexplicably cheers'ed our cartons of milk. We laughed and then reflected on how many dead camels we had seen on the side of the road as we drove around the Kuwaiti desert that day. It was clear the deployment was coming to an end: my second, his fifth, sixth, or maybe even seventh. The conversation turned to a recent mission our battalion had supported in Southern Syria and some of the difficulty we had faced in finding suitable landing sites for our aircraft. James said, "You know all those LZ [landing zone] restrictions are made up, right?"

Decision-Making Exercise – "Hot LZ": On a deployment in Afghanistan, James Jin was on a reconnaissance mission that was compromised by Taliban fighters. One of James's Marines was injured, and they immediately moved towards a planned landing site for extract. A British pilot was flying in the area and able to make the landing, but the landing zone was "hot," meaning James and his team were taking fire from the Taliban fighters in the immediate vicinity of where the helicopter was supposed to land. The pilot had to decide between the risk to him and his aircraft and the risk to James and his team. He could also try and find another site to land. What would you do?

The pilot thought he saw another clearing that could be used as a landing zone. James said he was able to break contact to that new clearing about 500m away. By standard operating procedures, the new landing zone was too small for the British helicopter: the pilot would be at risk flying in or out, in this case due to a steep decline halfway through the clearing and some boulders on the other side. The Taliban fighters were also not far away and would likely pursue James's team as they tried to get picked up.

The British pilot was young and inexperienced. James asked for extract at the new landing site; the pilot scanned the area and agreed. The helicopter landed, James and his team jumped in, and they pulled out of the landing zone. The Taliban fighters shot at them but did not significantly hurt the aircraft. James would say he owed the pilot his life.

James also knew he was lucky the British pilot had been on one of his first missions in his first combat tour. A more experienced pilot, who understood the risk and low probability of success in the landing, would have likely said no. James and his team would have had to continue to fight against a much larger force until a pilot could conduct a safer landing. I left the conversation with James wondering what probability of success would have been high enough for an experienced pilot. 25 percent? 50 percent?

Valuing human life in terms of estimative probability is difficult, even in abstract cases. It is also a dilemma faced widely outside of the military. Health-care workers have to weigh different courses of treatment, with cost defined not just in terms of dollars but also in emotional and physical strain on the patient and the patient's family. Judges and lawyers have to weigh different criminal sentencing, forecasting the likelihood for recidivism or re-offending against how long to keep someone behind bars.

The difficulty in these cases stems partly from the effort to quantify estimative probability. Outcomes can be considered binary: Did the pilot evacuate James's team? Did the patient become healthy? Did the criminal re-offend? Since every individual case has its own details and elements of chance, looking back and saying with certainty that the forecast of a 60 percent probability of success was correct, in any of those cases, is impossible. Remote outcomes still occur and near certain outcomes still do not happen, but that reveals little about the probability of the outcome unless the event can be repeated.

Generalization from similar data sets is a reliable way to estimate probability of specific outcomes. Pilots know how big a landing zone they need based on thousands of aircraft tests. As the size of the safe area to land decreases, the probability of a successful landing and takeoff decreases. While the tests were not under fire in Afghanistan, the pilot has enough of an understanding from this information to forecast what the aircraft can take. In rapid decision-making, this type of data trains "gut" reaction by improving recognition of patterns in complex circumstances.

Certain scenarios, like catching high-level terrorist leaders, do not have good generalized data sets to compare against. The requirement to understand probability of success of an operation to catch a terrorist though is still critical. The president will not want to take a risk for something unlikely to work. The question then becomes how estimative probability is determined for situations that have never been seen before.

Decision-Making Exercise – "Estimating Probability": In spring 2011, various intelligence agencies presented President Obama with their assessment of the likelihood that Osama bin Laden was living in a fortress-like compound the CIA had found in Abbottabad, Pakistan. President Obama was given many different assessments, and they all varied. For this exercise, we can focus on four of them: 40 percent, 60 percent, 80 percent and 95 percent. The CIA gave the assessment of 95 percent. President Obama had to decide what he thought the actual likelihood was before he made his decision on whether or not to authorize the raid. What would you do?

This moment is depicted in *Zero Dark Thirty*, as several intelligence analysts and officers from the CIA briefing the CIA director, Leon Panetta, who is frustrated by their lack of consensus. As described by Friedman and Zeckhauser in "Handling and Mishandling Estimative Probability: Likelihood, Confidence, and the Search for Bin Laden," President Obama received this brief himself and thought the set of four probabilities was confusing and unhelpful. President Obama decided the likelihood Osama bin Laden was living in the compound was around 50 percent. Friedman and Zeckhauser argue a set of probabilities is actually equivalent in meaning to the set's simple average, as long as each probability has the same trustworthiness. In this case, the average of the four probabilities weighted equally would be 69 percent. President Obama intuitively underestimated the true probability, perhaps due to caution or his own internal weighting of the lower assessments. Still, 50/50 odds were enough for President Obama to authorize the raid against the compound, and within a decade of 9/11, Osama bin Laden was killed. Looking back on the decision to authorize the raid, President Obama said: "One of the things you learn as president is that you're always dealing with probabilities."

Prior to President Obama receiving the set of probabilities, each intelligence agency had to compile information and determine a single estimative probability for something that did not have any reasonably comparative data set. Analysts can find clues or evidence that suggest an outcome, but outside of certainty or a "smoking gun," any forecast still relies in some way on past experience and comparisons. Bias, implicit or explicit, then easily confounds these projections. The fact that an analyst was wrong on previous work, unrelated to the current issue, could drive the projection to the center at 50/50, even if information could allow for more certainty; cynicism or naïve optimism could add certainty in a negative or positive direction, even if the information does not warrant it. If bias is explicit and known, a decision-maker like the president can weigh a specific probability differently in the set. Bias is more troubling when overlooked.

Rare disasters skew assessments of probability because they exist so vividly in memory. In this example, some key leaders may have weighed their likelihood estimates for the bin Laden compound towards unlikely, because of their memories of the intelligence community's incorrect assessment that Saddam Hussein had weapons of mass destruction in Iraq.

Intense images of plane crashes in the news skew assessments of safety in the same way. Many more people die by car crash than plane crash per year in the US, but that does not stop Americans from fearing planes disproportionally. Psychologist Daniel Kahneman argues that vividness is why planes seem scarier and why terrorism is so effective. The probability of dying from any terrorist attack in the US is extremely low, but most Americans remember where they were on 9/11 and that recall could make some think another terrorist attack is more likely than it is. Kahneman uses the thought experiment below to reinforce this point in *Thinking Fast and Slow*: "Suppose that two cities have been warned of the presence of suicide bombers. Residents of one city have been told that two suicide bombers are ready to strike. Residents of another city are told of a single bomber. Their risk is lower by half, but do they feel much safer?"

Emotional, clickbait-style headlines about rare disasters, ubiquitous during the COVID-19 pandemic, rely on vividness and another concept that Kahneman calls denominator neglect. While every death is a tragedy in its own way, deaths from COVID-19 in children were extremely rare. An analysis of the data in March 2021 from the US shows that COVID-19 accounted for 134 deaths in children (age 14 or below) out of an available population of over 60.8 million (.00022 percent). Still, headlines on the death of a child from COVID-19 made people picture a vivid and tragic death. Their ability to recall that death then generally made a child's death seem more likely, especially early in the pandemic.

Before the arrival of the Omicron variant in the winter of 2021–22, breakthrough cases, cases of infection after vaccination, were also rare, on the order of 750,000 out of more than 150 million fully vaccinated individuals in the US in July 2021 (~.5 percent). Headlines of a breakthrough case though, especially of a famous person, made people think breakthrough cases were more frequent. These clickbait headlines could have contributed to improper public-health precautions for children and initial loss of faith in vaccines, all because the denominator was overlooked.

Decision-Making Exercise – "Clickbait Misinformation": A journalist for a major media company is writing about side effects to one of the COVID-19 vaccines. Of 1,000,000 vaccines administered, 10 people had severe reactions that resulted in hospitalization. The journalist must write a headline that will grab readers' attention and make them read the article. What would you do?

A journalist would use vividness and denominator neglect in a headline, if the focus was only to get people to click. "TEN PEOPLE HOSPITALIZED DUE TO VACCINE SIDE EFFECTS" is much more effective than ".001 PERCENT OF 1,000,000 VACCINE ADMINISTRATIONS RESULTED IN HOSPITALIZATIONS." The first headline allows for vividness, since readers can picture a person hospitalized, rather than a percent. The second headline includes the denominator, revealing the rarity of the event, which makes readers more likely to ignore the article and see it as something they do not need to read.

Kahneman describes how framing information can manipulate opinion and influence certain actions. Vividness and denominator neglect are two examples of framing. Framing is used extensively in misinformation, which is defined as misleading information used to engender certain opinions or affect certain actions. The first headline is true, which means it does not fall to the level of disinformation or false information deliberately shared to deceive. It could, however, be considered misinformation, especially if used for a specific purpose like to decrease trust in vaccines. The line between misinformation and disinformation blurs and is mostly academic, as misleading, yet true information can be used under the same pretense of deliberate deception to create or support false opinions.

A product of framing and the cause for the prevalence of misinformation is "verification neglect." The tragic deaths of Kobe Bryant and his daughter Gianna in a helicopter crash in January 2020 exemplify the harmful effects of sharing compelling misinformation without verifying it. In the moments after the crash, many started speculating that all four of Bryant's daughters were on the helicopter, a vivid image stemming from the known fact that there were five passengers killed in the crash. This speculation even turned into official media outlets reporting their deaths before any information was confirmed. Sharing unconfirmed information, whether or not it was labeled as "unconfirmed," encouraged more to believe and share themselves, ultimately resulting in additional pain for Bryant's family and friends. Driven by emotion or sensation, verification neglect makes it easy for us to feel certain without checking additional sources. As Brooking and Singer write in *LikeWar: The Weaponization of Social Media*, "If you're not in doubt, then you are likely part of the problem."

In 1981, almost forty years before the COVID-19 pandemic, Kahneman created "The Asian Disease Problem" to demonstrate the power of framing. I used the variation below in my class.

An unusual disease that originated in Asia has appeared in your town of 600 people. The disease is so contagious that it is almost certain that everyone is infected. You are the mayor and are discussing two different treatments with your public-health officials that aim to save your afflicted population. Which will you choose?

Kahneman presents the potential treatments as two sets, worded slightly differently. A participant in the study only saw one of the sets, either A and B or 1 and 2.

Option A: 200 will be saved
Option B: ⅓ chance everyone is saved, ⅔ chance no one is saved

Option 1: 400 will die
Option 2: ⅓ chance no one will die, ⅔ chance everyone dies

Kahneman found that a statistically significant majority of respondents chose A and 2, even though A and 1 are equivalent and B and 2 are equivalent. The negative frame of Options 1 and 2, focused on death as an emotional loss, encouraged participants to take the riskier option in attempts to avoid that unfavorable outcome. This study also represents part of Kahneman's concept of loss aversion, the illogical way decision-makers tend to perceive losses over gains. A loss is so much more unfavorable than an equivalent gain that decision-makers will take larger risks to avoid the loss.

A financially incentivized treatment provider could manipulate public-health officials by presenting treatment options in a similar manner to "The Asian Disease Problem." Decision-makers therefore have to see through the frame and be aware of the tendencies of vividness, denominator neglect, and loss aversion to make proper decisions. If decision-makers do not see through the frame, they are succumbing to a form of misinformation and verification neglect, which is all too common in the world of social media.

Framing does not have to be a negative concept entirely. Understanding the probability of rare events can be made simpler through frames of comparison. Using the data on children's deaths from COVID-19, public-health officials and doctors could estimate a child is about as likely to get struck by lightning (.0002 percent) as to die from COVID-19 (.00022 percent) over a year. These tragic events are similarly unlikely but do differ in terms of the concept of "outrage." From a societal standpoint, a child dying from a preventable disease is a high-outrage event, while a child being involved in a freak accident like a lightning strike is strangely more acceptable and low outrage. Still with that difference in mind, using a comparison frame for low-probability events might help people make better risk-based decisions.

Framing can also be used to improve perspective on negative thoughts or outcomes. Repurposing or reconstrual are methods of reappraisal that assign meaning or purpose to events in order to decrease and take control of negative emotional responses. When my friend Antonio and I were on long field exercises in the woods of Quantico, we would share excitement most nights and tell each other, "We get to sleep tonight!" rather than complain that we only had a few hours to sleep. We naturally reappraised and changed the frame on the situation to make any amount of sleep seem like a win, which made us stronger to deal with sleep deprivation then and when it really mattered outside of training. Cognitive behavior therapy, an important treatment for depression and other mood disorders, teaches individuals reframing and reappraisal tactics to modify and take control of thoughts that could be negatively impacting behavior.

British Army officer Steve Pengilly was not affected by a frame when discounting the rare event of a wrong turn at the start of a convoy. The comparison frame for rare events is helpful because treating rare events like they will not happen is just as wrong as treating them like they are certain to happen. Steve would not have been correct to make us wargame a fire on a largely fireproof base every day. The difficult balance is preparing for a rare event without focusing too much time and effort on it.

James Jin might owe his life to framing too. The British pilot likely thought if he could not land, James and his five Marines all would die. That negative outcome was untenable to him, and he made the selfless, riskier decision to try and save them.

Option A: One person will be saved
Option B: 5 percent chance seven people will be saved, 95 percent chance no one will be saved

Option 1: Six people will die
Option 2: 5 percent chance seven people will not die, 95 percent chance everyone will die

The British pilot saw Options 1 and 2 and chose Option 2. What frame would you have seen? Would you have chosen any differently?

"You're Always Dealing with Probabilities" Summary and Discussion Questions

Hot LZ and Framing a Rescue

James Jin credits his life to a British pilot who took on significant risk to save him and his reconnaissance team. Daniel Kahneman's concepts of framing and loss aversion could explain why the British pilot took the risk he did. The pilot framed the decision around his safety and the loss of the Marines; he knew choosing his own safety and losing the Marines was something he could not live with.

1. How much risk could you expect a colleague to take on your behalf? A friend? A family member? How much risk would you take on for them?
2. How are framing and loss aversion used in marketing and propaganda?

Estimating Probability

President Obama had the difficult task of compiling analysis from several different intelligence agencies on the location of Osama bin Laden. He gave more weight to the lower probability estimates, rather than averaging all of them equally, but he still made the decision to authorize the raid. This example shows the difficulty of assessing likelihood for binary outcomes that do not have large, generalizable data sets.

1. How could assigning likelihood to a certain outcome help you weigh resources in planning and execution?
2. What analysis would be required after an event to determine whether your likelihood assessment was correct?

Clickbait Misinformation

The COVID-19 pandemic highlighted the damaging effect of clickbait-style, misleading headlines. Emotive information about deaths, breakthrough cases, or vaccine side effects were taken out of the context they deserved – the context that they were all rare events – and contributed to misunderstanding of risk in both the overly high and overly low manner. These misunderstandings helped fracture society even more, contributed to widespread mistrust of public-health officials, and led to improper public-health procedures. Media companies, driven by profits, do not have any incentive to stop this practice since it generates them clicks and advertising dollars.

1. How could society become more resilient to clickbait-style misinformation? Why is "verification neglect" so prevalent?
2. How could comparative probabilities improve communication of risk? How could they be misused?

PART III

LEADERSHIP

The humility, selflessness, empathy, and proficiency necessary to inspire the best in others

Learn to listen, and you'll have more friends to listen to you

"To whom much is given, much is expected."

Luke 12:48

"We are all ultimately saved by grace."

David Brooks

Chapter 11

SIFR WAHID

In September 2016, I boarded a military quad-propeller plane called a C-130 with 100 other Marines for our flight from Kuwait into Western Iraq. In the full combat gear of Kevlar helmets, flak jackets, gloves, and sunglasses, we jammed into the plane fuselage on four rows of mesh benches that stretched from the rear door to the cockpit. We had rifles draped across our chests and gas masks on our hips. I spent the two-hour flight wide awake holding my assault pack in front of me thinking about my platoon and all the men I was with. Some other Marines fiddled nervously. One older Marine sergeant across from me slept the whole way. By my second deployment, I would sleep that well on any military aircraft too.

We were from 3rd Battalion, 7th Marines Weapons Company, a mix of platoons of scout snipers, heavy machine-gunners, anti-tank missilemen, and mortarmen. Since early winter 2015, rotating Marine Weapons Companies from the Special Purpose Marine Air Ground Task Force-Crisis Response-Central Command held the mission to defend the base and support a small Task Force of Marines, soldiers, special forces, and allied troops who led the "Train, Advise, and Assist" mission in the War Against ISIS in Anbar Province.

I knew the war had improved since the base was re-opened in early 2015. ISIS had been pushed farther away from Al Asad by Iraqi forces partnered with the Task Force, and the frequency of attacks on base had decreased. We did not know how dangerous our mission would be though. Minutes from landing in Iraq, our executive officer, or XO, another lieutenant a year or so older than I was with the nickname Code Black due to his well-known temper, yelled for everyone to go Condition 3, which meant to insert a magazine into our rifles. I pulled a magazine from my chest and seemingly forgot how to make the magazine stick in the magazine well. I watched a young enlisted Marine struggle the same way until his sergeant helped him. I played off my own struggles and tilted the magazine in at an angle, so it would load. Our XO then yelled, "As you get off the bird, go condition 1!" I pictured all of us racking rounds into the chambers of our rifles as we jumped onto the airstrip of the desert base. We were landing in the middle of the day, and I wondered if the base was dangerous enough to warrant 100 Marines running off the plane with fully loaded weapons.

The plane landed and taxied to a halt. Our wise and experienced Company Gunny, who had several deployments to Iraq and Afghanistan himself, had convinced our XO that going Condition 1 was not necessary. I was met when I got off the plane by two members from the Train, Advise, and Assist Task Force, who felt safe enough on the airstrip that they were not wearing any body armor. I realized then that staying Condition 3 was probably the right call.

On my second day in Iraq, ISIS fighters attacked the base with Katyusha rockets fired from a protected firing site about 10km away near the Euphrates River. I had just returned from the command center and was sitting on my bed in the small shipping container where I slept. The alarms of "Incoming! Incoming! Incoming!" made me jump up, and I hastily began to throw on all of my combat gear. I was fumbling with my gas mask when I decided to jump out to the bunker. I almost barreled over a Marine sergeant calmly holding his helmet in his hands and sitting on a crate in the center of the bunker. He had spent enough time taking cover in bunkers on his first deployment to Iraq a year before to know we were probably going to be OK. He gratefully seemed to excuse my first-timer disheveled state too.

I settled into my role leading the command center over the next two weeks. Eventually, the competing feelings of danger and safety began to feel regular, even if the tenuous balance they created had been wholly unexpected. The base had an air of excitement to it, an electric tinge, that I could only describe as the gravity of combat. I felt it in every moment, the intense, like defending Iraqi soldiers on the ground with airstrikes, and the banal, like filling our daily allotment of sandbags outside of the base chow hall.

The extent of the medical mission was also different than I imagined. Our base commander and leader of the Train, Advise, and Assist Task Force was Marine Colonel Parker, who spent the majority of his career deployed in Western Iraq. He implored us daily in briefings that our center of gravity or our most important effort was our medical mission. He understood that Iraqi generals and soldiers were confident enough to fight ISIS on the ground, because they knew they could be treated on our base if they got injured. Without that confidence, the fight would stall, and ISIS would continue to maintain its territory.

The medical mission almost became personal for Colonel Parker during the deployment. I was working in the command center when a report came in that the police chief of Haditha, a town to the north of base, had been injured in an IED blast. I reported the event to Colonel Parker in a standard update when he arrived in the command center later that day. He stopped me immediately and said, "Anything about him, that's wake-up criteria. Add it to the CCIRs [Commander's Critical Information Requirements]. And let me know if he needs to be treated here."

I looked at him sort of puzzled. "Yes, Sir. Will do."

"He's a friend, Brooks. I've known him for a long time."

Luckily, the police chief's injuries were not that severe. He was treated at the Iraqi hospital in Haditha and returned to his duties the next day. That moment still was one of many that built my admiration for Colonel Parker and his compassion for the Iraqis.

The medical center treated more than just recent casualties of war. A prominent Iraqi general was seen monthly for a hand injury. It did not seem to matter that we did not have any hand specialists or orthopedic doctors on base. Our medical staff still examined him and gave him as much support as they could.

The nature of modern war required treatment for medical events more associated with the civilian world too. Not everyone on base was young or in what could be expected as military ready shape. A surprising proportion of the base civilian contractors, in roles of drone operations, aircraft management, or logistical functions, were middle-aged and overweight. One of these US contractors, who would not have been anywhere close to the front line in previous generations' wars, suffered from a heart attack on an otherwise forgettable night. The base medical center treated him and then transferred him to Baghdad for higher care.

By that point in my deployment, the base medical center had treated several cardiac events. The others though were even more unexpected: young Iraqi soldiers, mostly standing guard along the Euphrates and not in direct combat with ISIS. The first time this happened while I was on shift in the command center, I heard the Iraqi radio buzzing behind me and turned to my jacked interpreter Louie for the report.

"Jundi [a junior enlisted soldier]. He's having a heart attack near Dulab. Can we treat him?"

The Dulab Peninsula is a bend in the Euphrates River just outside of Al Asad. ISIS had been pushed miles away from there by then. "Heart attack? Really?" I responded.

"Sifr Wahid." Louie had been teaching me Arabic, so I knew that translated to 0-1. Louie could tell I still did not know what he meant. "Captagon. The drug. All the soldiers take it."

Captagon is an amphetamine that was originally marketed as an attention deficient disorder drug like Adderall. The drug found new use at war for its ability to increase alertness on guard or in battle. Some media outlets, including the *Washington Post* in 2015, described the drug as providing "superhuman" capabilities to soldiers. Users described fearlessness and a "great power" provided by the drug. However, other journalists reporting on the conflict, like German Lopez from *Vox*, argued that Captagon was generally thought to be a "run-of-the-mill" amphetamine. It is both addictive enough to be banned for therapeutic use and powerful enough to keep users awake and alert for more than twenty-four hours. Still, the drug does not truly reduce fear or make soldiers faster or stronger, outside of placebo effects tied to heightened awareness.

By the rise of ISIS in 2014, Captagon had begun to take hold of a new market. The *World Drug Report* from the United Nations in 2013 found that use appeared to be growing in the Middle East, due to increased demand for the drug. The denigration of the Syrian Revolution into a tri-state war helped fuel the need to keep soldiers alert and battle-ready. Some called Captagon the "Jihadists' drug" or "Jihad pill" as it was used prevalently among ISIS to sustain their fighters. However, Captagon was not limited to soldiers and fighters on the front line. Luggage carriers used it to work longer shifts. University students from Lebanon to Saudi Arabia found "Capti" a more acceptable party drug than alcohol, which is culturally unacceptable in many Arab countries. Some users thought Captagon was medicinal rather than a recreational drug since it appeared in prescription pill form. A medicine could not be banned by law, religion, or culture and should not have lasting negative effects like addiction. That line of thinking ensnared many vulnerable users across the Middle East and created a crisis of addiction. That addiction made many smugglers and producers extremely rich.

Soldiers taking drugs to manage their experiences at war has a long history. Toby Finney, the Vietnam veteran and focus of Chapter 2, encountered pervasive drug use in the Army in Vietnam. The most dangerous drug was heroin, although many drank alcohol in excess as well. Like I saw with Iraqi soldiers along the Euphrates, Toby saw more drug use the farther away he was from the front line. Part of the reason he enjoyed working on austere bases was the fact that he was then generally away from drunk and unruly soldiers or worse, heroin addicts.

Toby's experience with heroin became personal a few months into his time on Camp Granite. Toby and his friend Danny befriended a young kid named Kyle from Indiana during their daily duties in base defense. Toby never knew him well, but he found him despondent one day and learned that he had been dumped via letter by his girlfriend back home. Danny and Toby tried to console him, and he seemed to return slowly to his normal self. One night, Toby and Kyle stood watch on post together. Toby asked Kyle how he was doing and then let him take the first shift in the night, meaning Toby could sleep for three hours while Kyle manned the perimeter. Kyle never woke Toby up to change shifts. Toby jumped up when he woke up six hours later and found Kyle lying motionless on his rifle. He attempted to resuscitate him and radioed the sergeant of the guard, but help was too late. Kyle had never used heroin before, but he died that night of a heroin overdose.

Toby was furious, both at himself and at Kyle. Toby felt responsible for Kyle's death, for not realizing that his friend was not doing OK when they settled on shifts. Since no one had been guarding their sector while Toby slept and Kyle overdosed, they had also put the entire base at risk. Toby's commanding officer attempted to hide Kyle's cause of death from official reports, so that his unit would not appear to have a heroin problem. Toby was stunned. The officer did not seem to care for the well-being of his men and only wanted to protect his reputation and prospects for promotion.

Before heading home from Vietnam, all troops had to pass two tests: one for sexually transmitted diseases and one for drugs. Another young soldier, a consistent heroin user named Mike, approached Danny and asked for help. He had to get clean to go home.

> Leadership Exercise – "Get Clean to Go Home": Mike, a fellow soldier on Camp Granite, sought help from Danny to get clean from heroin. Mike had become a habitual and dependent heroin user during his time in Vietnam. Mike needed to pass his drug test, so that he could leave Vietnam. Danny asked Toby for help. They had to come up with a plan to get Mike clean, and they only had several days before Mike was due to ship out. Base services were limited, so Toby and Danny had to get creative. How would you lead in this moment?

Influencing someone to defeat an addiction ranks as one of the most difficult challenges in leadership. The choice to get clean has to start with the individual, but an addiction to heroin is so powerful that the individual usually cannot make the decision alone. Forced intervention is the first necessary step on the path to rehabilitation and recovery.

Toby and Danny knew they faced a difficult challenge with limited resources. They decided to take an unorthodox and risky approach. Mike needed to get through his initial period of withdrawal, so that he could be healthy enough to travel home substance free. Toby and Danny decided they would force him into withdrawal and monitor his recovery personally. They found an abandoned building on base, put some water and basic amenities inside, and then locked Mike in. Toby and Danny took turns talking to Mike through the locked door and never left him alone.

Mike's withdrawal was extremely difficult. For the first day, he protested continuously through the door and said he no longer wanted to get clean. Toby and Danny stuck to their promise and did not let him out. For the second day, he vomited for hours. He eventually dry heaved until he passed out. For the third and fourth days, he was quiet, although Toby and Danny made sure he was drinking water. They let him out at the end of the fourth day. He ate some food, drank more water, and then passed out again. He woke up and started to regain his strength. Two days later, he thanked Toby and Danny and left Vietnam drug-free.

Toby and Danny's unorthodox intervention reveals the physical dependency heroin users develop quickly on the drug. The first time heroin users decide to use is often considered the last time they are ever capable of saying no on their own without outside help. A drug like heroin had only one way of becoming more dangerous: if it appeared as a prescription pill, sanctioned and approved by the medical community.

At the turn of the twenty-first century, prescription opioids like OxyContin and Percocet were prescribed in increasing frequency in the US. The pain-masking effect of these drugs derives largely from their key ingredient: oxycodone. Oxycodone has a chemical structure and mechanism of action nearly identical to heroin. When used safely in small doses, OxyContin and Percocet mask pain for several hours and wear off. When abused, the drugs produce a euphoria very similar to heroin. These effects, whether from safe use or abuse, are highly addictive.

In 2011, President Obama published his government's strategy to combat the growing epidemic of prescription-drug abuse. The document calls prescription-drug abuse the "Nation's fastest-growing drug problem." For the first time, opioid overdoses from prescription drugs were increasing relative to overdoses from heroin. However, the document concedes the continued "great potential for relieving suffering" that opioids provide. This unavoidable juxtaposition of the harmful and beneficial effects of opioids delayed their national reckoning. Thousands and thousands more would die of opioid abuse before the US began to take the epidemic seriously.

A year or so after President Obama's epidemic declaration, Josh, a good friend of mine from high school, made a decision he thought he would never regret. He was a freshman at a college party, and a friend offered him a pill from an orange tube. While he drank and smoked marijuana occasionally, he had avoided "hard" drugs to that point. He remembered thinking that a prescription could not hurt him, and he popped the pill in his mouth.

Josh and I had spent most of high school running in the same circles with slightly different skills. Josh was the lead in all the musicals while I was background sailor #2; I was captain of the volleyball team while Josh was cheering from the bench. Our overlap in these different worlds made us fast friends and gave us some cherished adventures in adolescence. Gregarious, intelligent, and artistic, Josh had left Baltimore for college with limitless opportunities.

The first pill did not immediately change Josh's life. He slowly started to seek out opioids for further use as a party drug. He never felt a strong need to use: he just enjoyed it, and the prescriptions from friends were always available. Josh graduated college as a habitual user, but he had never experienced any sort of withdrawal to make him realize that he had a problem.

In 2014, Josh's access to opioids through college friends evaporated when he returned home to Baltimore. Further government pressure also finally started to make opioid prescriptions more difficult to obtain. As the supply dwindled, Josh felt his need increase. He began to take drastic steps to re-gain access to opioids. He would drive for hours to see college friends for the sole purpose of buying and using. Drugs from the streets in downtown Baltimore started to seem like much more convenient options.

Getting access to drugs on the streets of Baltimore was not a difficult task. Affluent and tourist neighborhoods of Baltimore are centered on the Inner Harbor and stretch for only a few miles. These neighborhoods are bounded on the east and west by poorer parts of town where crime, drugs, and murder are all prevalent. On the east side, Guilford Avenue represents one of these borders. Guilford Avenue was a red line, a relic of segregation that prevented both Blacks and Jews from owning property in the center of town until the 1970s. Today, that history lives on as economic disadvantages stark in contrast only hundreds of feet apart.

Josh had bumped into a drug dealer named Terrell outside of a bar where many college-aged and young adults drink on the weekends. Terrell might have noticed something in Josh's eyes when he began the conversation: Terrell knew he had found a new customer. When the supply of prescription opioids started running low, Terrell convinced Josh to try heroin and its more potent and deadly synthetic relative fentanyl.

When Josh made this transition to heroin and fentanyl, Josh's addiction started taking its toll on both his personal and work lives. Friends worried about his increased drinking and partying, but he had hidden his "hard" drug use from most of his friends. He managed to continue working for two years in several jobs that would have looked good for a law-school application. His transition to heroin and fentanyl, even if unknown to others, still started to scare him. He knew his time might be running out.

One day in summer 2017, he locked himself in a room and forced himself into withdrawal. He fought through the worst sickness he had ever felt in his life, sweating, vomiting, and dry heaving for twenty-four hours straight. He did not let himself leave the room until he had started to recover. Once he left, he decided he needed to leave Baltimore. He found a new job and started a new life in Chicago.

Josh thought a fresh start would help him beat his addiction. Josh would not have a Terrell in Chicago to buy from or an indulgent friend group to excuse his using. The "geographic cure" worked for more than year, and he stayed clean while he was in Chicago. Josh eventually though was pulled back to Baltimore. He would begin to represent the common addict misconception that the location is the issue not the person.

When he moved home, he took a taxi straight from the airport to the corner to meet Terrell. He was back using openly, and finally the lifestyle would start to catch up to him. Josh had returned home ostensibly for a prestigious assistant position for a local government leader. In his first few weeks on the job, he arrived at work several times unable to function due to withdrawal: his eyes were sunken, he was sick to the stomach, and he sweat profusely. His boss finally told Josh to go home and not come back.

One night that fall before Thanksgiving, some of Josh's close friends witnessed him take a speed ball: a mix of cocaine, heroin, and fentanyl. Horrified, they partnered with his parents to stage an intervention the next day. Josh thought he would stop briefly at his parents' house before heading downtown for a Ravens game, but his family, some close friends, and an intervention specialist waited for him. They planned to take him to rehab immediately.

Josh convinced his family to let him watch the Ravens game before going to rehab. He secretly used heroin one last time that night. In the morning, shaking as he came down from his high, he went willingly and checked himself into rehab.

Rehab introduced Josh to a new community and began to teach him about the nature of his addiction. He fought depression and anxiety and learned tools to overcome the patterns of thought and action that trapped him in the cycle of addiction. He stayed clean for a year and half before he relapsed for several weeks. He then checked himself into an outpatient clinic for two months of continued treatment. His recovery truly never would end.

I began to lose track of my friend when I moved to California and started deploying in 2016. But Josh hosted a pre-game party for me for the Ravens-Bills game on 9/11 in 2016 before I left for my first deployment and welcomed me home after my second deployment in 2019 at another party at my parents' house. By the time I was home in 2019, the long overdue national reckoning with opioids was well underway. The Sacklers, a billionaire family of philanthropists and pharmaceutical entrepreneurs, faced lawsuits for their efforts to minimize the dangers of their best-selling product Oxycontin. Their company Purdue Pharmaceuticals had promoted Oxycontin's ubiquitous prescription with aggressive advertising, even when the drug's addictiveness and abuse potential became apparent.

In the twenty-five years after Oxycontin was first introduced, the death toll would be staggering. In that timeframe, 450,000 Americans died of opioid-related overdoses. The perennial leader in accidental death in the US is auto accidents, resulting in almost 36,000 deaths per year; however, there are many more licensed drivers than opioid abusers. In accounting for that denominator difference, an estimate reveals an opioid abuser has a yearly risk of death from an overdose twelve times higher than the risk of death of any licensed driver in an auto accident.

We need seat belts to prevent deaths from auto accidents; the "seat belt" of opioid overdoses may be Narcan or naloxone, an emergency treatment for suspected opioid overdoses. By 2021, nasally administrated Narcan was widely distributed in efforts to prevent opioid overdoses. Implementing Narcan as a ubiquitous "seat belt" took far too long, but it did once save Josh's life.

In spring 2021 after another year without using opioids, Josh offered to speak to my class about drugs and addiction. Although he was back living on his own in Baltimore with a stable new job, he joined virtually, due to COVID-19 restrictions. As effervescent as I ever knew him, he began to tell his story. He spoke about his first use from that innocuous orange container, the path to addiction, the painful intervention, the relapse, and the continuous effort in recovery. He described chemically how opioids change the brain and take away the capacity for personal choice. He listed out all of his relatives that he learned had addiction problems too late for him to be more cautious himself.

Josh was open, honest, and courageous. He hoped only that my students could learn from his story. He had been in their shoes, steps away from college and life beyond high school only eleven years prior. He wanted to prevent them from making that terrible first choice, but he also wanted them to be better prepared to serve in a support system for others. It takes a village to help family, friends, and acquaintances avoid and recover from addiction.

Josh left my class that day with a line he had repeated several times: "Every day an addict stays clean is a miracle." I saw in his eyes when he spoke those words how much of a miracle it was. His eyes held pain, want, and regret and beseeched the young men and women before him to believe him.

Somewhat shaken after hearing my friend describe his struggles with addiction so openly for the first time, I did not have much more to say to my class. I dismissed the class quickly once Josh had finished speaking. Later after class, one of my students approached me. He said to me cautiously, "So, we just witnessed a miracle."

I looked at him in the eyes and nodded. "Don't forget it."

* * *

On October 13, 2022, a close friend from Baltimore, Sarah, called me. I was eating dinner, and I thought I might not even call back that night. Then, I saw her text:

"Call me back, Josh overdosed."

I stood up from the table and stumbled into a different room. Sarah's voice was calm when I called her back, calm enough that I thought all Josh needed was more support from close friends as he went back to rehab. But Sarah then described more of what she knew: Josh had been found by himself, and they had found him too late. He was on life support in the hospital, and he was not going to survive. I did not believe it.

"Oh, that's not true. That can't be true. That's not true," is all I could say.

Sarah calmly assured me that it was. I realized slowly that I had to start calling more of our friends.

A day later, on his 31st birthday, Josh was taken off life support. He, and we, ran out of miracles.

"Sifr Wahid" Summary and Discussion Questions

Center of Gravity

The Train, Advise, and Assist Task Force and base commander reminded us as often as he could that the most important effort we had in the war was our medical mission. We gained more from treating Iraqi soldiers than we did from killing ISIS fighters in airstrikes. This focus represented Colonel Parker's leadership philosophy for the overall mission and became part of my calling to return to war zones as a doctor.

1. The non-governmental organization Doctors Without Borders provides medical care to war zones and remains staunchly neutral. Their work attempts to find humanity in war by providing care to the wounded and afflicted on any side of a conflict. What are the positives and negatives of remaining neutral when providing medical care in war?
2. Our base had limited organic air-lift capability to transfer casualties to higher care in Baghdad. Still, the US contractor who had the heart attack was immediately transferred to Baghdad during the night. Our limited air lift meant that we could not use our aircraft to transfer Iraqi casualties. After being stabilized in our medical center, several Iraqis died in the ambulance on the long drive to Baghdad. Was that fair?

Get Clean to Go Home

Mike, a fellow soldier, turned to Toby and Danny for help getting clean from heroin before returning home from Vietnam. Toby and Danny had limited options to get him clean in only a few days and decided on a risky intervention. They would lock Mike in a building and force him to succumb to withdrawal symptoms. Toby and Danny monitored him as he struggled through physical withdrawal for four days. At the end of four days, Mike was able to start recovering and resist the urge to use.

1. How can you influence someone who is making bad decisions, whether in drug use or other contexts, to want to change and help themselves?
2. Leadership often starts with the example the leader sets. What personal habits of thought and action prevent you from risky behavior or succumbing to addiction?

What We Would Give For Another Miracle

The first time someone uses opioids is often considered the last time they have the capacity to say no on their own. My high-school friend Josh needed an intervention before he first decided to seek help and go to rehab. Even after rehab, Josh relapsed due to the strength of his addiction to opioids. He left my class with the line to remember, "Every day an addict stays clean is a miracle." Tragically, we lost him only eight months after he and I worked on capturing his journey in this chapter.

1. Which is the better way to influence the actions of a friend with a drug problem: indulging him to keep him close or cutting off your relationship with him entirely?
2. What could we have done better to save Josh? What can we learn from losing him?
3. Despite tendency for abuse, OxyContin, Percocet, and many other prescription opioids remain legal in 2022. Few pain-management alternatives exist. How should government officials and medical professionals lead to limit opioid abuse?

Chapter 12

THE WHEEL ON THE SCREEN

The US's involvement in the War Against ISIS in Western Iraq began in earnest in early 2015 when 2nd Battalion, 7th Marines Weapons Company returned to Anbar Province. The small force of Marines landed at Al Asad Airbase off the Euphrates River to begin the mission of support to the Iraqi Army.

As the US withdrew from Iraq in 2011, Al Asad had been transferred entirely to the Iraqi government. Marines in 2015 would arrive and discover some buildings had remained largely untouched since the withdrawal. Dusty papers and notes were strewn across former command centers and decaying bomb shelters. These remnants reminded the Marines they were in familiar territory, even if they were there to fight a very different war.

President Obama had promised Congress and the US people that the War Against ISIS would not be a repeat of the Iraq War. Rather than invading like in 2003, US troops were in Iraq at the request and invitation of the Iraqi government. Iraqis also would lead all elements of the war effort. Their troops would be the main forces on the ground fighting ISIS. Their generals and leadership would choose and approve every significant military action. Most visibly, the US and its allies provided airpower to strike ISIS targets and facilitate Iraqi ground maneuver. Behind the scenes, they trained the Iraqi Army, supported with intelligence, and helped plan the war campaign. Instead of fighting the war, the US would be "training, advising, and assisting" the Iraqis in their efforts.

One of my roles in the command center was to attain approval from our Iraqi partners for airstrikes. Once we found ISIS fighters on the battlefield through surveillance, I would turn to my interpreter or the Iraqi liaison officer and ask in English or broken Arabic, "We would like approval to strike ...". We did not move forward in the targeting process until we had their approval. The fact that we had to ask before we could blow anything up showed how different this war in Iraq really was.

President Obama knew that ensuring the war effort was Iraqi-led was the key to Iraq's long-term success. An Iraqi-led effort meant the president could largely count the cost of the US's involvement in dollars, rather than in US lives. The first validation of this adaptation of modern war came in 2015 and 2016 as Iraqi troops liberated towns on the Euphrates River with US and allied troops watching in support from relative safety.

When I arrived on Al Asad in September 2016, the Iraqis had already liberated the majority of the towns close to the base along the Euphrates River. The success had come slowly and painfully. Many Iraqis had died facing complex ISIS defenses that were intricately woven into the landscape. An Iraqi colonel, beloved by both Americans and Iraqis, was one of those casualties that many would remember. The entire command center had been focused on striking an ISIS fighter as he lined up a shot with a recoilless rifle towards the Iraqi line. The airstrike was delayed inexplicably, outside of the control of the command center that watched the battle. The fighter shot and destroyed the lead vehicle with the Iraqi colonel. The airstrike that finally came through minutes later to kill the ISIS fighter was little solace for the loss felt across the base.

A few weeks into my deployment, I happened to be working out in the gym next to Colonel Parker, the commander of the Train, Advise, and Assist Task Force and the entire base. For some reason, he decided to invite the young, nervous Marine lieutenant who was standing in front of him to a key leader engagement with Iraqi Army leadership. This meeting showed me in part why the train, advise, and assist model had been so successful against ISIS.

Leadership Exercise – "Influential Advising": The commander of Al Asad met regularly with his Iraqi counterparts to assess current efforts and plan future operations against ISIS. In early fall 2016, Colonel Parker pushed for a meeting to design operations after the potential catastrophic victory in Mosul. The plan revolved around the liberation of two important towns west of Lake Qadisiyah called Rawah and Anah. Rawah was larger, to the north of Anah, and along the main road to Al Qaim, another ISIS stronghold. Colonel Parker thought the towns should be surrounded and enveloped, so that no ISIS fighters could escape west towards Al Qaim and Syria. We went into the meeting thinking there could be resistance to this idea, as the Iraqis had been successful using simpler, frontal assaults against other towns along the Euphrates. Colonel Parker had to decide how he would influence his counterpart, an Iraqi general, to choose the envelopment option. How would you lead in this moment?

The morning of the meeting, we took a short drive in tactical vehicles from the US part of the base to the Iraqi headquarters. We parked outside and walked into the Iraqi general's office, leaving our rifles and body armor outside. The general's office felt more like a long and wide hallway. Ornate, deep-seated chairs with gold-plated upholstery lined the walls and a large desk sat centered at the end where the general stood to greet us. The wall behind him was almost entirely a map of Western Iraq with disposition of troops laid out with pins. Much of the western half of the map was dotted with red pins to show ISIS's remaining control.

The meeting began with handshakes and a long set of pleasantries I did not fully understand the importance of. Colonel Parker explained to me after the meeting that getting to work too quickly made partners feel unvalued and unimportant. A tribal sheik had been present for the meeting too, and Colonel Parker wanted to reinforce to him how much he respected the Iraqi general. I realized years later when I ran a meeting with Canadian partners in counterpropaganda that I still had not learned this lesson. While the Canadians had smiled and laughed because I had basically skipped any form of introductions in efforts not to waste time, I should not have overlooked the importance of friendly connection, even in a work environment.

The Iraqi general told Colonel Parker at the start of the meeting that he already had decided on a plan. He gestured to the map behind him on the wall with both hands, named several of his best units to serve at the front line, and swung his arm forward towards Anah and Rawah in what resembled a successive frontal assault. Our interpreter Saif translated for Colonel Parker, who already knew enough of what the Iraqi general had said.

Colonel Parker began a slow and careful process, starting with the benefits of a frontal assault and then closing with its costs. The main cost was the fleeing enemy who would retreat to a more fortified defense in Al Qaim. He then posed questions as to how they could prevent the enemy from fleeing. Some back and forth ensued as the Iraqi general continued with slight variations of the frontal assault. A few minutes later, the Iraqi general stopped the room and decided they would commit to a new plan with maneuver that resembled envelopment. We broke immediately for a formal Iraqi lunch in another room where I sat initially bewildered at platters of bread and chicken breasts.

The circuitous path to the envelopment plan was necessary because Colonel Parker could not offer advice too directly. If the Iraqi general took a plan from him and the plan had failed, the Iraqis would blame him, which would hurt their relationship and partnership. The important difference in the War Against ISIS was that the Iraqis owned responsibility. The US and allies had to respect that ownership and could not serve too much as planners more than advisers.

The success of this moment in leadership is uncertain. The plan in this form would never be executed, as either a frontal assault or an envelopment. The victory in Mosul would be slow and costly, which meant most of the maneuver by the Iraqi Army stalled completely. Even without the delay from Mosul, the Iraqi general also might have decided to stick with a frontal assault; he might have only ended the conversation with envelopment as his own form of pleasantries to a guest he respected.

The Iraqis would liberate Anah almost a year later in September 2017 before they liberated Al Qaim. In December, the Iraqi Army then pushed from Al Qaim to Rawah, the last remaining ISIS town in Iraq. This west–east advance blocked any ISIS retreat into Syria, while some of the Iraqi general's troops held the line east at Lake Qadisiyah. In that way, the most important part of the attack against Rawah would involve some elements of the planned envelopment.

I studied the leadership lessons I observed in Colonel Parker for my role in the command center. He was consistent and humble enough to learn publicly. He was empathetic to the Iraqis fighting and dying against ISIS. He worked incessantly and expected us to apply similar intensity to the mission, but he always made time to check in with everyone who worked for him.

In practice, I found the best way to lead the command center was to influence a consistent operational tempo. If we were moving too slowly, I felt we were missing opportunities; if we were moving too quickly, I felt we could be making mistakes. For example, if we were not actively targeting ISIS, I pushed to find opportunities for us to conduct airstrikes. If we had several airstrike opportunities at once, I made sure that we checked our work as we proceeded in the strike approval process.

Influencing the command center of civilians, Marines, and soldiers to put pressure on ISIS consistently became my leadership challenge.

Iraqi operations, when they fought to liberate ISIS towns or stir ISIS out of hiding places in the desert, represented the most important times to ensure that consistent pressure.

> Leadership Exercise – "The Wheel on the Screen": After a large Iraqi operation aimed to clear ISIS strongholds in the desert around Lake Qadisiyah, our command center tracked two pickup trucks of ISIS fighters retreat to a safehouse in the middle of the desert. Intelligence reporting indicated that a high-value ISIS target was likely present with them in this safehouse. However, airpower was limited, due to the ongoing effort in Mosul. We were forced to surveil the house overnight and plan for an airstrike in the morning.
>
> The command center began to make the familiar transition from operations to administration. I ensured the intelligence Marine named Terrence in charge of managing drone or aircraft surveillance operations understood we would watch the safehouse all night. He was young and talented with a cavalier streak, and I trusted him without any supervision. Later as I prepared to turn over shift to Lance, I looked up to the screen where I should have seen the safehouse and saw a wheel, the telltale sign of a drone returning back to base as the camera stows for safety. I knew without asking what had likely happened: there was a gap in observation on the safehouse as one aircraft replaced another. Unless there was a technical failure, this regular event should have been something we could have planned for. When the replacement aircraft arrived to observe the safehouse, both pickup trucks were no longer there. The ISIS fighters we had tracked from the desert had gotten away, and we had lost our lead on the high-value target. I had to ensure we would not make an avoidable mistake like this again. How would you lead in this moment?

When I first saw the wheel on the screen, I knew I needed to get surveillance back onto the safehouse as quickly as possible. There was not anything I could say or do to speed that up at that point. I still asked Terrence from across the room to explain why we were not looking at the safehouse and when we expected to get observation back. He explained the aircraft handover I suspected and said we would be back on the safehouse in twenty minutes. I said firmly, "You understand we just made a mistake, right?"

He paused but nodded and sat down. A handoff between aircraft was entirely predictable. We could have worked to get another aircraft up earlier to avoid the loss of time or shift a different drone platform to the safehouse in the interim. I wanted to reinforce the fact that Terrence had made a mistake, especially in not communicating. Though if we returned to the safehouse and the same two pickup trucks were parked outside, we might have gotten away with it.

The command center was largely silent as the aircraft returned to the safehouse and we all stared at the screen with no vehicles in sight. Terrence came over to me, and I yelled at him. I told him we cannot make simple mistakes like that and that he had to communicate if he needed help preventing foreseeable issues. A Marine who almost always had a smile on his face walked away upset and angry that I had yelled at him in front of the entire room.

There are many different ways I could have been a better leader in that moment. I could have found space with him alone and shown through tone and emotion rather than volume how disappointing the mistake was. If I wanted him to own the mistake publicly, I could have asked him to explain what happened to the room, take responsibility, and present his plan for making sure it would not happen again. Yelling only disrespected Terrence and all of his impressive work to that moment and broke the trust we had built together.

Years later in my work in counterpropaganda, I studied influence and social engineering from a different perspective. I came across another Marine veteran Robin Dreeke and the renowned social engineer Chris Hadnagy. Together, they summarized their life lessons in influence and leadership: "Leave people better off for having met you." I thought of Terrence and knew I had failed to leave him better off, even if my intent was to strengthen him and us for the next mission.

Terrence was resilient and back as a top-performing Marine the next day. We rebuilt our trust over time. Our command center never made a similar mistake again, although we did not get many similar opportunities.

I still wondered how Colonel Parker would have acted if he had been the young officer in my place. Respect and empathy, like he had for his Iraqi partners, were the key traits I lost in my moment with Terrence. Iraqi or American, we all had the same mission. Some sacrificed more than others, but everyone was committed to the defeat of ISIS. By December 2017, that commitment had resulted in a resounding victory for a sovereign and strong democracy in Iraq. Mutual respect and shared understanding would persist as lasting evidence for how the mission to defeat ISIS achieved that success.

"The Wheel on the Screen" Summary and Discussion Questions

Influential Advising

Colonel Parker knew Western Iraq, combat operations, and his Iraqi counterpart very well, but he also knew he could not give advice on the upcoming mission too heavy-handedly. The Iraqis maintained agency and responsibility over their war and only needed advisers, rather than planners. Colonel Parker influenced the creation of a plan he thought would work but ensured the Iraqis knew it was their plan.

1. When is it acceptable to give advice? How do you know when to be forceful or gentle in delivery?
2. What character traits and communication tactics make both "Influential Advising" and "Communicating and Receiving Trauma" successful?

The Wheel on the Screen

After an Iraqi operation, our command center had an important lead on a potential ISIS safehouse in the desert north of our base. However, one of my Marines made a mistake, and we lost the lead. When I chastised him publicly for it, I realized the mistake became my own.

1. In what situations are public reprimands required when leading a team or organization?
2. What are effective ways to maintain emotional control as a leader in high-stress scenarios?
3. What could I have done to rectify my lack of emotional control and improve Terrence's standing after the event?

Chapter 13

OWNERSHIP, SELFLESSNESS, PASSION

In mid-October 2016, Iraqi Prime Minister Haider al-Abadi, flanked by his military generals, declared the beginning of military Operation al-Fatah or "Conquest" to liberate Mosul, Iraq's second largest city. This announcement represented a turning point in the War Against ISIS. Two years and four months earlier, Abu Bakr al-Baghdadi, the terrorist leader of ISIS and former member of Al Qaeda in Iraq, had spoken from the minbar, or pulpit, of the Grand Mosque in Mosul and introduced his terrorist group to the world. After Baghdadi's speech, Iraqi forces would be forced to continue to retreat as ISIS advanced down both the Euphrates and Tigris rivers towards Baghdad. In fall 2014, Iraqi Security Forces, supported by a global coalition of allies under the banner of Combined Joint Task Force-Operation INHERENT RESOLVE, would slowly begin to push back.

Two years of hard fighting led to Prime Minister Abadi's speech, which was in a way a direct retort to Baghdadi's. Baghdadi's speech carefully evoked religious motifs from Islamic scripture in his gait to approach the minbar, the cleaning of his teeth, and his dress. Prime Minister Abadi wore the all-black military uniform of Iraq's Counter-Terrorism Services, its elite special forces trained by the US and other allies. He focused on unity, self-determination, and nationalist themes of the people of Mosul and Iraq. Prime Minister Abadi knew ISIS would be the ones retreating closer to defeat once the Iraqis won the Battle of Mosul.

How quickly the Iraqis would win that battle was uncertain. Mosul was home to over 1.5 million people and considered ISIS's capital in Iraq. Urban warfare had not reached a similar scale since the Second World War. The two main forecasts for the battle were on opposite ends of the spectrum: it was either going to be a catastrophic victory as ISIS turned in full-scale retreat or a costly victory as ISIS held in a complex, urban defense.

In Western Iraq, we had to prepare for a catastrophic victory. After the liberation of Mosul, the major cities in Western Iraq – Al Qaim and Rawah – would be some of the last ISIS strongholds in the country. We watched closely as the battle began, but it did not take long before the latter projection became the expected. A generation of Iraqi men would die in the long-fought liberation of Mosul over the next nine months.

As focus across the War Against ISIS turned to Mosul, our operations in Western Iraq dropped in priority. We received less air support to strike ISIS, and the Iraqis paused most clearance operations, since the focus of their Army was to the north. The problem mainly stemmed from logistics. There was not enough airpower to support both fronts against ISIS, and there were not enough hospital beds to treat the casualties from even one of those fronts. A few months into leading the command center on my deployment, I wondered if a long period of boredom awaited us.

That fear of boredom brought excitement to the concept of "no-shave November." Lance and I decided to try and grow mustaches. Mustaches are technically allowed by uniform regulations but rarely employed. I was embarrassed even a few days in with how feeble mine looked. Then unexpectedly, at least to me, part of my battalion showed up at our base for a training operation. One of the company commanders, a dedicated and caring leader I had grown to respect, came into the command center to check in and get an update. Gratefully, he pretended not to notice my poor attempt at no-shave November. I had already decided to shave when Daly yelled at me and told me I looked ridiculous later that night.

I might have been drawn to the concept of growing a mustache in a combat zone by a story my recruiter, Marcus Williams, told me years prior. He had been standing with a group of officers, including a younger version of that same company commander who ignored my poor mustache attempt, on a base in Helmand Province, Afghanistan, at the beginning of his second deployment. The executive officer in their battalion came up to them and told them they all had to shave their mustaches. The executive officer then pointed to Marcus and said, "It was because Marcus's mustache was so disgusting that you all can't grow mustaches anymore." Everyone laughed. Marcus told the story to me as a moment in leadership. The senior officer had to pass on an order that he knew and everyone knew was somewhat stupid. Admitting that it was stupid would just hurt morale, like any unproductive complaints about a boss or "higher" do. Instead, the senior officer owned it and broke the tension by making a joke with Marcus as the scapegoat. I would learn that Marcus faced a leadership challenge of his own later on that deployment when he had to confront one of his Marines who had decided to stop shaving altogether.

Leadership Exercise – "It Doesn't Make Sense to Shave": Lieutenant Marcus Williams was with his platoon of Marines near the Kajaki Dam, one of the most dangerous places in Afghanistan, in 2011. The Taliban attacked them regularly, and they had lost several Marines in firefights and IED blasts. They were sleeping outside in holes and did not have running water, showers, or laundry. All of their food came in the form of packaged Meals-Ready-to-Eat. Morale overall was low. Marcus then noticed one of his Marines stopped shaving. The Marine said to Marcus, "We don't have water. It doesn't make sense to shave." Shaving is a requirement in the Marines in most cases and represents one element of discipline. How would you lead in this moment?

Marcus knew that the facial hair was not the real issue. He knew his men though and thought not shaving could be a warning sign for something more troubling. Not shaving could mean the Marine would avoid other undesirable but perhaps unnoticed tasks. The Marine might stop cleaning his rifle after patrol because it would just get dusty again anyway. He might not fill up canteens or wear his body armor for patrol either because of the added weight. Marcus also knew that if he failed to enforce the standard of shaving, he would have set a new standard.

Marcus took on responsibility for his Marine and approached him empathetically. He asked him what was going on and tried to figure out if there were any deeper issues that he needed to address. Marcus ensured the Marine shaved, but he talked to him and listened to him while he did it. The Marine did not have any other issues in discipline for the rest of the deployment.

When Marcus faced this leadership challenge on his second deployment to Afghanistan, he had already seen the potential dangers of lack of discipline in combat. On his first deployment to Afghanistan, he served as the lead intelligence officer embedded within a route clearance platoon. Their mission was to clear bombs out of the road. Discipline, professionalism, and attention to detail became life or death when working in explosive ordnance disposal.

Marcus was one of the only intelligence officers in Southwest Afghanistan at that point and worked between Kandahar and Helmand Provinces. Kandahar was the spiritual center of the Taliban and the de facto Pashtun capital, the tribe that filled most of the Taliban's ranks. The Taliban and ISIS were similar in their desire to rule through a medieval interpretation of Islam but different in scope: the Taliban were entirely regional, focused only on holding and maintaining power in Afghanistan, while ISIS had global aspirations to rule and expand their vision of religious power.

After 9/11, when the Taliban refused to surrender Osama bin Laden, who had been working and planning from within their territory in Afghanistan, the US and its allies moved quickly to raise local leaders and fighters against them. One of those local leaders should have been Ahmad Shah Massoud, known as the Lion of Panjshir, which is a small province northeast of Kabul. The Panjshir Valley was the only land to remain independent through both the Soviet and Taliban occupation of Afghanistan in the 1980s and 1990s, respectively. Massoud was killed two days before 9/11 by Al Qaeda fighters posing as journalists. Nevertheless, US special forces in Northern Afghanistan used Massoud's network of resistance to defeat the Taliban militarily in the months after his death. The nation-building effort that followed in Afghanistan would last two decades.

At the beginning of President Obama's first term in 2009, he selected a "surge" strategy for Afghanistan that had been successful in pacifying Iraq from 2007–8. The "surge" deployed thousands of troops into the remote countryside of Afghanistan in largely peacekeeping rather than offensive roles. The effort sought to maintain Afghanistan as a unified country. The truth was and remains that Afghanistan is a collection of disparate tribes spread across territories that would be considered uninhabitable by modern standards. The surge would eventually wane and allow the Taliban to retake control of most of the countryside. On my second deployment in 2018, I would watch as US forces and allies transitioned even more to holding only major cities and bases in Afghanistan. Three years later when the US brokered a peace deal with the Taliban and retreated, Kabul and the rest of the country would fall at an astonishing pace by August 2021. The only area that remained independent was Panjshir Province. Massoud's son and another Panjshir native, the former Afghan Vice President Amrullah Saleh, led the resistance in Panjshir, invoking Massoud's legacy as a cause to fight and defend their freedom from the Taliban.

The "surge" was just building when Marcus arrived in Southwest Afghanistan for the first time in 2009. His mission was partly to prepare Southwest Afghanistan for a much larger presence of US and allied troops. Clearing logistical routes between Kandahar and Helmand province became the critical mission. On one patrol when Marcus was leading the platoon of route-clearance Marines, Taliban fighters had ambushed them from the other side of a canal they were patrolling along. Marcus and his Marines had located, closed with, and destroyed the Taliban fighters before continuing on with the patrol. After the ambush, Marcus spread out his patrol onto both sides of the canal. A few hours later, the sun began to set, and Marcus knew he had to consolidate his platoon on one side of the canal.

> Leadership Exercise – "Take the Bridge?": Lieutenant Marcus Williams was embedded within a route-clearance platoon of Marines on a patrol to find and clear IEDs along a canal. Marcus led a squad of Marines on the east side of the canal, and the rest of his platoon and their vehicles were on the west side. As the sun started to set, Marcus knew they needed to consolidate on the west side of the canal. The canal was about 30ft across and filled with water 10–15ft deep. Marcus and his squad came up to a small bridge across the canal made out of 55-gallon steel drums, welded vertically end-to-end. The bridge was rickety, could only support one Marine at a time to cross, and had a large thorn bush growing up through its center. When crossing, they would be completely exposed to the enemy, and they thought they were under surveillance because of the Taliban fighters they had encountered earlier. Most of the IEDs Marcus's platoon had found were noticed by visual cues: disturbed earth, above-ground wires, or other indicators. Marcus's platoon also had helicopters flying overhead who would only be available for the next twenty minutes. Marcus had to decide if he would take his squad across the bridge or try to find a more stable bridge farther down the canal. How would you lead in this moment?

The rickety bridge posed real dangers. Marcus and his Marines could fall into the water, and swimming with a hundred pounds of gear on is not easy. They would also be in a weak position if the Taliban attacked while they were crossing. However, Marcus decided crossing later without air support and patrolling in the dark in territory known for IEDs would be more dangerous.

Leadership Exercise – "Ordering the Cross": Marcus decided to cross the bridge with his squad to consolidate with the rest of his platoon. Marcus then had to decide where he should place himself as the leader during the crossing. Marcus could cross first to lead the way, cross last to remain in control of his squad separated from the platoon, or cross somewhere in the middle. How would you lead in this moment?

Marcus chose to cross in the last third of his squad. For his squad of eight Marines, he would be the third to last to cross. Marcus thought in the worst-case scenario if the bridge collapsed or the Taliban shot at them, he could lead and remain in control of his squad on the east side of the canal.

As Marcus's Marines started crossing the canal one by one, foot over foot, Marcus realized his last two Marines were terrified. They were not scared of getting shot at by the Taliban or dying; they were just scared of heights. The thorn bush in the middle of the bridge made the crossing even more of an uncomfortable balancing act. Marcus's plan then had to change because he needed to force his last two Marines across ahead of him. Marcus took some of the gear his Marines were carrying including a rocket launcher called an AT-4 and a radio to make it easier for them to cross. As Marcus crossed last across the canal, carrying the AT-4, two radios, his rifle, his pistol, and his pack, he would say he was terrified he was going to get shot at or fall in himself. Leaders make difficult decisions, though, and do what is right for those they lead. Marcus consolidated with his platoon, and they all returned safely to base.

Marcus's experience making difficult decisions like crossing the bridge prepared him for more trying moments in leadership he would face on his second deployment. He had been in several firefights during this first deployment, but his unit had suffered only several casualties. When Marcus landed by helicopter in Kajaki, the Taliban immediately attacked and fired on them as they exited the helicopter. Several Marines were wounded. Marcus knew from that moment that his second deployment would be different.

On one patrol outside of Kajaki, one of the vehicles in his unit hit a 200lb roadside bomb close to their base. As the patrol dismounted to provide security, the Taliban attacked and a long firefight ensued. Eventually, the patrol broke contact with the Taliban and started evacuating casualties back to base. A fellow Marine lieutenant had a broken back from the bomb blast, and another Marine had a surface-level gunshot wound to the shoulder. As they started treating the casualties, one of the Taliban fighters they had just been in a gunfight with showed up with two of their own casualties carried in a wheelbarrow.

Leadership Exercise – "When the Enemy Needs Aid": After a firefight with the Taliban that resulted in two friendly casualties, three Taliban fighters surrendered and requested medical aid at the US base. One of them had lost a leg and was bleeding to death. Several Marines were tasked with providing security to the surrendered enemy and moving them to the medical center. As the detail formed, the Marine in charge delayed their movement. A junior Marine asked him what was wrong. He responded, "This is bullshit. We shouldn't have to treat them." How would you lead in this moment?

Marcus and his Marines had just been shot at by these same fighters, but the fighters had turned themselves in. Laws of war require that available treatment must be given to enemy soldiers who surrender under standards of medical triage. The hard, right thing to do was treat them, regardless of the fact they had just been trying to kill Marines.

Marcus told the story saying that a junior officer faced the Marine in charge and took control of the security element. He led them quickly to the base medical center. The junior officer then went up to a medical officer who outranked him, pointed to the dying Taliban fighter, and said, "Sir, we need to treat him." The medical staff immediately responded. As the US casualties had already been stabilized, they elevated the care for the Taliban fighter and saved his life. It may not have been the popular decision, but it was the right thing to do. The junior officer returned to the Marine who protested and made sure he understood that.

I first heard Marcus tell that story in a brief he gave on leadership during a recruiting function while I was still in college. I asked him after the brief what happened to the junior officer who had spoken up.

Marcus looked at me and hid a smile. "He was fine, Brooks. Everyone knew it was the right thing to do."

Marcus turned to someone else who had come up to him to ask a question. I realized that the junior officer had to have been fine because he was standing in front of me. Marcus had known that he could not recover from moral indecision in that moment, and he would live with the knowledge that he had done the right thing when it mattered.

A little more than a year later, I sat in a classroom for initial officer training. We all went around the room to talk about the Marines who inspired us. Most said famous Marines like Elliot Ackerman or Doug Zembiec or named instructors in the school we were in. I was the only one to say my recruiter.

"Ownership, Selflessness, Passion" Summary and Discussion Questions

It Doesn't Make Sense to Shave

During one of the most dangerous parts of the Afghanistan War, Marcus Williams had to decide how he would manage one of his Marines who had stopped shaving. As the leader, Marcus set the standard: he knew that if he allowed the standard to slip, other more dangerous ways to cut corners could become common, like not cleaning weapons or not carrying enough water. Marcus also knew that not shaving could be a symptom of a bigger problem with his Marine.

1. As a leader, when is it acceptable to cut corners?
2. What could Marcus have done if more than one Marine had decided to stop shaving?

The Bridge in Taliban Country

After fighting off a Taliban assault, Marcus and the route-clearance platoon needed to consolidate on one side of a canal. Marcus then had to decide when and how to cross the canal. Marcus chose the nearest bridge they could find and crossed last, so that he could ensure all of his men got across safely first.

1. "Officers eat last" and "lead by example" are two mottos instilled in Marine basic officer training. Do these concepts align with Marcus's choice to cross last?
2. What leadership traits made Marcus effective in ordering and executing the cross?

When the Enemy Needs Aid

On his second deployment to Afghanistan, Marcus's unit took heavy casualties after a firefight with the Taliban. Several US Marines were wounded and were being treated in the base medical center. Taliban fighters then arrived at the base and surrendered, asking for medical aid. When Marcus saw a Marine protest against treating the Taliban fighters, he immediately escorted the fighters to the medical center and ensured they would get treatment.

1. The Taliban and many other adversaries of the US would not render aid to wounded US troops. Why is it important for US forces to provide aid to surrendered enemy troops anyway?
2. What guides or feelings do you rely on to make the hard, right choice in difficult scenarios?

Chapter 14

NOBODY CARES

When Jennifer's dad dropped her off in Annapolis for the six-day 2013 Naval Academy Summer Seminar, he told her with a smile, "I'll see you in two days." Jennifer glared and half smiled at her dad as they got out of the car. They hugged, and Jennifer took her first steps through the gate off King George Street that would start the most impactful journey of her life.

More than a hundred years after the first woman enlisted in the military in 1917, women have remained a striking minority in service. In 2020, women represented only 16 percent of the enlisted force and 19 percent of the officer corps. The reasons for this disparity are varied. Some is due to US and military culture, remnants of a male-dominated world that is hesitant to see women as valuable or desired contributions to the mission. Some is due to regulations, arcane rules that limit hairstyles or maternity leave. Some is due to logistics, the lack of facilities or gear like rucksacks that fit properly for women's bodies.

The most troubling issues involve sexual assault. The military estimates 5–6 percent of active-duty women experienced a sexual-assault incident each year from 2015–19. In 2015, the estimated prevalence of sexual assault against all US women was 4.7 percent. Women should be better protected from sexual assault in the military rather than in the civilian world. The military, with its own internal judicial system, also has failed sexual-assault victims by allowing commanders to judge punishment for perpetrators without an independent review. In July 2021, Defense Secretary Lloyd Austin endorsed legal procedures to ensure civilian review of all sexual-assault cases.

All of these issues have been improving, but at a pace painfully too slow for the many women who had to bear them. Until combat roles were opened to women in 2013, women were not even allowed to try out for infantry, special forces, or other combat-specific roles. Some specialty support roles, like Marine counterintelligence, only opened five years earlier in 2008. Throughout the wars in Afghanistan and Iraq, women deployed with support units like intelligence, logistics, and administration but never as organic support within the primary focus of the Marine Corps, the infantry battalion. The first Marine infantry battalion to deploy to a combat zone with women in support roles was mine in 2018. There were 2 women with us out of a unit of more than 700 Marines.

Jennifer faced all of these lasting issues when making her decision to join in 2013. At first, she felt a pride in trailblazing, being part of a minority of women breaking stereotypes and precipitating change for future generations. Years later, that pride was mixed with the painful question: "Why is this taking so long?"

Jennifer would hug her dad at the end of her six-day summer seminar and tell him immediately that she was going back to Navy for college. Her dad could not hide his excitement and pride for his daughter. She was starting a journey he himself had hoped to make at her age. Jennifer's mom would be the most nervous of the three.

Jennifer was a clear minority at Navy, as women would make up less than a quarter of her graduating class in 2019. She remembered looking around a math class of twenty students and realizing she was one of only two girls. The majority of her fellow male students would support her though; they motivated her to overcome challenges and never discounted her or assumed she was unable to meet the standard.

Plebe Summer, the first six weeks of military training before the first year of college, taught Jennifer the importance of doing the small things right. She always woke up early to do required menial tasks like taking out the trash and cleaning bathrooms. Her consistency and selflessness gained her trust with her peers. She learned trust built the foundation for influence and leadership that would facilitate her success in leadership roles with more complex and difficult tasks.

The training was never easy, as Navy seemed to find every student's weakness. In summer training between her first and second years, Jennifer found herself tying knots over and over again for hours into the night in preparation for a military evaluation. She looked at her phone only to see social-media stories of friends celebrating Fourth of July. As Jennifer put her phone away, the full weight of how much she was sacrificing hit her. A text from a friend later in the week saying they missed her at the party would mean more to Jennifer than that friend could know.

In her lowest moment during her second year, Jennifer considered transferring to another college. The sacrifices, the simple ones like missing parties and the complex ones like serving in an unknown capacity for years after college, were weighing on her, as were the challenges and discomfort of daily life. She had completed an application to transfer to University of Maryland and only had to let her leadership at Navy know via email to start the process. Sitting in her dorm room, she paused with her hand hovering over the enter key and remembered what an older student had asked her to do on her first day of Plebe Summer. He had said write down on a piece of paper why she came to Navy. She pulled it out of her desk and read it again: "Because I know that I can do this, and this is what I want to do." That "why" got Jennifer to close her laptop. She woke up the next day and never thought about transferring again. She would graduate with her class in 2019 and tell friends staying was the best decision she ever made.

Remembering a purpose or a "why" is critical in service like the military that has less immediate extrinsic rewards. Purpose gives meaning to sacrifice and suffering, a cause for why Jennifer had to tie knots for hours rather than see friends. For Viktor Frankl, a Holocaust survivor, a psychiatrist, and the author of *Man's Search For Meaning*, purpose is the essential element of life. Its loss is the main source of depression and even suicide. Frankl would ask his patients the blunt question of, "Why do you not commit suicide?" Their answers would provide clues to the unrealized purpose they felt made their lives worth living.

My sister came to me once years ago and told me she had just had an apocalyptic dream where she was running away from some unseen danger. She escaped to a rooftop in downtown Baltimore and looked over the burning city. The others she was with turned to her and said to jump, to commit suicide because their fate was set. She said she stopped and thought, "Jay could be alive somewhere." She did not jump, and she woke up.

Finding purpose through others, family, partners, or close friends, reveals how social the foundation of our lives can be. Seeking meaning through service to a community or a country is merely a larger representation of that social fulfillment. Inconsistency in the people or groups we find meaning in serves to damage our sense of "why." Inconsistency in ourselves works the same way.

When I was visiting that same sister at college, I overhead people who did not know me making fun of her. I was silent and stayed out of the conversation. I found an excuse eventually to walk away. I thought as I left, "Disowned her that quick, huh?" As Tim O'Brien writes in "The Lives of the Dead" in *The Things They Carried*, "Some practice at being brave might've helped a little." My inconsistency, even unseen to my sister, failed the purpose she and I felt in our relationship.

Consistency and reliability are what allowed for Colonel Parker's success in leading our base and influencing the Iraqis' progress against ISIS. Marcus maintaining his moral code even in the cognitively dissonant scenario of needing to heal the enemy who had just been trying to kill them showed his Marines he was unwavering in all situations. Consistency is essential not only to leading and influencing others but also to maintaining a meaningful life. Purpose and meaning can be damaged when those we rely on do not meet or live up to expectations. However, if that purpose and meaning derive from living up to a moral code, secular or religious, the only consistency we have to focus on is our own.

Leadership Exercise – "Mask Off": In spring 2021, the ongoing COVID-19 pandemic restrictions added to the sense of pandemic fatigue. Vaccines had slowed the rate of transmission and deaths significantly, but we were all still required to wear masks. I was teaching a class hybrid, with some students in person and some learning virtually. As class began, I turned to everyone in the classroom and said, "You mind if I take my mask off?" How would you lead in this moment?

This exercise might seem simple depending on personal experiences with the pandemic, as either a resounding no or even a yes. Some vocal seniors immediately said yes, and I paused, trying to act and wait to see if anyone else would speak up. The room was silent, and I eventually told everyone they had just failed a test. Regardless of personal feelings towards the restrictions, they knew we all had to follow the rules. If a rule is unjust, there are proper ways to protest it. That protest should be deliberate, planned, and coordinated and should not put others at potential risk. They should not have let me act cavalierly and break the rule on a whim, either explicitly through their permission or implicitly through their silence. Above masks, I received some very angry glares from students who felt I betrayed them.

Leadership Exercise – "Peer Accountability": Ahead of one quiz later in the semester, I planned another moral-courage exercise with two students who had stayed late after class one day. With my permission, the two students would cheat openly during the next quiz to see how their fellow students would react. When I gave the quiz a week or so later, I left the room and dawdled outside while the students worked. One student I had planned the exercise with turned to the room and openly asked for an answer on a multiple-choice question. The other student waited but then gave the answer. I came back into the room to start the lesson. The room was uncomfortable but silent, and I waited for anyone to speak up. How would you lead in this moment?

I continued class normally. One student, not part of the exercise, stayed behind after class to talk to me and let me know what had happened. Two others arrived later during lunch, but they admitted they thought it might be a test, especially considering the mask exercise from a few weeks prior. I opened the next class with a question: "What happened during the quiz on Tuesday?" No one spoke up, and I knew that no one had approached the two "cheaters" after class either. I told them again that what they had experienced was a moral-courage exercise and all but three of them had failed. I told the class that even the three who had alerted me missed part of the point of the exercise: checking in on their peers, the two "cheaters" making bad decisions, was the most important thing they could have done, more important than alerting the teacher. I did not receive any angry glares from above masks that time.

These efforts in acting were my small attempt to help my students build their own moral codes. Whatever mottos, thoughts, or decrees they wanted to follow did not matter. All that mattered is that the students developed a consistent foundation for improving leadership and achieving meaningful lives. Sports, volunteer work, employment, hobbies, education, all provide opportunities to define and refine this philosophy of leadership and living. Those philosophies provide the strength for action, to lead in and live through trying circumstances. Nobody cares what you think unless your actions match it.

Many experiences build successively on each other to reinforce existing beliefs in the face of difficult situations. Facing previous life-and-death decisions in the military prepared Marcus for the moment with the injured Taliban fighter. Some experiences, though, do not build linearly and require flexibility to determine the right action that would fit the moment. Ryan, a Special Forces officer, or Green Beret, faced such an unexpected decision in leadership when training Malaysian forces in the jungle.

Leadership Exercise – "The Lost Pistol": At the end of a week-long exercise in unconventional warfare, one of Ryan's soldiers came up to him and told him he had lost his pistol. They had just spent days "behind enemy lines" trudging miles through the jungle and conducting air assaults with a ten-man team of Malaysian soldiers. The soldier last confirmed he had the pistol before the exercise began, meaning the pistol could be anywhere. After having his team search through all of their packs for the pistol, Ryan told his leadership about the loss. His leadership said Ryan had to search through their Malaysian partners' packs. Ryan did not want to hurt the great relationship he had with the Malaysian troops, and it was very unlikely that they had taken the pistol. Still, he needed to follow his boss's orders. How would you lead in this moment?

Though Ryan had spent his life as a teammate and leader on the sports field and had seven years in the military before facing this decision, he had no comparable moment to guide his actions. He knew he could not lie to his leadership, since that would violate the trait of honesty he valued so much. Ryan decided he would bring all of his soldiers out with the Malaysian soldiers and search all their packs, US and Malaysian, together. He encouraged his troops to joke to lighten the mood and show they did not believe one of the Malaysian troops had stolen the pistol. After the search, they all sat down together to eat dinner, with Ryan and his Malaysian counterpart sitting next to each other at the head of the group. Ryan knew finding the pistol was less important than showing respect for his partners and maintaining their relationship.

Ryan and his team would never find the pistol. The loss of such sensitive equipment forced his team to rebuild their reputation within their command over the next year. Ryan's team's relationship with the Malaysians never wavered though. Respect and understanding, as with Colonel Parker in the War Against ISIS, were the keys for that success as well.

All of these varied experiences in the military are addictive. Jennifer could overcome challenges and gain strength that a sports field could never give to her. Ryan could lead troops at the forward edge of US influence and policy. And a young, 20-something kid could make decisions involving the life and death of ISIS fighters miles away. These opportunities for growth, the chance to define and refine who we are through suffering, are what drew us to the military. The sense of patriotism, of social fulfillment in serving your country provides meaning to these experiences seemingly impossible to match. The thought of missing these experiences is what makes it hard to leave.

Through my time in service, a Hemingway-loving intelligence officer named Pete served as my mentor. Wherever I was, Pete happened to be there. We found time to meet and eat together in Iraq and Kuwait, in California and Florida, and outside DC. He served through intense ground combat in Afghanistan early in his career and had a wisdom I could only hope to emulate. Over dinner, we talked of this struggle, of leaving behind the opportunities for growth and the sense of patriotism that drew me to the military initially. He left me with words I never forgot, a different but critical "why" and purpose for my life with its own challenges for growth.

"The most patriotic thing you can do, Jay, is raise a good family."

"Nobody Cares" Summary and Discussion Questions

Women in the Military

Many of the women I served with experienced discrimination during their time in service. Issues with regulations or ill-fitting equipment add extra burden on female servicemembers that their male counterparts do not experience. While slow progress on some of these issues has been made, including in maternity leave and in opening all service roles to women, women remain a minority in military service.

1. How should leaders ensure that women have equal opportunities to excel in the military as their male counterparts?
2. What issues in military culture continue to facilitate discrimination against women in service?

Remembering Your "Why"

During some of the most difficult training at the Naval Academy, Jennifer questioned why she had joined and wanted to serve in the military. Enduring support from her family strengthened her "why" – her purpose to lead a resilient, confident, and unselfish life.

1. Coach Wally, a mentor of mine in high school, once asked this question – I ask it the same way to you. How do you want to be remembered?
2. How did indecision play a role in strengthening Jennifer's resolve similar to the way it did for me?

Mask Off/Peer Accountability

I tested my class through two moral-courage exercises. Early in the semester, I asked them openly if they would let me break the rules and take off my mask. A few weeks later, I orchestrated two students to cheat in class. Both times, students hesitated and did not "pass" the tests.

1. In the words of Tim O'Brien, how can you get "some practice at being brave" in your daily life?
2. Why can it be more difficult to hold a peer accountable than it is to hold a subordinate or a leader accountable?

The Lost Pistol

As a Green Beret, Ryan led and trained forces all over the world. Maintaining strong relationships with all of these foreign partners was of chief importance. When one of his men lost a pistol, Ryan had to demonstrate humility, unselfishness, and empathy as a leader to ensure that the event would not hurt his relationship with his foreign partners.

1. What is more important when training a team: the skills you impart or the relationship you create? How do you balance the need for both?
2. What character traits and leadership principles are critical to success in scenarios like "The Lost Pistol" and "It Doesn't Make Sense to Shave"?

Chapter 15

THE ONE WE WANT BACK

When I returned to Al Asad Airbase in summer 2018, the electric air that once hung over the base was entirely gone. The command center had turned into a quiet meeting room. There were only a few red pins on the map on the wall on the near side of the room, mostly guesses of ISIS hiding places in the desert. I doubted anyone had been updating it anyway. The long tables that once stretched horizontally across the room were replaced with an oval table and eight leather desk chairs. An ornate rug stuck out prominently from under the table in stark contrast with the command center's plywood floor. A decorator might have been trying to match the style of the Iraqi general's office. The screens still hung on the wall in front, but most were blank. A few showed live feeds of somewhere away in the desert, as if combing for something long lost.

A coffee shop had opened up casually on base. One night, I met an Australian we were working with there for trivia night. He showed up unarmed in a Hawaiian shirt. I half laughed when I saw him. I felt overdressed wearing FROGs, camouflage gear designed to be worn with body armor, and holding a rifle across my chest. He said he might have still worn a Hawaiian shirt walking around in 2016, but he probably would have had a pistol on him at least.

The base shop, or PX, had tripled in size until it shared a wall with the small room that served as a chapel. The improved PX seemed to have all the amenities we had been lacking a year before, but the chapel looked unchanged. I remembered attending Mass once in that room when a rotating Catholic chaplain arrived on base. An older, special-forces advisor had shown up for Mass too, wearing pajama bottoms with dancing caricatures of Homer Simpson. I had not known he was Catholic, and I liked him even more after Mass because of our shared love of *The Simpsons*.

The base barber shop, a critical amenity for Marines even when the base was closer to combat, was in the same place. I walked in, and a few of the Nepalese barbers recognized me and smiled. I sat down for the standard haircut and bizarre head massage that involved them cracking their fingers on your scalp. I realized I should not have missed that head massage as much as I thought I did.

The barbers were only a few of many people I recognized. I passed and waved to the civilian manager of the gym I had seen almost every day a year before. He seemed to be using the WiFi to try and convince someone not to break up with him, so I did not interrupt. I exchanged smiles of recognition with some of the people who helped run the base chow hall. They had created a salad bar in the center of the room, which looked like an appreciated update. I ran into an interpreter I worked closely with too. He told me stories of the liberation of Al Qaim and how proud he was of all the progress we had made with the Iraqis. He would still be there in January 2020 when the base was attacked by Iran.

One of these chance meetings turned into a four-nation lunch. An Iraqi liaison officer who had sat behind me for months in the command center invited me and my friends to lunch with him in the shipping container that had been converted into his living room. We had seen each other outside of the command center, and he immediately came up to me. Through his interpreter, another friend from the year before, he said, "Look how much progress we made. This is because of you." I did not know if he or my friend was the one who greatly exaggerated. I invited the Hawaiian shirt-wearing Australian who surprisingly showed up in uniform, some Danes we were working with, and a few other Americans to join for lunch. We sat and shared stories and reflected on how grateful we all were that the war for Iraq was over.

The person I was most excited to see was Homer. I messaged Homer right when I landed. He was coming back from Baghdad, so it would be a few days before I could see him. "I'll pick you up, bro. First night I'm back. I'll be on night shift."

I woke up in the middle of the night a few days later and waited in the dark near the hangar that held the gym. I half expected I would turn around and go back to bed. A pickup truck then sped dangerously around the corner of the hangar and slammed to a halt in front of me. Homer left the truck running and burst over to give me a hug.

We hopped in the pickup truck. I told Homer he should think about slowing down. I couldn't really talk though since I had just put a few major scratches on a borrowed van earlier that day. I had been driving around coordinating drone training with the Danes and sideswiped a pole.

"Probably the dumbest thing I've ever done. Might get fired and sent home."

"Ah, I've done worse. And I'm still here."

Homer was more than "still here." By 2018, he could pass for a resident of Western Iraq. From the beginning of the war in fall 2014, Homer had spent almost three years in the country out of a possible three-and-a-half. He knew the towns and landscapes better than some of the Iraqis we worked with, all from flying a drone called a Scan Eagle and watching the live feed for hours and hours on end.

Homer had come home briefly to New York City after his first tour as a drone operator. At a small reunion, he told an old acquaintance that he had just returned from Iraq. She smiled and turned to him excitedly, "Oh my God. How was it??" He decided from that moment he was better off not coming home.

Years later, I would sit across from Homer in McSorley's, an old pub in New York City, and ask him the same question. But I wasn't talking about Iraq. I was talking about coming home, leaving the mission, becoming a civilian. My own transition had been mixed. On a professional level, it appeared ideal: I had won the award for officer of the year in counterpropaganda as I left my last job, had taught a high-school class, and was set to jump into medical school. On a personal level, it had gone terribly: the award I won came after burning out in a difficult mission and losing the love of my life. I was too immature to communicate all the emotions I felt in transition and too clouded to see myself and our future. Homer smiled at me, knowing all this, and said himself, "It was rough. It's still rough." He might have answered the same to the acquaintance years before, if he had thought she would understand.

On deployment, I learned to see the war in a similar way to Homer. Targeting ISIS was a necessary part of the war, exciting at times, yet demanding of seriousness and professionalism. It might have felt like a video game watching death on screens, but Homer knew from three years fighting ISIS that the death on the other end of the screen was real.

Homer was a fixture in the front left of the command center, where he operated the camera for his drone three rows ahead of my raised platform. He was a civilian contractor, but he had been in the Marines for a few years before that. The main thing I knew about his service was that "they couldn't faze" him and he had received enough disciplinary action that he could not re-enlist. The new job allowed him flexibility he liked though, deploying longer and more frequently than he ever would have as a Marine. He also could serve at the leading edge of the fight against ISIS, searching day in and day out to find ISIS fighters that we would strike and kill.

Homer was known as the savant of drone operations. He would even spend his free time studying ISIS propaganda to get inside the mind of the enemy. For all this, the Iraqis we worked with loved him just as much as we did. One of the Iraqi officers gave Homer traditional Iraqi clothing that he wore into the command center every so often. Most laughed at him, but Homer said he was just trying to get inside the mind of the enemy even more. Sitting late on shift with Homer one night, I asked him how he understood ISIS so well. "They're like my family."

I squinted at him, trying to figure out where the punchline was.

"No, really." He leaned in towards me. "My dad was in the cartel. He was a bad man. ISIS, they're just gangsters. All gangsters are the same."

I didn't know what to say and simply sat with him, staring forward at the screens that surveilled the suspected home of one of those ISIS gangsters by the river. Homer leaned in again, "Every time we kill one of them … I see my dad."

Homer's dad never treated his family well. He was flashy, quick to anger, and a heavy drinker: the combination of those three made him abusive, in ways Homer would never describe to me. Homer was born in one of the boroughs of New York City, but his younger brother Brando had been born in Mexico. Homer's mom got Brando across the border into Texas with the help of some coyotes. Brando gained his citizenship by following in Homer's footsteps and serving in the Marines.

Homer's dad died in a gunfight in Mexico, ambushed in a revenge killing, while Homer was still in the Marines. His Marine leadership had heard from the Drug Enforcement Agency that Homer's dad, a wanted criminal, was killed and called Homer into a meeting. Homer thought he was in trouble again, but his senior enlisted told him he had difficult news to pass on. It clicked when his senior enlisted started by mentioning the DEA. "My mom already told me. Good riddance."

With Homer's intimate understanding of ISIS, his work always turned into results, results that meant many opportunities for us to target and kill ISIS fighters. In that environment, we all quickly became very familiar with the law of armed conflict. Every opportunity was gauged against its four main principles: distinction, proportionality, military necessity, and unnecessary suffering. Distinction, most critically, meant we had to do everything within our power to avoid civilian casualties and collateral damage, distinguishing properly between combatant and non-combatant. Proportionality meant we had to use a weapon appropriate to the threat the target posed – our weapon's blast was constrained by the size of the target, which complemented distinction. Military necessity meant that there was no other option, non-lethal, diplomatic, or political. Unnecessary suffering meant that we killed the enemy quickly in the most humane way possible.

A few months into my first deployment, with the Battle of Mosul raging to the north, our command center settled into the daily operations of searching for and targeting ISIS fighters in front of the stagnant Iraqi line. A new base commander named Colonel Finn had taken over the mission, who was a caring and thoughtful leader with a different style from Colonel Parker. Colonel Finn knew that his time in command was likely to be uneventful, as we all waited for the Iraqis to win the Battle of Mosul.

Successful strikes became less frequent. We had fewer air sorties dedicated to us and fewer Iraqi operations to force ISIS out of hiding. Any strike we did have became an event on its own. When a strike was brewing, the command center started to receive unexplained visitors, who were otherwise bored without much to do. They sat on a bench along the wall like sports fans in cheap bleacher seats.

The constant level of seriousness in the command center due to of the life-and-death mission we ran waned as the opportunities to kill ISIS became less frequent. However, the Iraqi line far north of our base continued to be attacked by ISIS sporadically, which forced us to watch the Iraqi defense more closely. The most frustrating attacks involved quadcopters. In a relatively cheap and hard-to-prevent fashion, ISIS would deploy quadcopters to fly over the Iraqi line and drop makeshift bombs on their defensive positions. A few of those attacks had been successful and killed several Iraqi soldiers.

Homer applied new intensity to his role in the command center as the mission of targeting ISIS during this battlefield lull seemed to rest squarely on his shoulders. He was sharp as ever, and one day, he did the unthinkable. He recognized a tiny quadcopter flying almost imperceptibly in his video feed and followed it back to its landing point on the outskirts of a town held by ISIS. Two ISIS fighters stood on a roof to catch the quadcopter. Previous intelligence told us this building was a known ISIS safehouse. We had everything we needed to begin the strike process. Homer had once again found a dangerous threat not far from the Iraqi front line.

Colonel Finn and his key leadership entered the command center after I reported that Homer had found a few ISIS quadcopter pilots. Voyeurs filtered in soon after, as news spread from those who needed to know to those who did not. As I worked with the Iraqis and our command to approve the strike, we all watched as the ISIS fighters left their safehouse and packed up their pickup truck with several boxes of equipment. A dirt bike was tied up in the bed of the truck. We decided to follow the vehicle as they pulled out onto the street. The vehicle then approached a critical intersection. The ISIS fighters could either turn right and drive deeper into ISIS territory or turn left and drive towards the Iraqi defense. The command center was silent for a moment as the truck turned left. We had every indication to believe they were about to stage another quadcopter attack on the Iraqi front line. We were in the perfect position to prevent it.

Leadership Exercise – "That Ain't Right, Sir": With the command center full and Homer behind the controls of his drone feed, we all watched closely as a vehicle with two ISIS fighters armed with weaponized quadcopters drove towards the Iraqi defensive line. They pulled over and stopped on the side of the road to a secluded area in the desert hidden by large rocks and out of sight from Iraqi observation posts. There, they began taking propaganda photos. Nearing the end of the photo shoot, one of the ISIS fighters lay down on his side, crossed his legs, and propped up his head with his hand to pose like a model. The room erupted in laughter. I stood silently and made eye contact with a friend who then stopped laughing.

The ISIS fighters hustled back to the car, pulled the dirt bike and two boxes out of the back, drove until they found another secluded area less than a mile from the Iraqi defense. The two fighters huddled around the boxes and prepared their quadcopter for flight. Our air officer was in contact with a fighter jet that was preparing to drop bombs on them. The first bomb dropped, and both fighters disappeared in a cloud of dust. There were some slightly muted expressions of celebration and relief across the room.

When the dust cleared, we realized that the bomb had missed slightly. One of the ISIS fighters appeared to be dead; the other was brushing dust off himself and starting to stand up. When he regained his footing, he walked towards the dirt bike in an apparent attempt to flee. The air officer announced to the room the fighter jet only had one more bomb. Colonel Finn approved a re-attack, and we waited to see if the last bomb would hit its target. The air officer called "weapons away, forty seconds," which meant the fighter jet released the bomb and there were forty seconds to impact. On the screen, Homer zoomed in on the ISIS fighter as he struggled to kick start his dirt bike. I watched his foot frantically thrust down, one, two, three times. On the fourth kick, the dirt bike started, and he began to accelerate away. A cloud of dust then enveloped the whole screen, and we were zoomed in enough this time to know he would not survive. The room erupted in a cheer. Several officers who far outranked me fist pumped into the air. I stood rigid, hesitating just long enough that my radio operator Kitter on my right noticed. "That ain't right, Sir," he said in quiet agreement. I had to decide if and how I would address the room. How would you lead in this moment?

The feelings of relief and celebration seeing the second ISIS fighter killed were natural. The chase had taken time and effort, and we had successfully defended the Iraqi line from a certain attack. If we have a moment to appreciate a victory, we should, at least in a reserved way. As the junior officer in the room, I had no experience comparable to the senior officers who celebrated either. Most of them had been in combat on the ground and likely lost Marines at different points in their careers.

I still felt there was an issue of culture. First, the fight was never over. The Iraqis were still out on the front line, and we needed to continue to work to defend and support them. Second, I knew from previous strikes on that deployment that not every strike goes perfectly to plan. If we do make a mistake, if there is collateral damage or some other painful twist of circumstance, we need to rely on the fact that we took every action seriously.

In the moments after the strike, I could not address the room in any practical manner to criticize the unprofessional culture. The senior officers would have discounted me for my lack of experience and thought I was simply being disrespectful to them. Later that night, when the command center was quiet and only our main crew remained, I pulled everyone together and brought up the cheering. We discussed the culture, and I praised our team for always remaining professional, even in high-stress moments like the strike. I said I would work to keep uninvolved visitors out of the command center too.

I was only a few weeks away from returning home at that point. Leaving gave me the opportunity to sit down with Colonel Finn face-to-face in an exit interview on the day before I left. In between compliments, I brought up cheering and said I thought we needed to be more professional in the command center. He agreed. That was all I could hope for.

As I drove away with Homer that night in 2018 in his pickup truck, we caught up on everything from the year since we had last been together. He told me about supporting the liberation of Al Qaim and Rawah and the brief and uneventful trip home he had made. I talked about turning over my sniper platoon to a new platoon commander and seeing some old friends in Boston over Labor Day.

Homer took me over to their drone launch site and into a shipping container where he facilitated the takeoff and landing of their aircraft. The room was dark, lit only by tens of small buttons and a few screens on a command panel that monitored aircraft status. We talked as he worked. After some time, the conversation stalled into silence. Homer continued to plug away at his screens and controls, deftly floating between different metrics and analysis. I turned to Homer, somewhat nervously, "Do you remember the bad strikes?"

"Every single one, man."

"What about the one right before I ..."

Homer cut me off. "Yeah. I remember."

A week after the moment of cheering in the command center, Homer had found more opportunities for us to target ISIS. We started the routine strike process, and I felt the strike was likely going to be my last. My replacement had arrived that day, and I would begin training him the next. Lance and I had worked to create notes and "how-to" sheets for reference. We had learned a lot, and I wanted to pass on as much as I could.

The strike started like many others. Homer had found a few people "acting shady" outside an ISIS town and decided to follow them. They ended up driving to a large house protected by a square courtyard with walls that were about 8ft high. They entered the house and disappeared from view. Outside the house, Homer found a vehicle with a heavy machine gun in its bed, improperly hidden by an overhang. Intelligence reporting told us that the house was used to train suicide bombers. We felt again that we were in position to prevent a deadly attack on the Iraqi defensive line.

Colonel Finn and key staff in the strike process took up positions in the center of the room, two rows ahead of where I stood. To my chagrin, the typical group of voyeurs began to fill up the bench on the wall and other empty spots in the room. More than thirty faces jammed into the command center stared intently forward at Homer's screen as we prepared to destroy the vehicle, the ISIS safehouse, and all of its inhabitants.

The problem was the house was on the corner of a somewhat busy street. Once we were approved for the strike, the air officer talked a fighter jet into position to drop bombs on the house three times. Each time, a vehicle started driving by the house, and the air officer had to call "red," which meant the strike was paused. The fighter jet would have to re-set to make another bombing run.

The "red" call was usually obvious, part of a standard process called transient scans that were required before any strike. The air officer or his boss the fires chief would announce "red" quickly if a civilian was thought to be entering the determined blast area of our strike. Anyone in the room could call "red" though and sometimes I or others would, since all of our attention turned to the screens in this critical moment.

By the fourth bombing run, I turned to my computer and started finishing up the turnover document that Lance and I were working on. I was annoyed and frustrated. I was tired of feeling powerless when Colonel Finn and others who outranked me took command during a strike. I was tired of the voyeurs gawking at a job we all took seriously. I was tired of being stressed and on edge. I was tired of being away from family and friends. I was tired of being in Western Iraq.

I looked up from my computer. There was a road that came to a T intersection about 50m below the house on the screen. I saw a pickup truck slowly creeping along that road towards the T intersection. All eyes in the room were still focused forward. I turned to my radio operator Sully, another stalwart of the command center who had the later shift after Kitter, and said, "We're red still, right?" Sully just stared straight ahead.

The air officer announced to the room "weapons away, thirty seconds." The bombs had just been dropped. Those seconds seemed to stretch and bend, and the pickup truck arrived at the T intersection. A right turn would take the truck towards the house. A left turn would take it to safety. My eyes widened as the truck turned right. I begged the bombs to drop immediately, while the truck still had some distance away. The truck continued to inch forward, driving incomprehensibly slowly, as if it had nowhere in particular to be and by fate and chance just happened to be exactly where we did not want it to be.

The bombs finally landed. The explosion was one of the largest I saw throughout my deployment. Our bombs had ignited what was stashed in the house and created a massive secondary explosion that shook the entire street. The command center was silent. I waited in fear, staring at the cloud of dust.

> Leadership Exercise – "The One We Want Back": As the dust settled, Homer zoomed out to show the extent of the damage from our strike on the ISIS suicide-bomber training house. While the house was destroyed, the courtyard wall had protected the other buildings on the street. The vehicle with the heavy machine gun was on fire and slowly melting away. The pickup truck that had taken the wrong turn looked damaged and was not moving. Homer zoomed in to look closer. As he did, some people ran forward to the truck and pulled out three lifeless bodies: one adult male and two young children. I stared around the room at the various expressions of shock and disbelief. I needed to respond. How would you lead in this moment?

Murmurs and whispers began to break the silence in the room. Colonel Finn stood rigid himself, staring at the screens ahead. I jumped on the phone to call a counterpart in Baghdad, who supervised our strikes. I asked him, "The truck was out of range, right?"

"Yeah, that was secondaries."

I hung up. I had confirmed with him that under normal circumstances, our bombs would not have affected the truck. The truck had been out of the weapon engagement zone, or WEZ. If ISIS had not been storing their own bombs in the house that created secondary explosions, the dad and two kids would still be alive.

As most still stared at Homer's screen, I announced that I confirmed with Baghdad the truck was out of range. My words came out meekly as I attempted to explain what happened to the room. "It wasn't our fault the truck got hit. That was secondaries."

A British officer and friend who sat on my left almost every day in the command center asked me quietly, "Jay, why, why did you think you had to say that?"

I responded so only he could hear, "Because I know we just made a mistake."

Colonel Finn had looked back at me somewhat confused by what I had said too. He spoke up then, announcing to the room the importance of what we had done. He said we needed to focus on the lives we saved by destroying the vehicle with the heavy machine gun and the house that trained suicide bombers. Most faces in the room looked blank, a shock that would sit with the room for the rest of the day.

I had tried to console the room immediately after the strike. Colonel Finn had done the same in a much more eloquent way. Still on top of reinforcing the strike's necessity to save Iraqi lives from future ISIS attacks, he should have pointed to the pickup truck and said to the room, "That was my fault. That's on me. None of that is any of your responsibility, because I should have said something if I thought the truck was going to get hit. I didn't say anything, and that is not on any of you." By rank and position, he was the only one who could try to shoulder responsibility for everyone in the room.

After that day, an Army soldier who did shifts in the command center told his leadership he never wanted to do a shift there again. I remember thinking he was weak. As a junior soldier, that was probably the best protest he could make. His chain of command would have to address how they could better support their soldiers who had to deal with the bizarre collective responsibility of modern war.

That event should never have happened, but it did. We suffer only a fraction of the consequences in comparison with the civilians who died and their families. The pain of regret and guilt in the command center pales to the grief and loss experienced only miles away from us.

Of the hundreds of strikes I supported, my last stands out starkly from all the others. All in the room, decision-makers, those in support roles, and observers, remember the moment in their own ways. The truck inching forward after the T intersection will remain a lesson for me in the fragility of human decisions, especially those that lead to life or death. For Homer, the truck motivated him to volunteer at a New York City hospital at the beginning of the COVID-19 pandemic. He told me he just had to find more ways to serve.

A few days after the strike, I was shaving outside near the transient tents, where you sleep when you are on your way in or out. I overheard a senior enlisted from Daly's platoon, speaking somewhat to me but more to himself. "Oh. It's Monday. Yippee. Only time I like Mondays. On a deployment."

"Why's that?"

"Because it means I only have a few left."

We were finally headed home. When we landed, a swift transition would hit us that would make me question what I had actually been a part of. I would be recognized for the work I did on that deployment in an award. I was sick to my stomach as it was read to me to include "facilitating 101 strikes resulting in 143 enemy killed in action." There was no mention of the truck.

Before I left on my second deployment, I reflected in writing on my first. I seemed to have learned Judge Tucker's enduring lesson already by then: "For something we dedicate so much to – monuments, stories, gratitude – you learn every inspirational story of heroism or humanity in combat just should've been unnecessary and avoided altogether."

When I was back in the Middle East the second time, I was further removed from combat. I did not have to make or be involved in any life-and-death decisions. On a brief trip to visit some of our forward units, I walked into a command center in Southwest Afghanistan. I realized quickly that I was the voyeur to an ongoing strike. I turned around and showed myself out. I felt the same way in Syria and Baghdad. My most poignant moments from that deployment came the night with Homer, when we reflected on everything we had done more than a year before.

When I returned home, my friend Will met me on the field where families greet everyone coming home from deployment. The field was a small patch of green on the only part of the expansive desert base that resembled anything close to a town. A few miles of one-to-two-story buildings connected by small roads were guarded on the north by a steep set of hills and on the south by a man-made lake and the vast openness of the desert. I watched my friend's children and wife jump into his arms. He dropped all his bags but braced from toppling over.

I thought my second deployment would not be my last. My emotions were more subdued than the raw emotion I felt coming home the first time. I shook hands with a few of my Marines and then turned to Will, "Let's get out of here."

Will drove us on the east–west road that led out to the base gate and the small desert town beyond. Will was the only Marine officer I knew that I could describe as overly dramatic, and he planned to become a writer once he got out of the military. That future made him always want to "unpack" things, which was far from what I wanted to do at that moment. He kept his left hand on the wheel, turned to me slightly, and grabbed my left shoulder with his right hand. "Aren't you glad to be back home in old 29 Palms, Jay?"

I rolled down the window and stared at Lake Bandini, the sewage dump that wafted stench north up the base when the sun hit it just right. I saw the truck, with the dad and the two kids pulled out, bombed by us because I had had my head down writing notes for my replacement. I saw my platoon on a hill over the Pacific. I saw the air-traffic control tower in Kuwait. I saw the Kurdish garden in Northeast Syria and the endless expanse of desert during a sunset in Southwest Afghanistan. I saw the bend of the Tigris from a helicopter flying out of Baghdad, the Hands of Victory prominently raised to the sky. I kept staring at the lake. "I fucking hate this place."

I started falling asleep that night on the couch while Will described the entire plot of a fantasy series he had started to write. He was on Book Eight of Twelve gesticulating wildly over a map he had set up in the living room when I told him I needed to go to bed. I walked over into my bedroom, shut the door, and looked around: an old mattress in the corner, my guitar, and a few bags waiting to be unpacked.

"So, I'm back."

"The One We Want Back" Summary and Discussion Questions

How was It??

Homer answers the question "how was it??" referring to a deployment in Iraq or a transition into civilian life differently, depending on who is asking. If the person asking has personal experience with a deployment or is a veteran, Homer might answer honestly. If the person asking does not have any similar experience and asks in an uncompassionate way, Homer might wonder why the person asked at all.

1. Do you need personal experience with an event or difficulty to support someone through one?
2. How does "How Was It??" compare with "Communicating and Receiving Trauma"? What character traits are necessary for success in both scenarios?

That Ain't Right, Sir

In the command center, high-stress scenarios sometimes gave way to unexpected moments of levity. Still, the task we had – to inflict death on ISIS fighters miles away from us – required professionalism and seriousness. I tried to influence the command center to maintain that level of professionalism but largely failed.

1. What is the danger in being overly serious or overly professional? When is levity important and necessary?
2. What are the best ways to influence the culture of a team or organization?

The One We Want Back

A few days before I was to leave Iraq, a tragic instance of collateral damage shook our command center. The moment became one of several prominent memories that forever changed my outlook on war. By lenient analysis, the event was unavoidable, due to the release of the bombs before the truck was recognized in range and in any danger. That excuse is no solace to me, since I did not play the role I should have during the strike: I know there must have been some way to avoid it.

1. I was not lying when I tried to console the room after the strike, but perhaps I was a little misleading. Is lying or misleading someone ever an acceptable method of consolation?
2. What is the necessary and important role of guilt?
3. How does the responsibility of a leader remove the weight of guilt from subordinates?
4. What are critical behaviors in self-compassion that encourage growth after failure, moral injury, or traumatic events?

Epilogue

A NOTE TO MY FAMILY

The night prior to a routine patrol on my first deployment, I hastily penned a quick note to my family in my phone. It was a just-in-case-I-die letter, written in the style of one I had heard read at the Remembrance Day Ceremony we had just celebrated with our British counterparts. While part of a very different and much safer war, I still followed the tradition of the rifleman and the many before me who had died, not wanting to leave my family without taking one final chance to tell them I loved them.

Before my second deployment, I thought I was deploying to Syria to be part of the more active conflict against ISIS in a similar role to my first deployment. I took a moment during leave on a train to New York to write this letter. My mom sat next to me on the train and luckily did not ask what I was writing. The next day, I pushed it across a table to one of my best friends from college, who said to me, "You didn't do this last time …"

"I also didn't pack well and left the house I was renting in total disarray."

"Fair."

The letter thankfully remained unread until I read it aloud to my class on the last day of the semester, more than three years after the train ride when I wrote it. The theme remains true to me and represents my perspective as an American who fought in modern war.

Friends, resident aliens, countrymen, beloved family, and Max,

This sucks, huh? I cannot believe my keyboard became self-aware and electrocuted me to death. At least, they gave me a clean death, an intelligence officer's death.

Writing this letter now, I see myself 17 again with no scrap of facial hair at granddad's funeral crying listening to taps then wondering with friends by the pool whether the military was my path, 19 at college being handed my name tapes by an Army captain who saw more than the indecisive freshman I was, and 20 at boxing reading the TR quote on the back of a shirt then forever burned into my memory that made me realize I would only be able to look in a mirror again if I took the path traveled by so many I respected.

"Each time we face our fear, we gain strength, courage, and confidence in the doing."

And then I stepped out the door, stomach turning and homesick, onto a road that I would not know where it would whisk me off to. I wished often that the time had not come to me, only to learn through hardship that it was not my time for the choosing.

To set the record straight, I do believe that there are things in life worth dying for. I lived with that passion, a life wish I held close to me and a life understanding that gave me pain every time the bell tolled, on our side or theirs. And now the bell tolls again for me, but just once more, a last, final, and solemn time.

Call it fate. Call it a bad break. You can call it whatever you like. But with God's help, I know we will be a family again, stronger than ever even without me, with love and kinship that span and tie us together from Singapore to Baltimore.

Even in death, I still consider myself the luckiest man on the face of this Earth. And that great luck came from passing my life in the company of such amazing individuals – family that inspired me, friends that drove me, and all those in between that supported me tirelessly even when I acted like a dumb punk kid with nothing to lose. I had a whole lot to live and die for, and you, my beloved family and friends, do as well. The sun will shine in a new morning, first in a solemn toll of daybreak into a paean of full color and sound celebrating life's resilience, that seems to reveal the mystical oneness of all things in love and fellowship. Before you then will be the choice, the choice to see clarity, peace, and serenity, the choice to find meaning in chance and let chance speak to you. I hope you know I want nothing more than you to find that same just and lasting peace, intra and inter, and firmness in the right that drove my life.

The journey to find that meaning though will be better than the meaning itself, as the meaning folds and bends to the inconsistency of man and tumultuous times. Perhaps, if I could implore any of you to take on public service, a few will answer the latent call to support our political system with much needed open-mindedness. I do not have the hubris to believe my life means anything more than the next, but I do have the hubris to believe that some of you could help our wavering city on a hill retain its colossus, its ability to engender positive change in the world, as you will know personally that hill hides the bones of all of us who gave our lives to our country. My bones and handful of dust will rot in the Earth dedicated to the idea of self-evident truths not enough realized, without having voted for any of the elected officials I died for – it is your choice to see that as tragedy in current failure or beauty in hopeful, good things to come that will, one day, be realized. I have been smiling lately choosing the latter. Now, I pass the fire in a horn, the way people used to do, to you. I will be on ahead, and when you get here, I will be here.

I am young enough to say, but perhaps too young to be believed, that I really lived a wonderful life. While I had my teenage mopiness, as if my life was in a rut, I look back now with the sole wish to have caused harm only to me and to none else. As this was fate we could not cheat, I hope you call on each other, the large eclectic family we have become, to find home together, and to care for each other to face the cruel, emotionless bending arc of time that often seems to not be in tune. Remember, all that is gone, all our ups and downs, all our motivators and modifiers, are what we call living, now, and what we are so privileged to feel and experience in all that's to come.

I hope through all this that you remember me who I was – a mediocre singer who already blew his shot, a crying manager of a freshman basketball team who tried too hard in all rec activities, an inconsistent friend not in tune enough with others who could have been so much better – and do not paint my spirit too much in gold. But how you remember is your choice and yours alone.

I bid to all of you goodnight and the greatest joy in our memories and your future together. The angels in chrome by the doorway to a thousand churches ahead show me that this was my path and that is all there is to it. That's why they call it Golf. Right, Pop?

Tick. The bell tolls on the Nile. Or in Seville?

Tock. They say he never had an original thought.

I plead the fifth.

I love you.

And I am so sorry to leave you.

Peace. Peace. Peace.

Postscript

THIRTEEN MORE NAMES ON THE WALL

I heard about the attack in Kabul during lunch a few minutes before a cadaver dissection lab. I had sent out the first draft of this book only three days prior, so my thoughts had stayed close to the war, even as my distance from the military increased. I walked back into the rectangular cadaver laboratory with the hundred or so fellow medical students bustling around to the familiar smell of formaldehyde. It was comforting in a way, but jarring in others, that no one seemed to know the news.

While an instructor announced the day's lab to the class, I thought of the first mission I supported in Western Iraq which put US special forces under fire. The apparent steady facade I had maintained in the command center had devolved into me sitting on a bench press in the gym, staring at my feet with my heart racing. A song with the refrain "tell me that you're alright, everything is alright" was playing unheard from my phone, looping over and over again. I eventually stood up and walked into the night. Staring in the dark, I told myself to get my act together: there would be more missions to support with possible US casualties and deaths. I blinked and thought of the moment I thought I lost Aparicio and his team. I then pulled myself back into the lab, knowing still that the pain from the deaths in Kabul was something I could barely imagine.

The attack was clear evidence that the long-planned withdrawal had become a crisis evacuation. City after city had fallen to the Taliban in the first weeks of August, and Kabul, the capital, surrendered without a shot. Since all other US airbases had already been abandoned, a Marine Company from the latest iteration of the Special Purpose Marine Air Ground Task Force-Crisis Response-Central Command arrived to support evacuations from the main airport in Kabul. For days, Marines helped Americans and Afghans cross a small canal that served as a barrier to separate the US-controlled portion of the airport. Thousands of Americans, Afghans, and others had left the country safely because of their work.

In the early evening on August 26, a suicide bomber from ISIS-Khorasan, the Afghan brand of ISIS that had managed to persist despite the failings of the founding group in Iraq and Syria, blew himself up with a directional IED less than 15ft feet from the canal. The shrapnel cut through the crowd of Afghan civilians and hit the Marines, sailors, and soldiers helping Afghans across. More than 150 Afghan civilians and 13 US troops were killed. The thirteen would soon have their names chiseled onto one of the obsidian black plaques of the Global War on Terrorism memorial in Ft Benning, Georgia.

The thirteen who died in Kabul represent less than .2 percent of the more than 6,700 US military deaths in Iraq and Afghanistan. The question remains whether they will be the last, either in those countries or in the Global War on Terrorism overall. Their deaths will be marked as avoidable mistakes a patient enemy exploited, scarring the inadequate planning and execution of the withdrawal. The truth is the black plaques of the memorial have plenty of space for more names, for more mistakes we fail to avoid.

For my generation in the wars from 2014 on, a mass casualty event like this had never happened. For Marcus and others, it was all too familiar. We share some understanding of the loss and pain and suffering of war across generations. That understanding stretches only through empathy when the loss is a friend or fellow Marine or soldier, and we have never experienced that ourselves.

I remember coming home from Iraq the first time and seeing close friends, family, and veterans from earlier generations. I got in the habit of saying "good to be together" or "lucky to be here" whenever we would cheers or sit down to dinner. I did not think much of it or call attention to it. It was my way of reminding myself to be grateful for my life in the US, having lived in a war zone and knowing it could all be taken away in an instant.

The loss of the thirteen makes that feeling all the more important. Antietam veteran and US Supreme Court Justice Oliver Wendell Holmes, Jr once said, "in our youth our hearts were touched with fire. It was given to us to learn at the outset that life is a profound and passionate thing." We live forever with the memory of that fire, that death, that loss. Those memories play back when we see trucks that look out of place in the US or pictures of Marines killed who look so similar to ours we think we should know them. We force the memories away by reminding ourselves of the basic fact that we are living. The time we have, the decisions we make provide us the opportunity to assign meaning to what we have experienced. That meaning helps us recognize the profound gift still given to us that has been taken away from so many others.

So, with that I leave you.

"Good to be together. Lucky to be here."

Postscript II

TOUCHED WITH FIRE IN UKRAINE

"So, how did y'all become so close?"

I smiled at Sully and his girlfriend Nora, sitting across from me in a booth at a favorite Irish pub O'Connell's on King Street in Old Town, Alexandria. It was a legitimate question that Nora posed to me and Sully, but one neither of us seemed to have given much thought to previously.

"We were on deployment together, my first, Sully's second."

That was true. Sully sat next to me what felt like every day of that deployment as my radio operator and watch non-commissioned officer in the command center. He had done a previous deployment to Al Asad in 2015, not long after 2nd Battalion, 7th Marines re-opened the base at the beginning of Operation INHERENT RESOLVE. That first deployment was more intense for him, as ISIS attacked the base frequently. Sully would tell me his most meaningful parts of his first deployment came from handing out food weekly to displaced Iraqis who had fled the war to a camp on base. These initial experiences prepared him well for all we faced together at Al Asad a year and a half later.

What we did not realize until Nora asked the question was how short our time overlapping in Al Asad actually was. Sully was in a different unit, so he arrived in late January 2017 to the command center. My deployment ended in early April 2017. In a little more than two months, we built the foundation for a lifetime bond.

There were not many people in O'Connell's that night in Old Town. It was a regular Tuesday in mid-March, so King Street was relatively quiet. I had left medical school in New York earlier that day to say goodbye to Sully before his flight to Poland and eventual trip into Ukraine. I had been nervous for him, heading willingly into a combat zone more active and more dangerous than anything we had experienced in Iraq. My nerves partly had driven me to take him up on a last second reunion in Old Town. Yet once I arrived, I realized I had to put my feelings aside and take on a different role: I spent the majority of the time comforting Nora and telling her it was no big deal what Sully was doing. Nora did not need much comforting to begin with, but my acting seemed to pass the test that night.

When Sully and I reconnected in 29 Palms in summer 2017 after he returned home from deployment, Sully did not have much more time in the Marines. I would pin him to sergeant only a few days before he would start terminal leave and put 29 Palms in his rear-view mirror. Sully drove east home to Virginia and eventually moved close to Alexandria. He sent some care packages to our unit "for the boys" when we were back in the Middle East in 2018, and we kept in touch often about his transition into civilian life and my continued work in the military. We would reconnect in Alexandria when I moved there in 2019 to start my new job in information operations. The night at O'Connell's felt like the many nights we had together on King Street before our paths took us in different directions in 2020.

Sully's transition epitomizes some of the difficulty veterans face when leaving the military. From 2015–17, Sully had a critically important job, from both a global and a personal perspective. On deployment, he supported life-and-death operations in the War Against ISIS, the most powerful terrorist group at the time, who was then waging and inspiring attacks across the Levant and from Paris to California and Orlando. He knew his work every day helped protect innocent people around the world. On top of this strategic impact, Sully also could see a more direct effect of his work daily through his mentorship of junior Marines. He taught his Marines both radio and infantry skills and led them through the challenges of young adulthood. When Sully left the Marines, he lost the meaning and purpose both facets of his work had provided him. He tried out different jobs: he worked several security contracts before ending up at a department store selling flowers. While meaningful for the right person, this work left Sully unfulfilled and listless.

The lack of comparable intensity of the jobs Sully found in the civilian world also had a clear impact on the workplace relationships he could expect to create. Military culture, at its best, creates an atmosphere of camaraderie where everyone looks out for each other. On deployment, that feeling is amplified by the life-and-death nature of the mission. Sully and I both knew upon starting to work together that each of us would put his life on the line for the other, because it was what we were trained to do. Sully seemed to find very few coworkers he could trust to do anything at all for him, even the most mundane, common tasks, in the civilian world. Sully learned what he could expect from his new coworkers in civilian jobs was far less than what he could expect of the vast majority of people he worked with in Iraq. This mismatch in expectations prevented him from sustaining meaningful professional relationships in his initial jobs after the military.

Sully also lost a community of shared experiences when he left the military; I would feel something similar four years later when I moved on. We did not have to talk every day about our experiences at war, but we knew we were constantly with people who understood what it was like to go to war and come home. In Sully's and my generation, fewer of our peers deployed to combat zones. I always found comfort talking with those a few years older than me, who generally faced more life-and-death intensity abroad than I ever did. Once I left the military, I was immediately separated from these daily encounters. That isolation made me seek volunteer work in veterans' organizations like Team Rubicon and PB Abbate and drove me to connect more with veterans through my class and this book. I feel pulled now in medicine to work in a Veteran Affairs (VA) hospital and serve veterans as a doctor.

As Sully struggled to find purpose and community in his new life, his mental health suffered. He was quick to anger and felt constantly on edge. He was embarrassed to talk about the jobs he did not find any meaning in. At the beginning of the COVID-19 pandemic, he called me and said he needed a place to stay for a few days because he did not want to be alone. I asked my roommate and the girl I was dating if they would be happy to have him over, despite quarantine rules and the fact that he had also recently been sick. They both immediately said yes. While that decision is clearer with hindsight, I referenced it often as a good example of supporting friends when they needed it, even in the stress and anxiety of March 2020.

Around this time, Sully turned to writing and wrote the following poem, which he titled "On Transition":

My family gone,
It wasn't long before the sadness crept in,
An old feeling I hadn't felt in so long, alien to me,
I replaced it with something so familiar,
Anger.
The fights flew,

The drinks flowed,
Relationships splintered,
Friendships lost,
Lies told,
Vile flowed from my tongue,
Anger endured.
When I didn't suffer, I created suffering,
Life was too stale, bland,
I needed excitement once again,
I needed an escape from the sorrow,
I created my way,
Into the self-destruction and inevitable ruin,
A longing for the lost,
A failure to move forward,
A failure to advance upon the next objective,
I became warped by a war I no longer participated in.
You will spend so much time ready to die for something,
That you need to find something to live for.

As he grew through the struggles of transition to civilian life, Sully turned his passion for the military community into a purpose: he created an anonymous, military news-focused Instagram account that reported on daily happenings in the US military. While he had not yet attended college, Sully was a strong writer and a diligent student of history. His own experience in the military, compounded with these skills, made his reporting engaging and informative. The account slowly built followers over two years until world events forced it into the limelight. During the withdrawal from Afghanistan in August 2021, his account gained over 50,000 followers as his reputation for clear, honest, and unbiased reporting spread widely. He used some of this reputation to drive fundraisers for some of the veterans wounded in Kabul and refugees moving to the US. The beginning of the War in Ukraine in February 2022 would expose his account to even more people, as thousands sought to understand this coming war through the lens of a respected military veteran.

Sully could not watch and report on the war from home without feeling the pull to serve in conflict again. He missed the community of people who would have his back in an instant; he missed the electric feelings of intensity in a combat zone. He knew he could leverage his followers online and provide humanitarian support directly if he traveled to Ukraine. He also thought he could paint a clearer picture of the war to those watching at home and abroad once he was on the ground. Only two weeks after the war began, Sully told me he had booked his flights.

The grumblings of this war in Ukraine began in earnest in January 2022. Russia, like Iraq before it in the Gulf War on the borders of Kuwait, staged a large-scale training exercise along its and Belarus's borders with Ukraine. Before invading in late February 2022, Russia denied the troop activity was anything more than an exercise. This fallacy became apparent on February 24, 2022, when Russian President Vladimir Putin authorized a "special military operation" to demilitarize and de-nazify Ukraine. Russian forces moved quickly into Northern, Eastern, and Southern Ukraine with apparent aims to seize the Ukrainian capital Kyiv and create a land bridge from Russia to the Crimean Peninsula through Eastern Ukraine.

In the long arc of history, the true start date to this war likely will be considered eight years earlier in February 2014. Putin himself even alluded to this earlier start date in his speech to his country and the world on February 24, 2022: "[The special military operation's] goal is to protect people who have been subjected to bullying and genocide … for the last eight years."

In February 2014, Ukrainian President Viktor Yanukovych chose not to sign a trade agreement that would have strengthened ties with the European Union despite growing public support for alignment with the EU. Rallies filled the streets in Kyiv in what would be called the Euromaidan Protests. Ten years earlier in 2004, Ukrainians had similarly filled the streets in protest after Yanukovych had been declared winner of an election ripe with corruption and foreign interference. Yanukovych's rival Viktor Yushchenko suffered acute health issues in the months leading up to the 2004 election that later were determined to be the result of poisoning with a potent dioxin present in Agent Orange. Yushchenko was more friendly to the West, and his poisoning serves as another suspected attempt by Russia to interfere in Ukrainian politics and foreign elections. The protests of Orange Revolution led to a second election in December 2004 which Yushchenko won; however, he would lose a subsequent election in 2010, which allowed pro-Russia Yanukovych to become president.

On February 22, 2014, as Yanukovych fled Kyiv for Moscow ahead of a vote by the Ukrainian parliament to impeach him, Yanukovych's own security forces unleashed snipers on fellow Ukrainians protesting. The Ukrainian parliament voted 328–0 to impeach Yanukovych and installed a new acting president, Oleksandr Turchynov, although more than a quarter of the parliament abstained from the vote. Two days later, Russian forces, wearing no Russian insignia, moved into Crimea and began seizing key government buildings. By February 27, 2014, the Crimean Peninsula, a critical oil-trade hub and home to Russia's strategic naval base in the Black Sea, was in total Russian control. Two weeks after that on March 16, 2014, the pro-Russian forces then in power instigated a referendum with two options: one to accede into Russia or two to remain part of Ukraine with more autonomy.

Crimea was colonized by Russia in the late eighteenth century, and the people of Crimea remained Russian citizens until the mid-twentieth century. In 1954, the Soviet Union transferred Crimea to Ukraine as part of a long negotiation that received broad support among Ukrainian and Crimean representatives. The transfer still was somewhat unremarkable at the time as Ukraine remained part of the Soviet Union, and many ethnic Russians continued living in Crimea through the twenty-first century. If the referendum could be considered legitimate, perhaps these historical, ethnic, and political ties accounted for the referendum vote overwhelmingly in support of acceding into Russia. Though the fact that the referendum was held without impartial observers "under gunpoint" suggests the results are much more likely invalid.

Western Europe, then as dependent on Russian oil as they were in 2022, did not know how to respond to Putin's aggressive seizure of territory. Putin's actions were in direct violation of the Budapest Memorandum of 1994, a tri-party agreement signed by the US, the United Kingdom, and Russia to "reaffirm their obligation to refrain from the threat or use of force against the territorial integrity or political independence of Ukraine" in exchange for Ukraine's own de-nuclearization. However, the Russian government, in a weak attempt to hijack the principles of self-determination, pointed to its referendum as proof the people of Crimea wanted to accede into Russia. The international response to Russia was blunted as Western governments weighed options, and economic sanctions with uncertain effects became the only meaningful retort.

Crimea was taken before Ukraine was able to mount significant defense, but its leadership and the international community would never acknowledge Russian control of Crimea as lawful. A long struggle against Russian-backed separatists in Ukraine's Donbas region on its eastern border with Russia then began and would continue into February 2022. Like Crimea, these regions did house some Ukrainian citizens sympathetic to Russia, although most polling would suggest that separatists are a small minority.

This war precipitated the budding discipline of open-source intelligence, as civilians used technology and social media to publish truth outside of government-controlled channels. The "Live Universal

Awareness Map," or "LiveUA," was created by two Ukrainians to track the war in Donbas. Eventually, the site expanded to track social media in Iraq and Syria during the rise of ISIS. The war in Eastern Ukraine also brought tragedies in loss of life, among Ukrainians, Russian separatists, and civilians in sporadic fighting in the region over eight years. Malaysia Airlines Flight 17 would become one more passenger jet mistakenly shot down in a war zone, this time by a surface-to-air missile on July 17, 2014. All 298 people on board were killed. Bellingcat, another open-source intelligence group that gained traction supporting fact-finding in Ukraine, provided clear evidence that the shooter was part of the Russian military, but Russia never would accept responsibility for the attack.

The Winter Olympics in Sochi in 2014 had just ended when Russia invaded Crimea and began supporting separatists in Donbas. Russia again had the focus of the entire world at the end of the Winter Olympics in Beijing in 2022 when Putin began his total invasion into Ukraine. Like in 2014, Putin feared Ukraine was becoming too closely allied with the West and wanted to disrupt any possibility that Ukraine could join the European Union or the North Atlantic Treaty Organization. The Russian government thought they would achieve a quick victory and receive a heroic welcome in Kyiv. However, Ukrainians fighting for their freedom and independence pushed back and stalled some of the initial Russian advances. The cost of war was immediately evident for the world to see, as Russian targeting of civilian infrastructure led to thousands of Ukrainian civilians displaced, wounded, and killed in the first weeks of the war.

Sully and I watched from home and felt the pull to serve again like many other veterans. I decided I would be more useful serving in a war zone as a doctor with Doctors Without Borders once I was fully trained; the sad realization hit me that this war would not be the last one I would watch start in my lifetime. Sully felt too much of a call himself to ignore and knew he had to make the journey into Ukraine. In mid-March, 2022, he landed in Poland.

When Sully arrived in Poland, he did not come empty-handed. He had packed as much medical gear as he could, including bandages, tourniquets, and other military first-aid kit supplies. He and several other US volunteers he had only recently met slowly made the journey from Warsaw to the Ukrainian border, tracing the Vistula River south and east to a crossing point west of the Ukrainian city Lviv. There, Sully donated food, water, and toiletries purchased through his social-media fundraising to several refugee camps. In Iraq, he had supported men, women, and children in the camp on Al Asad. On the border of Ukraine, he remembered only seeing women and children. All the men had to fight.

Only several days before he first crossed into Ukraine, Russian long-range missiles destroyed a military training facility in Yavoriv, 10 miles from Ukraine's border with Poland. The death count ranged from nine to thirty-five and hundreds were injured. The base housed many foreign volunteers who had just made their first steps into joining the war. Sully remembered several training camps that we had destroyed on our deployment in 2017, including one hidden along the Euphrates River that we watched for hours waiting for strike approval. ISIS fighters were shooting at targets outside of their tunnels when the fighter jets dropped their bombs. Sully wondered if ISIS felt similarly to the Ukrainians and foreign volunteers he was with then, outgunned by a larger and more well-funded force that could strike at any time from complete safety miles away.

At the border crossing, Sully made camp in makeshift quarters with his small team of volunteers in the attic of an emergency volunteer center. He continued supporting refugee camps and began the first of several trips across the border into Ukraine. He documented and captioned photos on his social media of the many Ukrainians, men, women, and children, thrust into involvement in the war effort. Both Ukrainian military and civilians did not seem phased by the constant air raid sirens that echoed over the city. Their resilience made Sully proud to be there to try to support their cause and elevate their stories.

Sully also documented his fellow foreign volunteers. The majority were professionals, but a few Sully viewed as LARPers, or live-action role players, either without usable or relevant skills or unwilling to apply them. The LARPers were in Ukraine for naïve or selfish purposes. Some were unaware of the true costs of war; some were there only to seek attention through staged pictures for social media. The LARPers were more likely to be startled by the constant air-raid sirens.

These volunteers, the good and the bad, followed a long tradition of service in foreign wars, dating back as far as men and women volunteering as soldiers, nurses, and ambulance drivers in the First World War before the US joined the war in 1917. Many US volunteers in Ukraine were former military or trained in medicine. Their most important work was training Ukrainian military and civilians in tactical combat casualty care or TCCC ("T-triple-C"). With air raids and missile strikes a constant threat, every man, woman, and child needed to learn how to "stop the bleed."

As Sully watched a TCCC practical application one day in a converted classroom in Lviv, he saw a US volunteer get agitated when his Ukrainian counterpart tightened his tourniquet. Sully thought the American was merely pretending to be a casualty in pain, until he heard him yell, "Take it the fuck off me right now!" Later, another American would apologize to the Ukrainian and say, referring to the man who yelled, "He's had a rough week. He's just stressed out." Sully felt the painful irony in two ways: first, an American had traveled all this way only to yell at the people he was supposed to be supporting, and second, the Ukrainian's week was almost certainly worse. His past eight years since Crimea were likely the same, and his future totally uncertain. The American could go home to his country whenever he wanted.

After Sully donated most of the gear he had brought, he knew his best way to make an impact and support Ukrainians was to document more of their story. For that, he knew he needed to live and work more closely with Ukrainian soldiers. However, as the war intensified in Kyiv and Donbas, the Ukrainian military wanted more from Sully and his fellow volunteers.

Decision-Making Exercise – "Joining the Fight": As Sully attempted to work more directly with the Ukrainian military, he witnessed an argument between two Ukrainian military officers, one from the Ukrainian Army and one from the Ukrainian Territorial Defense, the equivalent of the US National Guard. The Territorial Defense officer saw value in Sully's experience to the existential threat he and his unit faced. He wanted Sully and his team to surrender their supplies and gear and accompany him to a joint camp for international volunteers. Sully was not sure entirely what purpose he would have in the camp, but he knew he was quickly losing control of his own destiny. What would you do?

Sully first thought of the other Americans he was with. Most of them did not have military experience: they were medical professionals, and they were not there to be soldiers. While Sully knew he could fight if he needed to, he also knew he had Nora and family waiting for him at home. Sully decided quickly his goal of documenting the experience of Ukrainian soldiers was not worth the known and unknown risks he and his team would have to undertake in traveling outside of Lviv. He communicated to the Territorial Defense officer that he and his team could not help, but he did donate the remaining medical gear and supplies he had.

While he thought he might travel into Eastern Ukraine or Kyiv when planning his trip, the realities of the conflict on the ground made him realize his own abilities as an independent journalist in a war zone were extremely limited. Sully decided he had to go home before he felt like one of the LARPers. He could not let himself and his own basic needs become a distraction from the life-and-death mission he had wanted to support. Soon after he witnessed the confrontation between the two officers arguing over his team's destiny, Sully made final plans to travel back to Warsaw.

Our night in Old Town before Sully left ended at Murphy's, another favorite Irish pub that had a later crowd. We found a table close to the stage where Justin Suede, a regular performer at Murphy's, was a few songs into his set. I had been playing my guitar for Sully and Nora down by the river early in the evening and still had it with me. Sully and Nora immediately pointed to Justin and asked him to invite me on stage. Justin did not need much convincing. I jumped up and jammed along while he played a cover of Give Me One Reason by Tracy Chapman. I was probably pretty out of key, but Justin and the crowd did not seem to mind.

On a moment when Nora was out of earshot, Sully told me how happy and calm he felt in his relationship with her. He was looking forward to their future and their immediate plans of moving in together when he returned from Ukraine. After walking home with them around 1 a.m., I said bye to Sully and Nora at the door of their hotel room. I told Sully I was proud of him and looking forward to our next reunion.

I texted Nora occasionally over the next few weeks to see how she was doing, but I thought better not to bother Sully while he was abroad. Then in mid-April, I got a text from Sully I was not fully expecting. I thought he might be heading back home around then, but I was not sure if he had extended his trip. He told me he was sitting in the airport waiting to board his flight back to DC. His heart was racing out of control, and he did not know what to do. He felt so crushed by anxiety and panic that he almost did not board the plane. I did not think I could help, but I told him what he was experiencing was natural and that he would be with family and friends who loved him soon. He received my last text before he took off, "I'm with you Sully. And always will be."

Sully turned to Nora and his friends and family when he returned. Nora served with him while he was abroad, like all do when they love someone in a war zone. Sully sought new ways to improve his anxiety and continued reading and writing, even if he distanced himself more from the daily happenings of the war. Sully's social-media presence continued to grow, and he made plans to attend college and publish more of his writing.

The two months Sully and I spent together in a war zone bonded us more than we could ever have foreseen. We came home and looked the same to our family and friends. Yet in different ways, we carried the weight of some innocence lost, amorphous moral injury of unsettling victories in killing ISIS remotely and horrifying mistakes in collateral damage. Sully carried additional weight home from a new war zone, different in cause, time, and place, but similar in the worthlessness of the suffering.

Although our winding paths diverged after Old Town in 2020, the parts of us we lost in combat zones call us back to each other now. They compel us to pick up the phone and talk when we read news of Marines dying in training or at war; they drive us to reminisce about war again when we watch a new one start from afar. Sometimes, that talk becomes wistful, as we remember the electric feelings of camaraderie and purpose only combat seems to build instantly among strangers. This wistfulness drives some friends to return to war, either in the military or out of it like Sully did. Coming home, we are older, disenchanted and detached at times from the purpose that first drove us to serve and to war. We seek then to rebuild all that we lost at war in the complexities of civilian life.

In the face of new and old wars, our past grasps hold onto us forever. Yet in time, and with help, we learn ways to loosen its grip.

Appendix 1

ADDITIONAL DECISION-MAKING GAMES AND THOUGHT EXPERIMENTS

Negligent Discharge

SGT Toby Finney spent part of his last months in Vietnam in a job familiar to what he did in Germany: driving a water tanker to fill up water cisterns around base. After surviving countless patrols and VC attacks, Toby had one more near-death experience in this "safer" job. One afternoon, he was sitting on the tanker filling up a cistern when he felt the whiff of a bullet fly past his ear. The crack was the last noise he heard before silence took over. He turned to see several recently arrived soldiers cowering to the side of the truck looking at him. Toby paused only for a moment to gather himself and decide how to respond. What would you do?

Suggested Reading: Toby Finney's *Through These Eyes*

Framing a Loss

You lead public affairs for the US State Department. The US embassy in Islamabad has just been attacked by students from a nearby university, and one US Marine has been killed. Three weeks ago, Iranians stormed the US embassy in Tehran, beginning the Iranian Hostage Crisis.

The Secretary of State (Cyrus Vance) turns to you and asks you to write a public-affairs statement for release to news agencies. He says quickly as he walks away, "We need to make this look better than what happened in Tehran."

You must write a short statement on the event (two to three sentences) to present to him for review before release. What would you do?
Suggested Reading: Steve Coll's *Ghost Wars*

Go and No-Go Criteria

During Operation EAGLE CLAW, the attempted rescue of the hostages held in Iran during the Iranian Hostage Crisis of 1979–81, US special forces had to fly into Tehran in six helicopters to be able to rescue all fifty-two Americans from the embassy. Imagine President Carter had the opportunity to cancel the mission when the first of the eight total helicopters on the mission turned back due to mechanical failure. President Carter had to consider the fate of the hostages, the troops on the ground, and his own political future in an election year. With the hindsight of the two other helicopters failing at Desert One, this decision seems obvious; however, in the moment, it is more complicated. What would you do?
Suggested Viewing: "Desert One": Inside the failed 1980 hostage rescue in Iran, CBS *Sunday Morning*, accessed 8 August 2021, https://www.youtube.com/watch?v=-m7nZA-VlI

Drone Going Down

A drone operator reported a critical issue with a surveillance aircraft. The aircraft had expensive cameras and equipment that we would not want to hand over to ISIS. The drone operator turned to me as the command-center leader and asked if he should crash on land or in the lake. I was still new to my role in the command center, but I had to answer immediately. What would you do?

Discussion: I said lake and luckily the drone operator was not able to comply. The aircraft crashed on the land. An hour or so later, we would drop a bomb on the aircraft to keep ISIS from getting it. Dropping a bomb on an aircraft in a lake would not have worked, and ISIS was known to paddle in rowboats out to crashed aircraft and try to pick them up.
Suggested Viewing: Gavin Hood's *Eye in the Sky* (2015)
Suggested Reading: Phil Klay's *Missionaries* (2020)

Drone Overhead

Shia Militia Groups had an overt presence on Iraqi Army bases in Western Iraq during the War Against ISIS. Tenuous allies against ISIS,

Shia Militia Groups and US forces were on the brink of conflict as the threat of ISIS waned. These tensions culminated in the assassination of Qassem Soleimani in 2021, as described in Chapter 9. During my second deployment in 2018, I led our infantry battalion's small unmanned aerial system (SUAS) section, consisting of quadcopters, RQ-20B Pumas (large model airplanes), and the palm-sized PD-100 Black Hornets. One night on a base in Western Iraq, one of my quadcopter operators and I joined a night security patrol with the Iraqis. Our plan was to practice night flights with the quadcopter and enhance the security of the Marine and Iraqi patrol. During the patrol, we paused and prepared to launch. My quadcopter operator turned to me and asked if he could fly overhead and observe the Shia Militia Group position on the outskirts of base. Unlikely to provide meaningful intelligence, the move could be a "show of force" and highlight the capability of our forces to observe. It could also be seen as escalation. What would you do?
Suggested Viewing: Gavin Hood's *Eye in the Sky* (2015)

9/11 Response

Fifteen Saudi nationals fly airplanes into the World Trade Center and the Pentagon. The US decided to invade Afghanistan. What would you do?

Discussion: This question was posed by one of my guest speakers to the class. It forces us to think about the accountability behind 9/11 and the decision-making that led to the US's twenty-year war in Afghanistan.

Not Better Off

Robin Dreeke, a renowned social engineer, coined the phrase that in every conversation, meeting, or engagement you should "leave people better off for having met you." Building rapport in this "truthful" way, even if based on a selective presentation of the truth, helps both you and the person you are interacting with establish a meaningful and potentially lasting connection.

When would you be faced with a situation where you would not want someone to feel better off for having met or engaged with you? When would you want someone to feel hurt?
Suggested Reading: Robin Dreeke's *It's Not All About "Me": Ten Techniques For Building Rapport With Anyone*

Defusing Arguments

You are at a family reunion, and a relative is expressing loud political opinions you disagree with. Your goal is to get them to change the subject without engaging them in a debate, which they are prone to do. How do you do it? Include (make up) necessary details about the scenario in order to show how you would use Dreeke's techniques to achieve your goal.
Suggested Reading: Robin Dreeke's *It's Not All About "Me": Top Ten Techniques For Building Quick Rapport With Anyone*

Building Rapport

Imagine you are in a coffee shop or restaurant. A friend challenges you to make conversation with someone you don't know and establish meaningful connection. How do you do it? Include (make up) necessary details about the scenario in order to show how you would use Dreeke's techniques to achieve your goal.
Suggested Reading: Robin Dreeke's *It's Not All About "Me": Top Ten Techniques For Building Quick Rapport With Anyone*

Offensive Cyber Weapon

You are the president of the US. It is 2039, with an upcoming election in 2040 (your re-election). You are surrounded by the members of the national security council who have provided their assessment on the effectiveness of an offensive cyber weapon. The cyber weapon is designed to destroy North Korean long-range missile systems that can carry nuclear warheads. North Korea, seeing the end of the Kim regime in sight, has been threatening to attack Seoul and is massing troops on the DMZ in an unplanned military "exercise." Worried about the potential for a nuclear strike, the military is eager to conduct the operation. Your diplomats are warier, thinking that there could be a political solution. After review, the NSC has three spokespeople, and they give you their ideas of the probability of success.

Your Secretary of Defense states the operation has an 80 percent probability of success.

Your Director of National Intelligence states the operation has a 70 percent probability of success.

Your Secretary of State states the operation has a 30 percent probability of success.

Success would mean the missile systems would be destroyed; North Korea would suspect US involvement but be unable to prove it. Failure under all assessments would leave the missile systems intact but reveal the US's attempt to destroy them to North Korea. Both success and failure have risks of escalation, but in failure, it can be assumed North Korea will retaliate.

As president, how do you understand the actual probability of success? What is your decision?

Suggested Reading: Friedman and Zeckhauser's *Handling and Mishandling Estimative Probability: Likelihood, Confidence, and the Search for Bin Laden*

Election Interference Debate

In *Sneakers* (1992), Cosmo (Ben Kingsley) and Martin Bishop (Robert Redford) have philosophical debates on how manipulation of information can drive people's actions. One example is below:

Cosmo: Posit: People think a bank might be financially shaky.
Martin Bishop: Consequence: People start to withdraw their money.
Cosmo: Result: Pretty soon it is financially shaky.
Martin Bishop: Conclusion: You can make banks fail.

Complete the following debate with the posit (which means take this to be true), consequence (immediate response), result (effect on the system), and conclusion (what should/can we do knowing all of this?) below.

Posit: Foreign actors pretending to be Americans spread lies and misleading information on social media to influence public opinion during US elections.
Consequence: Reports on election interference circulate in the aftermath of the elections.
Result: People begin to lose faith in electoral processes, their elected leaders, and democracy.
Conclusion: ???

Answer the conclusion in several sentences with "what should we do" knowing the posit, consequence, and result above in the face of the manipulation of information surrounding elections.

Suggested Viewing: Phil Alden Robinson's *Sneakers* (1992)

Appendix 2

SCOUT SNIPER PLATOON LEADERSHIP PHILOSOPHY

Below, I share the leadership philosophy I wrote for my scout sniper platoon in May 2016. I was 24 when I wrote it, and I see references to it still five years later in the writing of this book. It was the honor and challenge of my life to lead Marines. I will always be grateful for the men I was privileged to lead and the gift of perspective the challenge of leading them gave me.

Subj.: LEADERSHIP PHILOSOPHY

1. Wise men who came before us have said that leadership doesn't change; only leaders do. Below, I describe my vision for the foundation of what we Marines know well as leadership. I expect all of you to embody these traits at all times and hold each other, as much as you hold me, to them.

2. **HUMILITY**. "The only wisdom we can hope to acquire is the wisdom of humility: humility is endless." You are in this platoon because you represent the most proficient infantrymen in V37. Overconfidence in this fact, however, will not be tolerated. You must continually seek to learn, understand, and better your faults. Only through constant evaluation of our imperfections can we truly strive towards self-betterment and earn our roles as leaders. Be the man you yourself would want to follow and earn it every moment.

3. **SELFLESSNESS**. To be truly selfless is to win a hard-fought battle against human nature. Live and fight for your family and friends back home, but most importantly, live and fight for each other and your brothers in arms. Your pain will always be lessened by helping

someone else. At times, we all will need help; at times, we all will give help. The bond we form in helping each other provides the strong base on which effective leadership relies.

4. **EMPATHY**. "You never really understand a person until you consider things from his point of view." Take the time to learn about your brothers in the platoon and feel the pain they feel. Our bonds of camaraderie will serve and guide us well through any and all of the difficulties we will face together.

5. **TECHNICAL AND TACTICAL PROFICIENCY**. Your proficiency will be visible in both the clear and concise way you task subordinates and the faith and confidence you inspire in those around you. Ambiguity at any level will not be tolerated; the confidence you inspire will bind us together. You must fight to earn the trust of the men of this platoon, and never break it.

6. These traits, when woven together tightly, form the rope that guides and carries us to **MISSION ACCOMPLISHMENT**. Succeeding in the missions ahead will always be a challenge. However, the way we meet that challenge will be defined wholly in our ability to express and carry these traits. They are the bedrock of our character, and they will define you as scout snipers, us as Marines, and, more importantly, us as men.

7. We hold the great honor of once again representing our country in a combat zone this fall. First, however, we must earn our role as a battalion asset. Carry yourselves as **QUIET PROFESSIONALS**; everything we do or fail to do will affect what role we hold on deployment. How do you want to be remembered?

Appendix 3

CHARACTER MAP

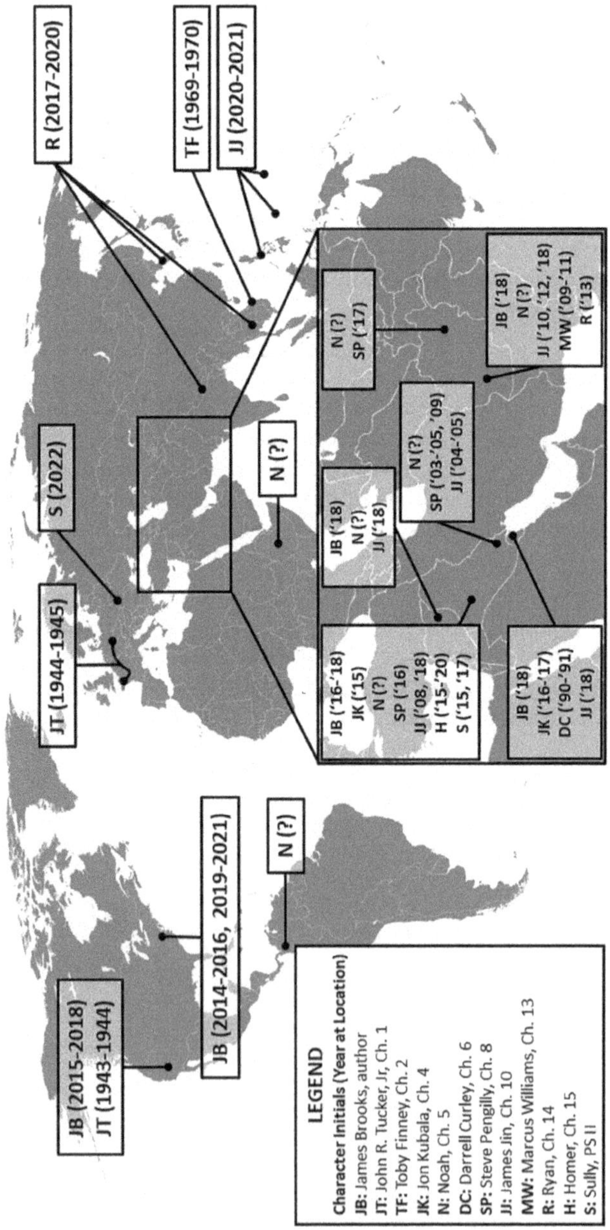

SOURCES, NOTES, AND INSPIRATION

Below, I include references for all historical events discussed in the book and the writings, songs, and movies I either directly or indirectly reference myself. I include books on the history of the Middle East and US foreign policy that discuss the historical details I highlight in this book. I am most grateful to all the guest speakers to my course who shared their experiences with my class and allowed me to attempt to communicate their stories in this book. I also am grateful to Toby Finney for allowing me to add in his memoir and experience in Vietnam. I only wish I had reached out to have Toby as a guest speaker. All attempts at empathy fail to capture what my guest speakers and Toby gave in lessons, but I am lucky to be able to try.

In the re-telling of history and personal stories, some characters in the book, including guest speakers, wanted to remain anonymous for security, personal, or other reasons. Some, out of humility, wanted to distance themselves from their stories and downplay any perceived heroism of service in combat. As I state in the Introduction, stories of personal experience are true to experience even when obscured through changes to personal details, time, or place, and I maintain larger historical accuracy throughout. I obscure personal details most prominently in Chapters 5 and 6 and minimally in Chapters 8 and 14. Elsewhere, the book remains true to factual experience to the best of my ability, outside of the continued use of pseudonyms.

Preface: Finding Meaning

I wrote this unconventional "about the author" portion on the twentieth anniversary of 9/11, as the book started to be shared outside of my immediate circle of friends and family. I reference the writings and song below.

Stewart, James. "The Real Heroes Are Dead: A Love Story," *New Yorker*, February 3, 2002, https://www.newyorker.com/magazine/2002/02/11/the-real-heroes-are-dead.

Fitzgerald, F.S. *The Great Gatsby*. New York: Charles Scribner and Sons, 1925.

Tedeschi, Susan and Mike Mattison. "Midnight in Harlem," *Revelator*, Song, 2011. Stream.

Introduction: The Night of the Base Blood Drive

The opening story is based off my experience as a Watch Officer on my first deployment in Western Iraq from September 2016–April 2017.

O'Brien, Tim. *The Things They Carried*. New York: Houghton Mifflin Harcourt, 1990.

Eliot, T.S. *The Waste Land*. New York: Houghton Mifflin Harcourt Publishing Company, 1922.

Part I: Self-Awareness

As with Parts II and III, I include some quotations that I used on the last day of the course to summarize the three main sections of the course.

"Ask for Help, but Salvation Lies Within": Somewhat a reference to *Shawshank Redemption* (1994). You need to be humble enough to ask for help, but you need to want to be helped too. Those two feelings are not equivalent.

The Shawshank Redemption. Directed by Frank Darabont, Castle Rock Entertainment, 1994.

"You have to carry the fire": From Cormac McCarthy's *The Road*. Hold onto and maintain a personal sense of goodness and strength in the face of evil and temptation.

McCarthy, Cormac. *The Road*. New York: Alfred A. Knopf, 2006.

"Take the foot": From the Marine Corps Infantry Officer Course. If you can bear someone else's suffering, take it on. This phrase is derived from a story about young Marines in Iraq who were tasked with cleaning up the scene of a suicide bombing that targeted civilians. A young Marine, confused and shocked at seeing so much death up close, picked up a foot and held it out to his lieutenant. The lieutenant walked on, unsure what to do. The officer would reflect that he should have taken the foot and shouldered part of his Marine's pain.

Chapter 1: Don't Go to War

The story of Judge John R. Tucker, Jr is based off his war memoir written in 1990, used with the permission of his son. Some information after 1990 is confirmed in his obituary written in 2015. I also reference some of the works below. *Tribe* by Sebastian Junger was one of two major books I had my students read for the semester.

Bacque, P. "J. Randolph Tucker Jr., retired Richmond Circuit Court judge, dies at 101," *Richmond Times-Dispatch,* November 27, 2015, https://richmond.com/obituaries/featured/j-randolph-tucker-jr-retired-richmond-circuit-court-judge-dies-at-101/article_30c7c13e-6312-505d-985e-247e7c1ec716.html.

Junger, Sebastian. *Tribe: On Homecoming and Belonging*. New York: Hachette Book Group, 2016.

Ghost Army. Directed by Rick Beyer, Plate of Peas Production, 2013.

Ambrose, Stephen. *Eisenhower and Berlin, 1945: The Decision to Halt at the Elbe*. New York: W.W. Norton Co., 2000.

1 Corinthians 13:12

Chapter 2: You Got Heart, Kid

The stories in this chapter are based off my experiences boxing in college; meeting Vietnam veteran Toby Finney, a childhood friend of my dad's, and other Vietnam veterans in Baltimore; and Toby's own moving memoir *Through These Eyes*, used with Toby's permission. *Through These Eyes* covers much more than the few stories I highlight in this chapter and challenges some of the prevailing societal issues over the past sixty years. I highly recommend his book for a touching tribute to a life seeking self- and collective-betterment. I use the official Department of Defense resources below for casualty statistics, two websites for casualties in Okinawa and Iwo Jima, and a study of the draft from University of Michigan to discuss yearly changes in numbers of men drafted. I reference the article "The Vietnam War and the Media" and "Vietnam War: Looking Again at Larry Burrows' Photo, 'Reaching Out'" for the paragraph on how anti-Vietnam fervor was understandable due to the near real-time nature of the reporting. I reference two primary sources, "The Long Telegram" and NSC-68, and one secondary source by Gaddis to discuss Kennan's and Nitze's views on "containment." The direct quotations are from Kennan, p. 17 and Nitze, p. 11. The concept of Boyd's OODA Loop is described well in Coram's *Boyd: The Fighter Pilot Who Changed the Art of War*. I also reference Hadyniak's work on journalism during the Vietnam War to discuss the timing of the My Lai massacre and its appearance in media. The basic facts about the Vietnam War, including the Gulf of Tonkin incident and the Tet Offensive, can be found in many different sources, including Hadyniak. I reference the article on "Soviet Aid to North Vietnam" to show that their aid increased over the duration of the war. Several of the movies and songs I reference in the chapter are listed below as well.

Finney, Toby. *Through These Eyes*. Toby Finney, 2021.

"Induction Statistics," *Resistance and Revolution: The Anti-Vietnam War Movement at the University of Michigan, 1965–72*, accessed January 8, 2022, http://michiganintheworld.history.lsa.umich.edu/antivietnamwar/items/show/73.

"OPERATION IRAQI FREEDOM U.S. CASUALTY STATUS" as of January 3, 2022, 10 a.m. EDT" (PDF), retrieved January 8, 2022, https://www.defense.gov/casualty.pdf.

History.com Editors. "Battle of Okinawa," A&E Television Networks, updated March 30, 2021, accessed January 8, 2022, https://www.history.com/topics/world-war-ii/battle-of-okinawa.

"75th Anniversary of the Battle of Iwo Jima," National Museum of the Marine Corps, accessed January 8, 2022, https://www.usmcmuseum.com/battle-of-iwo-jima.html.

"U.S. Military Casualties – Korean War Casualty Summary," Defense Casualty Analysis System, accessed January 8, 2022, https://dcas.dmdc.osd.mil/dcas/pages/report_korea_sum.xhtml.

Cosgrove, Ben. "Vietnam War: Looking Again at Larry Burrows' Photo, 'Reaching Out'," *LIFE*, accessed January 8, 2022, https://www.life.com/history/life-behind-the-picture-larry-burrows-reaching-out-vietnam-1966/.

Spector, Ronald H., "The Vietnam War and the media," *Encyclopedia Britannica*, April 27, 2016, accessed January 8, 2022, https://www.britannica.com/topic/The-Vietnam-War-and-the-media-2051426.

"George Kennan's 'Long Telegram'," February 22, 1946, History and Public Policy Program Digital Archive, National Archives and Records Administration, Department of State Records (Record Group 59), Central Decimal File, 1945-1949, 861.00/2-2246; reprinted in US Department of State (ed.), *Foreign Relations of the United States, 1946*, Volume VI, *Eastern Europe; The Soviet Union*. Washington, DC: United States Government Printing Office, 1969, pp. 696–709, https://digitalarchive.wilsoncenter.org/document/116178.

"National Security Council Report, NSC 68, 'United States Objectives and Programs for National Security'," April 14, 1950, History and Public Policy Program Digital Archive, US National Archives, http://digitalarchive.wilsoncenter.org/document/116191.

Gaddis, John Lewis and Paul Nitze. "NSC 68 and the Soviet Threat Reconsidered," *International Security*, Vol. 4, No. 4, The MIT Press, 1980, pp. 164–76, https://doi.org/10.2307/2626672.

Coram, Robert. *Boyd: The Fighter Pilot Who Changed the Art of War*. Boston: Back Bay Books, 2004.

Hadyniak, Kyle, "How Journalism Influenced American Public Opinion During the Vietnam War: A Case Study of the Battle of Ap Bac, The Gulf of Tonkin Incident, The Tet Offensive, and the My Lai Massacre." University of Maine, 2015, https://digitalcommons.library.umaine.edu/honors/222.

"Soviet Aid to North Vietnam," Globalsecurity.org, accessed January 8, 2022, https://www.globalsecurity.org/military/world/vietnam/hist-2nd-indochina-ussr.htm.

West, Kanye et al. "All of the Lights," *My Beautiful Dark Twisted Fanstasy*. Roc-a-fella, 2011. Stream.

Young, Neil. "Ohio," Single, Atlantic, 1970. Stream.

Dr. Strangelove: Or, How I Learned to Stop Worrying and Love the Bomb. Directed by Stanley Kubrick, Stanley Kubrick, 1964.

Full Metal Jacket. Directed by Stanley Kubrick, Stanley Kubrick, 1987.

Chapter 3: It's Your Turn Now, Fucker

The stories in this chapter are based off my travel to my first deployment in Western Iraq, the struggles I had deciding whether or not to join the military in college, my experience at Officer Candidate School in Quantico, Virginia, in June 2012, and the difficulty

I had dealing with the reality of war that I experienced on my first deployment. Volunteers of America is a useful resource for further discussion of moral injury in and out of war. The PTSD screening tool is useful to determine if someone may meet criteria for further evaluation for PTSD. *The Diagnostic and Statistical Manual of Mental Disorders*, 5th edn (DSM-5) provides the full criteria for PTSD dagnosis (>1 month of symptoms, hyper-vigilance, avoidance, etc.). Kessler et al.'s study provides the figure that 46.4 percent of Americans experience any mental-health disorder over the course of their lifetime. Szasz's article, while potentially downplaying chemical imbalances that exist within depression and other forms of mental illness, is an important framework for normalizing mental health. I reference Stein et al. for the definition of mental disorder, and the WHO's 2004 summary report for the definition of mental health. The 17 percent figure is quoted widely but derives from the Surgeon General report in 1999. I was first introduced to this research on mental health in a lecture by Dr Guy Montgomery. McDermott-Murphy's article on the Global Flourishing Study is a succinct overview of an ongoing study to define why that 17 percent is so low and how it can be improved scientifically, the same way we study hypertension or other physical ailments. I also reference or allude to the works below.

Lone Survivor. Directed by Peter Berg, Universal Pictures, 2013.

"Survivor Story: Navy SEAL Tells Story of Battle That Killed Team," *CBS This Morning*, with Anderson Cooper and *60 Minutes*, CBS, 2013, https://www.youtube.com/watch?v=FTuf5PRnbFg&t.

Eliot, T.S. *The Waste Land*. New York: Houghton Mifflin Harcourt Publishing Company, 1922.

Brown, Brendan. "Teenage Dirtbag", Wheatus, Columbia, 2000. Stream.

McNamara, Michael. "3 Goals & 10 Commandments of Post-Traumatic Winning," *Post-Traumatic Winning*, accessed August 8, 2021, https://posttraumaticwinning.com/3-goals-10-commandments.

Kessler, R.C., P. Berglund, O. Demler, R. Jin, K.R. Merikangas, and E.E. Walters. "Lifetime prevalence and age-of-onset distributions of DSM-IV disorders in the National Comorbidity Survey Replication," *Arch Gen Psychiatry*, 2005 Jun; 62(6), pp. 593–602, doi: 10.1001/archpsyc.62.6.593. Erratum in: Arch Gen Psychiatry. 2005 Jul; 62(7), p. 768. Merikangas, Kathleen R. [added]. PMID: 15939837.

Szasz, Thomas S. "The myth of mental illness," *American Psychologist*, 15 (1960), pp. 113–18, doi: 10.1037/h0046535.

World Health Organization. *Promoting mental health: concepts, emerging evidence, practice (Summary Report)*. Geneva: World Health Organization, 2004, https://apps.who.int/iris/bitstream/handle/10665/42940/9241591595.pdf.

Stein, D.J. et al. "What is a mental/psychiatric disorder? From DSM-IV to DSM-V," *Psychological Medicine*, Vol. 40, 11 (2010), pp. 1759–65, doi: 10.1017/S0033291709992261.

US Department of Health and Human Services. *Mental Health: A Report of the Surgeon General*. Rockville, MD: US Department of Health and Human Services; Substance Abuse and Mental Health Services Administration, Center for Mental Health Services, National Institutes of Health, National Institute of Mental Health, 1999.

Prins, A., M.J. Bovin, R. Kimerling, D.G. Kaloupek, B.P. Marx, A. Pless Kaiser, and P.P. Schnurr. *Primary Care PTSD Screen for DSM-5 (PC-PTSD-5) [Measurement instrument]*. 2015

McDermott-Murphy, Caitlin. "Healthy? Maybe. But are you flourishing?" *The Harvard Gazette*, January 11, 2022, accessed February 1, 2022, https://news.harvard.edu/gazette/story/2022/01/new-global-survey-looks-at-health-well-being/.

Chapter 4: Bird Down

This story is based off my experience as a scout sniper platoon commander from May 2016–August 2017. I also reference the song below. I list an article that describes the tragic death of Major Richard Norton in July 2016, the event behind "Bird Down."

Glover, Ben, Joe Leathers, and Rachel Thibodeau. "Love Don't Run," *Love Don't Run*, Curb, 2011. Stream.

Garske, Monica. "MCAS Miramar Pilot Killed in F/A-18C Hornet Crash in California," July 29, 2016, accessed August 18, 2021, https://www.nbcsandiego.com/news/local/mcas-miramar-pilot-killed-in-aircraft-crash-in-california/56562.

Chapter 5: No One is Built for Captivity

This story is based off my experiences on two deployments in Western Iraq from 2016–18 and an individual I worked with in my role as a counterterrorism information operations planner. With Noah's permission, I included some of his life story, although most is obscured for security reasons. Noah did work in hostage rescue, but to my knowledge, he was not part of either hostage rescue mission that I mention in the chapter, again obscured for security reasons. The "shine" comment is based on a conversation I overhead in 2017, not 2003, which serves as one small example of the pervasiveness of racism in the military. I include a reference below from 2021 that discusses racism in the military. The second decision-making exercise is based on historical events, although the exact timing of talks with the Syrian government on Austin Tice is unknown. A reference is included below for more information on those talks.

Legend, John and Toby Gad. "All of Me," *Love In The Future*, Columbia, 2013. Stream.

"Race in the Ranks: Investigating Racial Bias in the U.S. Military," *60 Minutes* with David Martin, CBS, 2021, https://www.cbsnews.com/news/us-military-racism-60-minutes-2021-08-22/.

"Austin Bennet Tice Collection," *Veterans History Project*, accessed August 8, 2021, http://memory.loc.gov/diglib/vhp/bib/loc.natlib.afc2001001.66650.

"The Assad Regime's Use of Chemical Weapons on April 4, 2017," accessed August 8, 2021, https://fas.org/irp/news/2017/04/wh-assad.pdf.

Farley, Robert. "Obama's Blurry Red Line," FactCheck.Org: A Project of the Annenberg Public Policy Center, accessed August 8, 2021, https://www.factcheck.org/2013/09/obamas-blurry-red-line/.

Fox, Ben, Eric Tucker, and Matthew Lee. "Inside Secret Syria Talks Aimed At Freeing Marine Vet Austin Tice And Other US Hostages," *MilitaryTimes*, April 8, 2021, https://www.militarytimes.com/flashpoints/2021/04/08/inside-secret-syria-talks-aimed-at-freeing-marine-vet-austin-tice-and-other-us-hostages/.

Part II: Decision-Making

"Be comfortable with the gray": A riff built from Brooking and Singer's *LikeWar: The Weaponization of Social Media*. In the age of clickbait headlines and the overt manipulation of information, "[i]f you're not in doubt, then you are likely part of the problem."

Singer, P.W. and Emerson T. Brooking. *LikeWar: The Weaponization of Social Media*. New York: Houghton Mifflin Harcourt, 2018.

"And right action is freedom / from past and future also": Taken from T.S. Eliot's "The Dry Salvages." Focus on action in the present to cure guilt of the past and anxiety of the future.

Eliot, T.S. *The Four Quartets: The Dry Salvages*. New York: Houghton Mifflin Harcourt Publishing Company, 1941.

"In the end, the decision you make makes you": Attributed to University of California Los Angeles Basketball Coach John Wooden. Taking responsibility for our actions has elements of fear and freedom. Focusing on our choices lets us define ourselves in the manner we want to.

Chapter 6: When Inaction Becomes a Decision

This story is derived from some of the life lessons that Darrell provided my class during the semester. The story is obscured and based off Darrell's experience with his permission. I am extremely grateful to Darrell for allowing me to share his experience with a larger audience. Like Noah's story, I am an outsider to Darrell's experience of race, but I am glad to be able to encourage more discussion of the history of racism and the history of segregation and redlining. Some of my interactions with Darrell in the story are a compilation of other veterans, especially those from Vietnam, who welcomed me with open arms when I left the service. I reference Robinson's article for details and timing of President Reagan's speech in 1987 at the Berlin Wall. The first decision-making exercise is conjecture; I do not have evidence that someone from the media asked that question. The exercise is meant to examine the laws and policies of the military in information operations and influence. I include references to Jon Krakauer's *Where Men Win Glory: The Odyssey of Pat Tillman* to show that the US has not always lived up to these laws and policies. I include some further references below.

Reagan, Ronald. "The Berlin Wall Speech." Delivered June 12, 1987, the Ronald Reagan Presidential Library, https://www.youtube.com/watch?v=8KQ9DSbuv5g&t.

> Mr. Gorbachev, open this gate.
> Mr. Gorbachev. Mr. Gorbachev, tear down this wall!
> I understand the fear of war and the pain of division that afflict this continent, and I pledge to you my country's efforts to help overcome these burdens. To be sure, we in the West must resist Soviet expansion. So, we must maintain defenses of unassailable strength. Yet we seek peace, so we must strive to reduce arms on both sides.

Marriot, Michel. "Tupac Shakur's Death A Product Of His Lifestyle." *The New York Times*, September 16, 1996, https://www.southcoasttoday.com/article/19960916/NEWS/309169972.

Shakur, Tupac. *The Rose That Grew From Concrete*. New York: MTV Books, 1999.

Marine Corps Warfighting Publication 3-32. "Marine Air Ground Task Force Information Operations," April 4, 2018.

Ross, Robert. "Truth and Deceit: Media Relations and Military Deception," Naval War College, 1998.

Aukofer, Frank and William Lawrence. *America's Team: The Odd Couple. A Report On The Relationship Between The Media And The Military*. Nashville: The Freedom Forum First Amendment Center, 1995.

Krakauer, Jon. *Where Men Win Glory: The Odyssey of Pat Tillman*. New York: Doubleday, 2009.

Collins, Shannon. "Desert Storm: A Look Back," US Department of Defense, January 11, 2019, https://www.defense.gov/Explore/Features/story/Article/1728715/desert-storm-a-look-back/.

Chapter 7: I Can Hear You

The stories in this chapter are based off my time in college, on deployment in Western Iraq from 2016–17 targeting ISIS, and my work in intelligence studying terrorist organizations. I include my conversation in 2013 at the end of the chapter to highlight how interpretations of different events change over the years. I rely on many references listed below to provide the historical details. I reference Arnett's original CNN interview with Osama bin Laden as shown in the link below. I also include bin Laden's fatwas as primary sources. Peter Bergen's analysis of bin Laden in his book in *The Rise and Fall of Osama bin Laden* describes how bin Laden's initial desire to remove Americans from the Middle East remained his steadfast goal. Steve Coll's *Ghost Wars* details the Soviet invasion of Afghanistan and the initial US support of the mujahideen. Blaber's *The Mission, The Men, and Me* and Evans's *Foxtrot in Kandahar* provide more background on the Battle of Tora Bora and the beginning of the War in Afghanistan. Warrick's *Black Flags: The Rise of ISIS* describes Zarqawi, the partnership between US and Jordanian intelligence agencies to defeat him and AQI, and the subsequent rise of ISIS. Ricks's *The Gamble* is a comprehensive discussion of the "surge" and the "Sunni Awakening" in 2007. Ackerman's *Places and Names* discusses the beginning of the

"Arab Spring" in more detail in his chapter "In Dara'a, The Spark and the Fuel." I use official government resources for discussion of the embassy attack and USS *Cole* death totals. Byman's article describes why the US and its allies have been so successful in dismantling Al Qaeda and preventing further attacks. Wolfe's article in *Defense Daily* provides a detailed description of non-combatant casualty cut-off value. Horton's article provides the dissenting voice to the argument that bin Laden's primary goal was to force US soldiers to leave the Middle East through his article "Peter Bergen is Mistaken about bin Laden's Strategy."

Bergen, Peter. *The Rise and Fall of Osama bin Laden*. New York, Simon & Schuster, 2021.

Coll, Steve. *Ghost Wars: The Secret History of the CIA, Afghanistan, and bin Laden, from the Soviet Invasion to September 10, 2001*. New York: Penguin Books, 2004.

Blaber, Pete. *The Mission, The Men, and Me: Lessons from a Former Delta Force Commander*. New York: Dutton Caliber, 2010.

Evans, Duane. *Foxtrot in Kandahar: A Memoir of a CIA Officer in Afghanistan at the Inception of America's Longest War*. New York: Savas Beadie, 2017.

Ricks, Thomas. *The Gamble: General Petraeus and the American Military Adventure in Iraq*. New York: Penguin Books, 2010.

Warrick, Joby. *Black Flags: The Rise of ISIS*. New York: Penguin Random House, 2016.

Ackerman, Elliot. *Places and Names: On War, Revolution, and Returning*. New York: Penguin Press, 2019.

Britannica, The Editors of Encyclopedia. "Soviet invasion of Afghanistan." *Encyclopedia Britannica,* May 11, 2020, accessed January 14, 2022, https://www.britannica.com/event/Soviet-invasion-of-Afghanistan.

Bergen, Peter L. "September 11 attacks," *Encyclopedia Britannica,* September 24, 2021, accessed January 14, 2022, https://www.britannica.com/event/September-11-attacks.

Bin Laden, Osama. "Declaration of War against the Americans Occupying the Land of the Two Holy Places," first published August 1996, accessed January 14, 2022, https://is.muni.cz/el/1423/jaro2010/MVZ203/OBL___AQ__Fatwa_1996.pdf.

Bin Laden, Osama. "World Islamic Front's Statement Urging Jihad Against Jews and Crusaders," first published February 1998, accessed January 14, 2022, http://www.mideastweb.org/osamabinladen2.htm.

"Exclusive Osama Bin Laden – First Ever TV Interview," CNN, first published August 1997, accessed January 14, 2022, https://www.youtube.com/watch?v=dqQwnqjA-6w.

"Transcript of President Bush's address: September 20, 2001," CNN Politics, first published September 21, 2001, accessed January 14, 2022, https://www.cnn.com/specials/politics/bush-transcript-september-2001.

"George W. Bush – 9/11 Bullhorn Speech," AmericanRhetoric.com, first published April 3, 2009, accessed January 12, 2022, https://www.americanrhetoric.com/speeches/gwbush911groundzerobullhorn.htm.

"The 1998 Bombings of the US Embassies in East Africa," Central Intelligence Agency, first published August 7, 2018, accessed January 14, 2022, https://www.cia.gov/stories/story/us-embassy-bombings-in-east-africa/.

"USS Cole Bombing," Federal Bureau of Investigation, accessed January 14, 2022, https://www.fbi.gov/history/famous-cases/uss-cole-bombing.

"Bill Clinton's Lost Tape: I Could Have Killed Osama Bin Laden," *NBC News*, first published July 31, 2014, accessed January 14, 2022, https://www.nbcnews.com/news/world/bill-clintons-lost-tape-i-could-have-killed-osama-bin-n170111.

"US pulls out of Saudi Arabia," *BBC News*, first published April 29, 2003, accessed January 14, 2022, http://news.bbc.co.uk/2/hi/middle_east/2984547.stm.

Wolfe, Frank. "Pentagon Removed Non-Combatant Casualty Cut-Off Value From Doctrine in 2018," *Defense Daily: Homeland Security Report*, first published June 11, 2021, accessed January 14, 2022, https://www.defensedaily.com/pentagon-removed-non-combatant-casualty-cut-off-value-doctrine-2018/pentagon/.

Reinares, Fernando. *Al-Qaeda's Revenge: The 2004 Madrid Train Bombings*. New York: Columbia University Press, 2016.

"Al Qaeda Claims London Attacks," *CBS News*, first published September 1, 2005, accessed January 14, 2022, https://www.cbsnews.com/news/al-qaeda-claims-london-attacks/.

Byman, Daniel. "Why There Hasn't Been Another 9/11," *The Wall Street Journal,* first published September 11, 2021, accessed January 14, 2022, https://www.wsj.com/articles/why-there-hasnt-been-another-9-11-11631332860.

Picheta, Rob and Reuters. "Tunisian democracy in crisis after president ousts government," CNN, updated July 27, 2021, accessed January 14, 2022, https://www.cnn.com/2021/07/25/africa/tunisian-president-sacks-prime-minster-intl-hnk/index.html.

Horton, Scott. "Peter Bergen is Mistaken about bin Laden's Strategy," The Libertarian Institute, first published August 23, 2021, accessed January 14, 2022, https://libertarianinstitute.org/articles/peter-bergen-is-mistaken-about-bin-ladens-strategy/.

Chapter 8: Punching Your Plan in the Face

This story is based primarily off my experience on my first deployment in Western Iraq from September 2016–April 2017 with several officers from the British Army. With Steve's permission, the story follows the lessons he provided to my class during the semester closely. I include a short article about Dhofar, the war Steve's father fought in in the 1970s. The discussion of wargaming is built from both US military and UK military doctrine. Although I do not reference Colonel John Boyd's Observe-Orient-Decide-Act (OODA) Loop concept directly in this chapter, Steve himself used the concept in combat to focus on seizing the initiative. I include some references below. Most of the historical detail derives from Steve's personal experience.

Carter, David. "'Oman (Dhofar) 1969–1976', Britain's Small Wars: The Preservation of British Military History." Accessed January 23, 2022, http://britains-smallwars.com/campaigns/oman/page.php?art_url=dhofar.

Coram, Robert. *Boyd: The Fighter Pilot Who Changed the Art of War.* Boston: Back Bay Books, 2004.

Marine Corps Warfighting Publication 5-1 "The Marine Corps Planning Process," August 24, 2010.

Iraq's 55 Most Wanted Scoreboard, accessed August 8, 2021, https://www.angelfire.com/ultra/terroristscorecard/IraqDeck.html.

Flower, Kevin. "Iraqis Riot in Basra over Petrol," CNN.COM/WORLD, August 9, 2003, http://www.cnn.com/2003/WORLD/meast/08/09/sprj.irq.basrariot/index.html.

Chapter 9: The Tale of Two Passenger Jets, Mistakenly Shot Down
This chapter, like other discussions of history in this book, is meant to encourage a deeper inspection of US history and policy. I attempt to be as equal as possible at all times, but my bias is as an American who worked in intelligence and often saw Iran as a threat. The final decision-making game about the radar technician is conjecture, and I have no way of knowing if that is what happened when the Iranians shot down the passenger jet. I also include some of my personal experience on my second deployment to the Middle East from March–October 2018 and working in counterterrorism from 2019–20. Bacevich's *America's War* and Nsar's *The Shia Revival* serve as references for much of the discussion of US and Iranian relations from 1980 to 2014. I include some other online references below, including a perception of life under the Shah. The *BBC News*, MSN article, and official video release from US CENTCOM describe the early warning US forces had prior to the missile attack on Al Asad and the damage from the attacks.

LA Times Staff and Wire Reports. "Kermit Roosevelt; Arranged Iran Coup," *Los Angeles Times*, June 11, 2000, https://www.latimes.com/archives/la-xpm-2000-jun-11-me-39909-story.html.

Horton, Alex. "Soleimani's Legacy: The Gruesome, Advanced IEDs That Haunted U.S. Troops in Iraq," *The Washington Post*, January 3, 2020, https://www.washingtonpost.com/national-security/2020/01/03/soleimanis-legacy-gruesome-high-tech-ieds-that-haunted-us-troops-iraq/.

Names Withheld. "Life Under The Shah," *The Harvard Crimson*, December 6, 1979, https://www.thecrimson.com/article/1979/12/6/life-under-the-shah-pit-was/.

Bacevich, Andrew. *America's War For The Greater Middle East*. New York: Penguin Random House, 2016.

Nasr, Vali. *The Shia Revival: How Conflicts Within Islam Will Shape The Future*. New York: W.W. Norton, 2006.

Daftari, Amir. "Holy Defense Museum in Tehran – Iran's War Memorial For The Digital Age," CNN Travel, April 1, 2017, https://www.cnn.com/travel/article/iran-holy-defense-museum/index.html.

NBC News. "Read The Full Transcript of Trump's Iran Speech," *NBC News*, January 8, 2020, accessed August 8, 2021, https://www.nbcnews.

com/politics/donald-trump/read-full-transcript-trump-s-iran-speech-n1112456.

Martin, David and Mary Walsh. "The inside story of the Iranian attack on Al Asad Airbase," MSN, February 28, 2021, accessed February 4, 2022, https://www.msn.com/en-us/news/world/the-inside-story-of-the-iranian-attack-on-al-asad-airbase/ar-BB1e6duL.

BBC News. "Iran missile attack: Did Tehran intentionally avoid US casualties?" *BBC Middle East News*, January 8, 2020, accessed February 4, 2022, https://www.bbc.com/news/world-middle-east-51042156.

United States Central Command Public Affairs. "Al Asad TBM Attack 08JAN20," The War Zone, Youtube, accessed February 4, 2022, https://www.youtube.com/watch?v=SOLEPq40Kdg&t.

Chapter 10: You're Always Dealing with Probabilities

This story is based off James's experience getting evacuated in Afghanistan during one of his deployments and my experience working with him in 2018. The title of the chapter quotes President Obama as seen in Friedman and Zeckhauser's paper referenced below. Daniel Kahneman in *Thinking Fast and Slow* uses a similar example for vaccine hesitancy in his "Rare Events" chapter that I adapted for my third decision-making exercise. My description of "gut" decision-making as pattern recognition also derives from Kahneman's concept of "fast" thinking. Both the suicide-bomber thought problem and the Asian Disease Problem appear in Kahneman's *Thinking Fast and Slow*.

Every death is a tragedy, and a discussion of the rarity of children's deaths from COVID-19 is no solace to a parent who lost one. However, the data helps raise an important discussion of the use of "comparison frame" or comparative probabilities. The CDC reports that the odds of being struck by lightning in a given year are 1/500,000 or .0002 percent, which is similar to the percentage of US children who died from COVID-19 from March 2020–February 2021. A counterargument could be made that a child is not as likely to get struck by lightning as much as an adult. I could change the estimation then and say to a parent, "you are about as likely to get struck by lightning as your child is to die of COVID-19." While merely an estimation either way, the comparison allows for deeper understanding of the actual risk, especially when the concept of societal "outrage," derived from Dr Peter Sandman and the CDC's CERC manual cited below, is considered as well.

Public-health officials generally use "risk," "attack rate," and "case fatality" to describe the generalized progression of a disease at a societal level. The effectiveness of a vaccine (or any public-health measure) could be measured with risk, for example, by showing a difference in case load in the unvaccinated and vaccinated population. Risk is described as (number of cases)/(population at risk). Attack rate shows how many people develop a disease, usually in the case of an epidemic, who share a specific risk factor like attending a concert. Attack rate is described similarly as (number of cases)/(population at risk, e.g. who attended the concert). Case fatality shows the severity of a disease. Case fatality is described as (number of deaths)/(number of cases).

The measurement I used was the total numbers of children's deaths from COVID-19 as a proportion of the whole population of children in the US (134/60.8 million). "Risk of death," as I described it, could be seen to make the disease look less deadly since many of those 60.8 million did not have COVID-19. A case fatality rate for children in the US would be higher, although case data is not available from the study I used (Bhopal et al.). Bhopal et al. research sought "to put the deaths into a context that would help the understanding of parents, clinicians, and policy makers." The Bhopal et al. research paper compares the number of deaths from COVID-19 to all-cause mortality for children in the same timeframe, showing that less than ~1 percent of all children's deaths were caused by COVID-19 in the timeframe. That number of ~1 percent should be understood as "of children who died, ~1 percent died COVID-19." "Risk of death" is useful in this way by showing "of all children, .00022 percent died from COVID-19." I believe "risk of death" communicates a clearer understanding of generalized risk, than either Bhopal's 1 percent figure or case-fatality in the case of something as prevalent as COVID-19. Asymptomatic presentation also skews a case-fatality ratio, when many cases are not counted, due to lack of symptoms.

Current public-health messaging has been criticized throughout the pandemic. Public-health officials would do better defending their decisions to increase or decrease public-health measures with more straightforward language and risk estimates. The use of a comparison frame or comparative probabilities would then help communicate abstract percentages into understandable terms. After writing, I came across the article below about the likelihood of an asteroid hitting earth. If we can use comparative probability to help people understand that rare event, why should we not with public health? The counter-argument, listed in some public-health messaging guidance, is that comparison frames do not provide a fully accurate picture as estimations and can be misleading, again partially due to the concept of "outrage." Public-health messengers must consider both the positive and negatives of comparison frames.

I included discussion of the rarity of breakthrough cases, using data from the Kates et al. paper and *The Atlantic* article below. By August 2021, breakthrough cases were becoming more common, as vaccine effectiveness in preventing infection seemed to wane. By January 2022 due to the Omicron variant, breakthrough infections had become even more common. I still include my argument as another example of Kahneman's concept of "vividness."

I list an important study below on the positive impact of the "reappraisal" methods of "repurposing" and "reconstrual" during the beginning of the COVID-19 pandemic (Wang et al.). Beck's book is also a useful reference for teaching cognitive behavior therapy.

Kahneman, Daniel. *Thinking Fast and Slow*. New York: Farrar, Straus & Giroux, 2011.

Friedman, Jeffrey and Richard Zeckhauser. "Handling and Mishandling Estimative Probability: Likelihood, Confidence, and the Search for Bin Laden," *Intelligence and National Security*, July 2013.

Zero Dark Thirty. Directed by Kathryn Bigelow, Columbia, 2012.

Singer, P.W. and T. Emerson Brooking. *LikeWar: The Weaponization of Social Media*. New York: Houghton Mifflin Harcourt, 2018.

"Lightning: Victim Data," Centers for Disease Control and Prevention, accessed August 8, 2021, https://www.cdc.gov/disasters/lightning/victimdata.html.

Bhopal, S.S., J. Bagaria, B. Olabi and R. Bhopal. "Children and young people remain at low risk of COVID-19 mortality" [published correction appears in *Lancet Child Adolesc Health*, 2021, Mar. 24]. *Lancet Child Adolesc Health*, 2021; 5(5): e12-e13, doi:10.1016/S2352-4642(21)00066-3.

Kates, Jennifer, Lindsey Dawson, Emma Anderson, Anna Rouw, Josh Michaud, and Natalie Singer. "COVID-19 Vaccine Breakthrough Cases: Data from the States," *KFF*, July 2021, accessed August 8, 221, https://www.kff.org/policy-watch/covid-19-vaccine-breakthrough-cases-data-from-the-states/.

Yong, Ed. "How the Pandemic Ends Now," *The Atlantic*, accessed August 18, 2021, https://www.theatlantic.com/health/archive/2021/08/delta-has-changed-pandemic-endgame/619726/.

Siliezar, Juan. "Like hitting a bullseye with closed eyes," *The Harvard Gazette*, accessed August 31, 2021, https://news.harvard.edu/gazette/story/2021/08/statisticians-put-odds-of-bennu-hitting-earth-into-perspective/.

Wang, K., A. Goldenberg, C.A. Dorison et al. "A multi-country test of brief reappraisal interventions on emotions during the COVID-19 pandemic" [published correction appears in *Nat Hum Behav.*, 2022 Sep.; 6(9):1318–19], *Nat Hum Behav*, 2021; 5(8):1089–1110, doi:10.1038/s41562-021-01173-x.

Beck, Judith S. *Cognitive Behavior Therapy: Basics and Beyond*. New York: The Guilford Press, 2021.

Center for Disease Control and Prevention. *Crisis and Emergency Risk Communication Manual*. Center for Disease Control and Prevention, 2018.

Part III: Leadership

"Learn to listen, and you'll have more friends to listen to you": Somewhat derived from the lessons of Robin Dreeke. Dreeke's book, cited below, was the second major book we read and studied during the semester. Build rapport with others and you will have more support when you need it too.

Dreeke, Robin. *It's Not All About "Me": The Top Ten Techniques for Building Quick Rapport with Anyone*. Virginia: People Formula, 2013.

"To whom much is given, much is expected": A quotation attributable originally to the Bible. I remember hearing it in my first week of college. I wrote it on my board on my desk and it followed me for the next ten years. The quotation describes the sense of personal responsibility that come with the powers of leadership.

"We are all ultimately saved from grace:" From David Brooks's *The Road To Character*. Recognize the importance of forgiveness. One of my strongest memories initially returning to my high school to teach came from walking past the soccer fields. Two elementary students got into a large argument over the game as I walked past. I continued walking, but I realized neither of those students would likely remember the argument later that day or that night. Why do adults hold onto arguments for so much longer? Weeks? Years? Decades? Are our problems that much bigger than children's that we need to hold onto grievances or pain for that long?

Brooks, David. *The Road to Character*. New York: Random House, 2015.

Chapter 11: Sifr Wahid

This chapter is based off my arrival into Iraq in September 2016 and the work of base medical center during my deployment. Few official sources exist to discuss ISIS and Iraqi soldier use of "Sifr Wahid" or Captagon, but I use investigative reporting, several news articles, and blogs as background for the writing of this chapter. The Bazmi et al. study discusses the common cardiovascular complications of amphetamine abuse. I found the main reference for amphetamine use increasing in the Middle East before ISIS – United Nations's *World Drug Report* from 2013 – through an older post on a WordPress blog that I list below. Rawan Mortada's reporting provides the detail on the use of Captagon by more than just fighters on the front line, including luggage carriers and university students. I reference Toby Finney's memoir *Through These Eyes* with his permission to discuss heroin and drugs in Vietnam. His forced withdrawal method with Mike might sound extremely dangerous, but a fact taught in medical school is that you can't die from heroin withdrawal (you can die, however, from alcohol withdrawal, which should suggest more of its dangers in comparison). I reference official statistics from the National Institutes of Health and Centers for Disease Control and Prevention. I highlight President Obama's 2011 declaration of prescription drug abuse as an "epidemic" to demonstrate the slow beginning to the US's reckoning with opioid abuse. I use resources from Johns Hopkins and Opiate Addiction and Treatment Resource to compare the mechanism and chemical structure of oxycodone and heroin. Keefe's *Empire of Pain: The Secret History of the Sackler Dynasty* is a compelling history of the opioid crisis that I reference for the paragraph on the Sackler family.

The figure of 450,000 Americans dying by 2021 is quoted by the CDC and Keefe. I use Hedges Company for the 230 million figure of licensed drivers (2019 as reference), and Department of Transportation statistics for deaths in auto accidents. The 2019 National Drug Use Survey provides the figure of 10 million opioid abusers in 2019. The 12x figure derives from estimates in 2019. The leader in accidental death in the US is auto accidents, resulting in almost 36,000 deaths a year. The number of drivers in the US totaled almost 230 million in 2019, which accounts for .00015 deaths per licensed driver. The Centers for Disease Control and Prevention estimated that 10 million people abused opioids and 18,000 died from opioid overdoses in 2019. Those figures result in .0018 deaths per opioid abuser.

I close the chapter with discussion of one of my best friends and his struggles with opioids. Josh gave one of the most impactful lectures in my class and was proud to include his story in the book in the hope it might help others. Tragically, eight months after he and I collaborated on the chapter, he succumbed to his addiction and died. I left the chapter almost entirely the same from the version he read – the references to the pre- and post-deployment parties are the only changes prior to the scene break. I cherish my memories with him: a kind, caring, empathetic, and hilarious human. On my transition out of the military, he consoled me and made me proud to have done what I did, even when I was questioning why I served at all. While we were talking on the phone to work on the chapter, I remember trying to empathize with him when he talked of his struggles by briefly sharing some of my own (perhaps clumsily). He immediately pivoted to share support for me. He was just that kind of person, always on the lookout for his friends and family, despite everything he himself was going through. His twin brother Billy closed his moving eulogy for him with an imagined conversation between the guardian angel Clarence (who got his wings from George Bailey) and God. "Josh is coming to us now. Weren't those people down there lucky to have him?" We certainly were lucky.

Of all the chapters and lessons in the book, Josh's is one I hope I can learn from the most. I love you brother.

The Cockroach Factory. "Captagon ISIS: Drugs in Warfare," Wordpress, March 21, 2017, accessed February 2, 2022, https://cockroachfactory.wordpress.com/2017/03/21/captagon-isis/.

UNODC. *World Drug Report 2013*. United Nations publication, Sales No. E.13.XI.6, 2013, accessed February 2, 2022. https://www.unodc.org/unodc/secured/wdr/wdr2013/World_Drug_Report_2013.pdf.

Holley, Peter. "The tiny pill fueling Syria's war and turning fighters into superhuman soldiers," *The Washington Post*, November 19, 2015, accessed February 4, 2022, https://www.washingtonpost.com/news/worldviews/wp/2015/11/19/the-tiny-pill-fueling-syrias-war-and-turning-fighters-into-super-human-soldiers/.

Lopez, German. "Captagon, ISIS's favorite amphetamine, explained," *Vox*, November 21, 2015, accessed February 2, 2022, https://www.vox.com/world/2015/11/20/9769264/captagon-isis-drug.

Griffiths, Josie. "War on Drugs: What is Captagon? Isis drug dubbed 'chemical courage' intended to treat sleeping disorders abused by terrorists," *The Sun* (UK), August 18, 2017, accessed February 2,

2022, https://www.thesun.co.uk/living/3688057/captagon-isis-drug-chemical-courage-sleep-disorders-terrorists/.

Mortada, Rawan and Emanuele Pasquale. "The Drug Fueling Conflict in Syria," Journeyman.TV, Youtube, September 21, 2015, accessed February 3, 2022, https://www.youtube.com/watch?v=7ke13JNlpBQ.

Bazmi, Elham et al. "Cardiovascular Complications of Acute Amphetamine Abuse: Cross-sectional study," *Sultan Qaboos University Medical Journal,* Vol. 17, 1 (2017), e31–e37. doi:10.18295/squmj.2016.17.01.007.

Finney, Toby. *Through These Eyes*. Toby Finney, 2021.

"Opioid Overdose Crisis," National Institute on Drug Abuse: Advancing Addiction Science, March 11, 2021, accessed February 4, 2022, https://nida.nih.gov/drug-topics/opioids/opioid-overdose-crisis.

"Prescription Opioids and Heroin Research Report: Introduction," National Institute on Drug Abuse: Advancing Addiction Science, January 2018, accessed February 4, 2022, https://nida.nih.gov/publications/research-reports/prescription-opioids-heroin/introduction.

Office of National Drug Control Policy Washington. "Epidemic: Responding to America's Prescription Drug Abuse Crisis," Executive Office of the President of the United States, April 2011, accessed February 4, 2022, https://obamawhitehouse.archives.gov/sites/default/files/ondcp/issues-content/prescription-drugs/rx_abuse_plan.pdf.

"Opioid Chemical Structures," Opiate Addiction and Treatment Resource.Com, Rehab Media Network LLC, accessed February 4, 2022, https://www.opiateaddictionresource.com/media/images/opioid_chemical_structures/.

"What Are Opioids?," Johns Hopkins Medicine, accessed February 4, 2022, https://www.hopkinsmedicine.org/opioids/what-are-opioids.html.

Keefe, Patrick Radden. *Empire of Pain: The Secret History of the Sackler Dynasty*. New York: Doubleday, 2021.

"How Many Licensed Drivers Are There In The US?", Hedges & Company, accessed February 4, 2022, https://hedgescompany.com/blog/2018/10/number-of-licensed-drivers-usa.

"NHTSA Releases 2019 Crash Fatality Data," US Department of Transportation's National Highway Traffic Safety Administration, December 18, 2020, accessed February 4, 2022, https://www.nhtsa.gov/press-releases/nhtsa-releases-2019-crash-fatality-data.

Substance Abuse and Mental Health Services Administration. "Key substance use and mental health indicators in the United States: Results from the 2019 National Survey on Drug Use and Health" (HHS Publication No. PEP20-07-01-001, NSDUH Series H-55). Rockville, MD: Center for Behavioral Health Statistics and Quality, Substance Abuse and Mental Health Services Administration, 2020, retrieved from February 4, 2022, https://www.samhsa.gov/data/.

Chapter 12: The Wheel on the Screen

These stories are derived from my experience as a Watch Officer on my first deployment in Western Iraq from September 2016–April 2017. The tragic death of Iraqi Colonel Nasr, which I describe in the opening of the chapter, remains felt by many who served in partnership with the Iraqis for the beginning of the War Against ISIS in Anbar Province. The references below highlight the eventual liberation of Anah, Al Qaim, and Rawah. I also reference Robin Dreeke's mantra for leadership and influence: "Leave people better off for having met you." The renowned social engineer Chris Hadnagy also uses the mantra for his company Social Engineering, LLC.

Antonopoulos, Paul. "Iraqi Forces Liberate Anah District From ISIS in its Drive to Reach the Syrian Border," FRN, February 19, 2018, https://fort-russ.com/2017/09/iraqi-forces-liberate-anah-distric/.

The New Arab & Agencies. "Iraqi PM Declares al-Qaim Liberated from IS after Lightning Offensive," *The New Arab*, November 3, 2017. https://english.alaraby.co.uk/news/iraqi-pm-declares-al-qaim-liberated.

"Last Iraqi Town Held by ISIS Recaptured, Officials Say," *CBS News*, November 17, 2017, https://www.cbsnews.com/news/last-iraqi-town-held-by-isis-recaptured-officials-say/.

Dreeke, Robin. *It's Not All About "Me": The Top Ten Techniques for Building Quick Rapport with Anyone*. Virginia: People Formula, 2013.

Hadnagy, Chris with Seth Schulman. *Human Hacking: Win Friends, Influence People, and Leave Them Better Off for Having Met You*. New York: Harper Business, 2021.

Chapter 13: Ownership, Selflessness, Passion

This chapter begins with my experience watching the beginning of the Battle of Mosul from Western Iraq in 2016. With Marcus's permission, I used the lessons he provided to my class during the semester for the rest of the chapter. The illustration included in the plate section is based off of Marcus's description of the bridge and some of the photos he took during his patrol that day. I include a reference below that shows the beginning of the Battle of Mosul and a discussion of Baghdadi's speech. The brief discussion of the history of Afghanistan derives from Coll's *Ghost Wars*, Evans's *Foxtrot in Kandahar*, and the articles below.

Austin, Henry and Sarah Burke. "Iraqi Forces Launch 'Operation Conquest' To Retake Mosul From ISIS," *NBC News*, March 24, 2016, https://www.nbcnews.com/storyline/isis-terror/iraqi-forces-launch-operation-conquest-retake-mosul-isis-n544826.

Rubin, Alissa. "Militant Leader in Rare Appearance in Iraq," *The New York Times*, July 5, 2014, https://www.nytimes.com/2014/07/06/world/asia/iraq-abu-bakr-al-baghdadi-sermon-video.html.

Coll, Steve. *Ghost Wars: The Secret History of the CIA, Afghanistan, and bin Laden, from the Soviet Invasion to September 10, 2001*. New York: Penguin Books, 2004.

Evans, Duane. *Foxtrot in Kandahar: A Memoir of a CIA Officer in Afghanistan at the Inception of America's Longest War*. New York: Savas Beadie, 2017.

Behan, Richard. "The Taliban Surrendered in 2001," *Common Dreams*, accessed August 18, 2021, https://www.commondreams.org/views/2021/08/18/taliban-surrendered-2001.

Reuters. "Son of slain Afghan hero Massoud vows resistance, seeks support," Reuters, August 19, 2021, https://www.reuters.com/world/asia-pacific/son-slain-afghan-hero-massoud-vows-resistance-seeks-support-2021-08-19/.

Chapter 14: Nobody Cares

The chapter begins with a story Jennifer relayed to my class during the semester. With her permission, I used some of her story and lessons to open the chapter. I am also grateful to be able to highlight some of the experience of women in the military. Some of the most dedicated and impressive Marines and soldiers I knew at home and from deployment were women. They faced many more challenges in military than I ever did. I include some of the references I used in the discussion of women in the military below. I reference the preface from Frankl's *Man's Search For Meaning* and some of Frankl's themes after Jennifer's story. I did use the moral courage decision-making games within my class, but I had come back to the room too quickly for the second decision-making exercise. Luckily, I then received a call from Noah, which got me back out of the classroom and allowed the students to "cheat." With Ryan's permission, the chapter concludes with the lessons he provided to my class during the semester.

"Demographics of the US Military," Council on Foreign Relations, last updated July 13, 2020, accessed August, 8, 2021, https://www.cfr.org/backgrounder/demographics-us-military.

Hays, Keith. "These Were the First Women to Join Each U.S. Military Service," Military.com, accessed August 8, 2021, https://www.military.com/history/womens-history-month/first-women-join-military.

Allen, Jonathan. "Biden, Pentagon Endorse Major Change to Military Sexual Assault Law," *NBC News*, July 2, 2021, https://www.nbcnews.com/politics/politics-news/biden-pentagon-endorse-major-change-military-sexual-assault-law-n1273006.

"National Intimate Partner and Sexual Violence Survey: 2015 Data Brief – Updated Release," Centers for Disease Control and Prevention, accessed August 8, 2021, https://www.nsvrc.org/sites/default/files/2021-04/2015data-brief508.pdf.

"SAPRO Report Metrics Overview," Department of Defense Sexual Assault Prevention and Response Office, accessed August 8, 2021, https://www.sapr.mil/sites/default/files/public/docs/reports/SAPRO_Report_Metrics_Overview_ReferenceCopy.pdf.

Frankl, Viktor. *Man's Search For Meaning*. New York: Beacon Press, 2006.

Chapter 15: The One We Want Back

This chapter is based off my experience deploying to Western Iraq from September 2016–April 2017 and visiting my old base a few times over the course of my deployment from March–October 2018. I frame the story around Homer with his permission and include an illustration of a photo he sent to me in 2020 at the beginning of the COVID-19 pandemic in the plate section. I close the chapter and book with a direct reference to the end of Tolkien's *Return of the King*, the same line that

Sam says when he returns to the Shire. I allude indirectly to Eliot's "The Waste Land" and Frankl's *Man's Search For Meaning* in the chapter as well.

"Introduction to the Law of Armed Conflict," International Committee of the Red Cross, accessed August 8, 2021, https://www.icrc.org/en/doc/assets/files/other/law1_final.pdf.

Eliot, T.S. *The Waste Land*. New York: Houghton Mifflin Harcourt Publishing Company, 1922.

Frankl, Viktor. *Man's Search For Meaning*. New York: Beacon Press, 2006.

Tolkien, J.R.R. *The Lord of the Rings: The Return of the King*. London: George Allen & Unwin, 1955.

Epilogue: A Note to My Family

This chapter describes the writing of my just-in-case-I-die letter, and I include the letter unchanged from 2018. I wrote it as I wrote my standard attempt-at-humor correspondence to my family, with many allusions and some direct quotations of my favorite movies, songs, and books. Below is a list of the references I caught when rereading, although I likely have missed some.

Gladiator. Directed by Ridley Scott, Dreamworks, 2000.

Khalifa, Wiz. "Young, Wild and Free," *Mac & Devin Go To High School*, Atlantic Records, 2011. Stream.

Gottwald, Lukasz, Jessica Cornish, and Claude Kelly. "Party in the USA," *The Time of Our Lives*, Hollywood Records, 2011. Stream.

Tolkien, J.R.R. *The Lord of the Rings: The Fellowship of the Ring*. London: George Allen & Unwin, 1955.

Reagan, Ronald. "A Time For Choosing," speech given October 27, 1964.

Tice, Austin. "It's nice and all, but please quit telling me to be safe," *The Washington Post*, accessed August 8, 2021, https://www.washingtonpost.com/world/middle_east/austin-tice-its-nice-and-all-but-please-quit-telling-me-to-be-safe/2012/08/23/984488ba-ed4b-11e1-a80b-9f898562d010_story.html.

Hemingway, Ernest. *For Whom the Bell Tolls*. New York: Scribner, 1943.

Gehrig, Lou. "Farewell Speech," given July 3, 1939.

Angels in the Outfield. Directed by William Dear, Walt Disney Pictures, 1994.

Holmes Jr, Oliver Wendell. "In Our Youth Our Hearts Were Touched With Fire," Memorial Day speech in New Hampshire, 1884, accessed August 8, 2021, https://freerepublic.com/focus/news/690119/posts.

Wallace, David Foster. "This is Water," commencement speech at Kenyon College, 2005.

No Country for Old Men. Directed by Joel and Ethan Coen, Miramax, 2007.

Fergie and Toby Gad. "Big Girls Don't Cry," *The Dutchess*, A&M, 2006.

Kundera, Milan. *The Unbearable Lightness of Being*. New York: HarperCollins, 1984.

Stevens, Cat. "Peace Train," *Tease and the Firecat*, Paramount Studios, 1971. Stream.

Park, Patrick. "Something Pretty," *Loneliness Knows My Name*, Hollywood Records, 2003. Stream

Waters, Roger. "Eclipse," *The Dark Side of the Moon*, Harvest, 1973. Stream.

Pohl, Frederick. *Gateway*. New York: St Martin's Press, 1977.

Mumford, Marcus. "I Will Wait," *Babel*, Markus Dravs, 2012. Stream.

"The Parting Glass," traditional Scottish song.

Thompson, Richard. "1952 Vincent Black Lightning," *Rumor and Sigh*, Mitchell Froom, 1992. Stream.

Gabriel, Peter. "In Your Eyes," *So*, Geffen, 1986. Stream.

Mountcastle, George. "The Wanderstill Time," *Blue and Gray, Fall 1967*, accessed August 8, 2021, https://www.gilman.edu/academics/upper-school/lectures-leadership/mountcastle-lecture.

Eliot, T.S. *The Waste Land*, New York: Houghton Mifflin Harcourt Publishing Company, 1922.

Postscript: Thirteen More Names on the Wall

I wrote this chapter after I completed the book in mid-August. I reference the attack in Kabul and the song below. I have included a link to a charity organization that supports US families who lose family members to war.

Pierre, Justin. "Everything is Alright," *Commit This To Memory*, Epitaph Records, 2006. Stream.

Holmes Jr, Oliver Wendell. "In Our Youth Our Hearts Were Touched With Fire," Memorial Day speech in New Hampshire, 1884, accessed August 28, 2021, https://freerepublic.com/focus/news/690119/posts.

Whitman, Walt. "O Me! O Life!," *Leaves of Grass*, 1892, https://www.poetryfoundation.org/poems/51568/o-me-o-life.

NPR. "The Attack Outside Kabul Airport Pushes the U.S. Exit Into Deeper Disarray," August 26, 2021, accessed August 28, 2021, https://www.npr.org/2021/08/26/1031428645/the-attacks-outside-kabul-airport-pushes-the-u-s-exit-into-deeper-disarray.

Tragedy Assistance Program for Survivors. "Caring for the Families of America's Fallen Heroes," https://www.taps.org.

Postscript II: Touched with Fire in Ukraine

The War in Ukraine started two weeks after I turned the full manuscript of this book into my publisher. I wrote this chapter six months later in the summer in between my first and second years of medical school. As the book slowly became more personal, both for me and my friends who asked me to include their real names and less obscured versions of their stories, I realized more that I would want to write about transition from the military and my close friend Sully. It took me some time to put transition in perspective, so I probably would not have been able to write as much if I had tried in the first few months after leaving the military. Sully's and my transitions from the military were different in many ways, but his feelings and experiences were similar to mine. My hope is the transition portion of this chapter can prepare other veterans for some of the difficulty faced in transition. Everyone in the military wants to help you get out on the right foot (at least the good people), but none of them have done it themselves. Working and talking with other veterans helped me make sense of some of the confusing feelings I had upon leaving. When Sully returned from Ukraine, I asked him if he would be willing to help me capture his experience in a final chapter, both focused on transition, the drive to return to war, and the War in Ukraine. I am grateful he was willing to share such a personal story. The portion on his time in Ukraine is adapted directly from a memoir he provided to me with his permission. His poem "On Transition" is also used with his permission. The history of the 2014 and 2022 invasions of Ukraine are built from many different sources, as they remain such recent events. Mike Auten, a friend, fellow Marine, and fellow medical student, who has done significant work in Ukraine since 2016, helped me provide a more nuanced perspective on the history of Ukraine and Crimea with additional sources and detailed edits. I studied the invasion of Crimea in a "Laws of War" class at Harvard in my senior year in spring 2014, which was taught by a mentor and fellow Marine Gregg Peeples. I thought of the final pages of both Willa Cather's *My Antonia* and Fitzgerald's *The Great Gatsby* when I wrote the concluding paragraphs about me and Sully.

Osborn, A. and P. Nikolskaya. "Russia's Putin authorises 'special military operation' against Ukraine," Reuters, February 24, 2022, accessed 10 July 2022, https://www.reuters.com/world/europe/russias-putin-authorises-military-operations-donbass-domestic-media-2022-02-24/.

Morello, C., Will Englund, and Griff Witte. "Crimea's parliament votes to join Russia," *The Washington Post*, March 17, 2014, accessed July 10, 2022, from http://www.washingtonpost.com/world/crimeas-parliament-votes-to-join-russia/2014/03/17/5c3b96ca-adba-11e3-9627-c65021d6d572_story.html.

Deeks, A. "Russia in Ukraine: A Reader Responds," Lawfare, October 31, 2019, accessed July 10, 2022, from https://www.lawfareblog.com/russia-ukraine-reader-responds.

"The Budapest Memorandum of 1994," Memorandum on Security Assurances, signed December 5, 1994, accessed July 10, 2022, from https://larouchepub.com/eiw/public/2014/eirv41n08-20140221/34-35_4108.pdf.

Christie, E.H. "Sanctions after Crimea: Have they worked?," *NATO Review*, July 13, 2015, retrieved July 10, 2022, from https://www.nato.int/docu/review/articles/2015/07/13/sanctions-after-crimea-have-they-worked/index.html.

"The Orange Revolution and the Yushchenko presidency," *Encyclopedia Britannica*, retrieved October 30, 2022, from https://www.britannica.com/place/Ukraine/The-Orange-Revolution-and-the-Yushchenko-presidency.

Bellingcat. "Identifying the Separatists Linked to the Downing of MH17," Bellingcat, October 13, 2020, retrieved October 30, 2022, from https://www.bellingcat.com/news/uk-and-europe/2019/06/19/identifying-the-separatists-linked-to-the-downing-of-mh17/.

Bershidsky, Leonid. "Who Killed Ukraine's Heavenly Hundred?," *Bloomberg*, retrieved October 30, 2022, from https://www.bloomberg.com/opinion/articles/2014-03-05/who-killed-ukraine-s-heavenly-hundred?.

Marson, J. "Poll Finds Ukrainians Favor EU Pact," *WSJ*, November 12, 2013, retrieved October 31, 2022, from https://www.wsj.com/articles/poll-finds-ukrainians-favor-eu-pact-1384287839.

Boghani, P. "Putin's Attack on Ukraine," FRONTLINE, October 26, 2022, retrieved October 31, 2022, from https://www.pbs.org/wgbh/frontline/documentary/putins-attack-on-ukraine-documenting-war-crimes/.

"Malaysia Airlines flight 17, Background, Crash, Investigation, & Facts," *Encyclopedia Britannica*, retrieved July 10, 2022, from https://www.britannica.com/event/Malaysia-Airlines-flight-17.

"Live Universal Awareness Map." Accessed July 10, 2022, from https://liveuamap.com/.

ABC News. "Russian missile strike near Poland raises tough questions for Biden," March 15, 2022, retrieved July 15, 2022, from https://abcnews.go.com/Politics/russian-missile-strike-poland-raises-tough-questions-biden/story?id=83436540.

Zinets, N. and M. Saito. "Multiple rockets hit Lviv city in western Ukraine," Reuters, March 26, 2022, retrieved July 15, 2022, from https://www.reuters.com/world/europe/three-powerful-explosions-heard-near-ukraines-western-lviv-city-says-governor-2022-03-26/.

INDEX

"I wrote down what I would have preferred not to remember, for it is these recollections that help me forget."

Ai WeiWei, A Thousand Years of Joys and Sorrows